The Longest Winter

The Longest Winter

*The Epic Story of World War II's
Most Decorated Platoon*

ALEX KERSHAW

MICHAEL JOSEPH
an imprint of
PENGUIN BOOKS

MICHAEL JOSEPH

Published by the Penguin Group
Penguin Books Ltd, 80 Strand, London WC2R ORL, England
Penguin Group (USA) Inc., 375 Hudson Street, New York, New York 10014, USA
Penguin Group (Canada), 10 Alcorn Avenue, Toronto, Ontario, Canada M4V 3B2
(a division of Pearson Penguin Canada Inc.)
Penguin Ireland, 25 St Stephen's Green, Dublin 2, Ireland
(a division of Penguin Books Ltd)
Penguin Group (Australia), 250 Camberwell Road,
Camberwell, Victoria 3124, Australia (a division of Pearson Australia Group Pty Ltd)
Penguin Books India Pvt Ltd, 11 Community Centre,
Panchsheel Park, New Delhi – 110 017, India
Penguin Group (NZ), cnr Airborne and Rosedale Roads, Albany,
Auckland 1310, New Zealand (a division of Pearson New Zealand Ltd)
Penguin Books (South Africa) (Pty) Ltd, 24 Sturdee Avenue,
Rosebank 2196, South Africa

Penguin Books Ltd, Registered Offices: 80 Strand, London WC2R ORL, England

www.penguin.com

First published in the USA by Da Capo Press 2004
First published in Great Britain by Michael Joseph 2005
1

Set in 13.5/16 pt Monotype Garamond
Typeset by Rowland Phototypesetting Ltd, Bury St Edmunds, Suffolk
Printed in Great Britain by Clays Ltd, St Ives plc

A CIP catalogue record for this book is available from the British Library

ISBN 0–718–14745–6

For veterans of the Bulge –
and those who sacrificed their lives
defeating the Third Reich

Contents

PART FOUR Last Battles

MAPS

Acknowledgments

Thanks must first go to my astute and hugely supportive editor at Da Capo Press, Robert L. Pigeon, who wondered whether I would be interested in writing a book that focused on a small unit but that also gave a broad overview of the Battle of the Bulge – the greatest battle in U.S. history. A call to longtime supporter Michael Edwards at the Eisenhower Center led to my discovery of the Intelligence and Reconnaissance platoon of the 394th Infantry Regiment of the 99th Division. Edwards outlined a fantastic story and said that the commanding officer was still alive, as were others from what is thought to be the most decorated platoon of the entire Second World War.

The commanding officer, Lyle Bouck Jr., was indeed still alive – very much so. An author could not have hoped for a better relationship with the main character in his book. I would like to thank Lyle – a true American officer and gentleman – and his wife, Lucy, for their hospitality on several occasions. Without Lyle Bouck's assistance, this book would have been impossible. I was especially lucky because Lyle also handed over years of careful documentation, press clippings, and many remarkable written accounts by platoon members who were deceased.

The following platoon members also provided generous help, and some suffered many hours of questioning: Vernon Leopold, who spent days checking over the manuscript and directing me toward new information; James Fort; Louis Kalil; Risto Milosevich; Samuel L. Jenkins; Robert Lambert,

ix

who sadly passed away during the writing of this book; Joseph McConnell; James Silvola; and Robert Preston.

Helga Druxes, a professor at Williams College, did an outstanding job of translating colloquial German from the 1940s into pristine English. Once more, Lindsay Sterling provided crucial advice and help with the manuscript. She has no equal.

The following relatives, experts, and veterans also helped a great deal: John Creger Jr., Delfina Fernandez, the Silvola family, Kurt Vonnegut, James Fort Jr., Bill Meyer, Will Cavanagh, Peter Gacki, Emma Sue Creger, Lt. Warren Springer, Hans J. Wijers, Bob Thompson, William H. Merricken, Paul Tsakanikas, Larry McBreyer, Abe Baum, William Nutto, Barbara Anderson, Bill Slape Jr., Mike Slape, John Lambert Jr., Ward Silvola, Roberta Catlett, Jean Silvola, Jim Price, Agnes McGehee, and Anna Tsakanikas.

My wife, Robin Loerch, acted as researcher, picture editor, technician, and transcriber. The book would have taken twice as long to complete without her amazingly good-natured help. She and my son Felix have allowed me to pursue my fascinations far more than most writers could hope for.

My agent, Derek Johns, and his colleagues at AP Watt again provided all the assistance they could. The superb team at Da Capo Press was yet again also a delight to work with. And without the late Peter Burchard, there would have been little joy in endless weeks of library research at Williams College.

Roster of the Intelligence and Reconnaissance Platoon,
394th Infantry Regiment, 99th Infantry Division
at the Battle of the Bulge

At the village of Lanzerath, Belgium

First Lieutenant Lyle Bouck, commanding
Private Robert Adams
Private Robert Baasch
Private John Creger
Sergeant William Dustman
Private Clifford Fansher
Technician Fourth Class James Fort
Private Bill James
Corporal Sam Jenkins
Private Louis Kalil
Private Joseph McConnell
Corporal Aubrey 'Schnoz' McGehee
Private First Class Risto 'Milo' Milosevich
Private First Class Robert 'Mop' Preston
Sergeant George 'Pappy' Redmond
Private First Class Jordan 'Pop' Robinson
Private James 'Siv' Silvola
Sergeant Bill Slape

At regimental headquarters in Hünningen, Belgium

Private Vic Adams
Private First Class Carlos Fernandez
Private First Class John Frankovitch
Technician Fifth Class Robert Lambert
Private Vernon Leopold
Private First Class Elmer Nowacki
Private Sam Oakley

Es geht alles vorüber
Es geht alles vorbei
Nach jedem Dezember
Gibt wieder ein Mai.[1]
– Popular German song played on
the radio throughout spring 1945

PART ONE
Watch on the Rhine

1. The Wolf's Lair

The Wolf's Lair, East Prussia, Nazi Germany –
July 20, 1944

Count Klaus von Stauffenberg, chief of staff to General
Friedrich Fromm, commander of the Army of the Interior,
tried to keep his nerve as he stood alone, holding open a
briefcase, in a bathroom deep inside Adolf Hitler's Prussian
headquarters – the so-called Wolf's Lair. Stauffenberg carefully grasped a fuse with the remaining three fingers on his
only hand and began to stuff it into a bomb. He had lost
the other two fingers, an eye, and an arm in fierce fighting
at the Kasserine Pass in Tunisia in 1942.

Stauffenberg gingerly placed the bomb in the open briefcase and activated it. A small glass capsule inside the fuse
device broke, allowing burning acid to drip onto a thin wire.
It was 12:26 P.M. He had exactly fifteen minutes before
the wire burned through and the bomb exploded. Quickly,
Stauffenberg left the bathroom and walked down a long
corridor toward a conference room. If he succeeded in
blowing up Hitler, the Germany he had once loved would
be saved and millions of lives would be spared; the hell of
the Third Reich would soon be history.[2]

The meeting with senior generals had already started
when Stauffenberg slipped unnoticed into Hitler's tea house,
constructed of wood rather than reinforced concrete like
the usual conference room in a nearby bunker. The windows

had been opened in the stuffy room; outside, it was a sweltering summer day.

The generals examined maps spread out on a long oak table. Hitler sat behind the table toying with a powerful magnifying glass, his spectacles lying on a map. His face was gaunt and deeply lined. Rumor had it that his latest personal physician was overprescribing cocaine and other stimulants.

Other generals looked intensely at areas where millions of Red Army soldiers threatened to engulf several German divisions like some vast red tide. Since early June, the Russians had broken through virtually the entire eastern front. More than thirty German divisions languished in Stalin's POW camps.

In France, the Allies had finally broken out of Normandy after several weeks of fierce fighting and were now eliminating tens of thousands of Hitler's best troops in the Falaise Pocket.

Only the Führer among the assembled group believed that the war could still be won. His much-vaunted miracle weapons, including the atomic bomb, could not now be developed or brought into the field in sufficient numbers to stop the Allied onslaught from east and west.

Stauffenberg placed his brown leather briefcase under the table, a mere six feet from Hitler, then excused himself, mumbling that he had to take an urgent phone call. He slipped out of the room unnoticed and hurried down a corridor to make his escape.

At 12:42 P.M., there was a massive explosion. Smoke filled the room as splinters and plaster flew everywhere. Stauffenberg heard the explosion as he made his way through a security perimeter. Surely, this time, it was all over.

Back inside the Wolf's Lair, one of the generals scrambled out of the conference room and lay bleeding in the corridor.

Suddenly, he saw a ghostly figure emerge from the plaster dust and smoke. The man's face was blackened by the smoke, and his trousers were shredded.

The ghostly figure was Adolf Hitler. Miraculously, the Führer was still alive. In a daze, he stumbled out of the destroyed tearoom. The force of the explosion had been dissipated because of the open windows and the adjoining corridor, which had acted as a vacuum, sucking away the blast.

Aides rushed to the Führer and led him toward a bunker. '*Was ist los?*' (What is wrong?) they asked Hitler.

Someone suggested that it was a Soviet bomb dropped from a passing plane. However, it was soon clear that Hitler had not survived an attack by Stalin's air force but an assassination plot by his own senior Wehrmacht officers.

Once he had regained his senses, Hitler allowed himself to be treated by his personal doctor, Dr. Hanskarl von Hasselbach. Hitler had a bad cut on his head and had lost the hearing in one ear. But he looked ecstatic. 'Now I have those fellows!' he shouted. 'Now I can take steps!' He had long suspected a conspiracy among senior officers. Now he would wipe them out, purge German society of other subversives, and reassert his power.

Another doctor arrived, gave Hitler an injection, and examined his heart. Hitler's pulse was normal.

'Think of it,' said Hitler. 'Nothing has happened to me. Just think of it!'

Hitler's three secretaries rushed into the bunker. His plaster-dusted hair stood on end as he held out his left hand. The women clasped it carefully.

'Well, my ladies,' Hitler grinned, 'once again everything has turned out well for me. More proof that Fate has selected me for my mission. Otherwise I wouldn't be alive.'

Meanwhile, Stauffenberg was on a plane headed for Berlin. He arrived later that afternoon and immediately set about ordering his co-conspirators to secure Berlin. Rumors flew across Germany: some reported that Hitler was dead, others that he had survived.

Stauffenberg manned a telephone at his office in the Bendlerstrasse headquarters of the Army of the Interior, answering calls from fellow plotters wanting confirmation that the assassination attempt had indeed succeeded.

By coincidence, thirty-six-year-old SS Major Otto Skorzeny was also in Berlin that afternoon. A six-foot-four-inch blond Viennese with a large scar across his face from a duel over a ballerina, Skorzeny carried himself with the élan and confidence of a man who had yet to experience failure or defeat and was considered by British intelligence to be the most dangerous of all Hitler's elite SS Kommandos. In late 1943, supported by a small unit of parachutists, he had pulled off one of the most daring raids of the war – rescuing Mussolini from under the nose of the Allies.

'On 20 July, I was preparing to leave for Vienna,' recalled Skorzeny. 'At six o'clock I arrived at the Anhalt Station and settled down in a reserved compartment and prepared for the night. But at the Lichterfelde Station, the last within the city limits of Berlin, I heard my name called: "Major Skorzeny! Major Skorzeny!" On the platform an officer was running alongside the train, shouting at the top of his lungs. I opened the window and beckoned to him; completely out of breath, he rushed forward: "Major, you must return immediately. Higher orders. The attempt on the Führer was intended to start a putsch!"'

The young officer drove Skorzeny back into Berlin and then toward the central office of the Waffen SS, where he learned that the chief plotters were holed up at the

Bendlerstrasse. Before long, he received a call from the Wolf's Lair: 'Orders for Major Skorzeny to report with all troops at his disposal to the Bendlerstrasse in order to support the action of Major Remer, commander of the Greater Germany Guard Battalion.' Major Remer has already begun the encirclement of the ministry.

In his office, Stauffenberg was suddenly seized by several Luger-waving loyalists who had decided to save their necks by turning against the plotters. Stauffenberg was quickly placed under guard with other conspirators. His superior, the obese General Fromm, soon arrived and pulled out his Luger: 'I am now going to treat you as you treated me.' (Earlier that day, Fromm had been imprisoned by some of Stauffenberg's supporters when they thought the assassination plot had succeeded and then later released as news spread that the attempt had failed.)

One of Stauffenberg's co-conspirators, General Ludwig Beck, asked to be allowed to shoot himself. Fromm nodded his agreement.

Beck placed his pistol to his head and fired, but the bullet merely wounded him. He slumped back in his chair, blood pouring from his head.

Fromm looked at Beck with contempt and then turned to Stauffenberg and the others. 'Now, gentlemen . . . if you have any letters to write you may have a few minutes to do so.'

Fromm returned five minutes later. In the name of the Führer, he announced, they were to be executed.

A German sergeant dragged the unconscious Beck from the room. A shot rang out. Beck was now dead – killed by a bullet through the neck. A few minutes later, Stauffenberg and his co-conspirators were lined up in front of a pile of sand in a courtyard. It was midnight, less than twelve hours since his bomb had exploded in Hitler's tearoom.

'Long live our sacred Germany!' shouted Stauffenberg as the firing squad took aim. A few seconds later, Stauffenberg's riddled body slumped to the ground.

Fromm reviewed the firing squad. Satisfied with their work, he shouted 'Heil Hitler!' and left the courtyard.

Thirty minutes later, Otto Skorzeny arrived with his men and confirmed with Gestapo officials that the Bendlerstrasse headquarters were secure.

It was a few seconds before 1:00 A.M. on July 21, 1944, when a loud blast of military music interrupted all broadcasts on German radio.

'I was spared a fate which held no horror for me, but would have had terrible consequences for the German people,' Adolf Hitler solemnly declared. 'I see in it a sign from Providence that I must, and therefore shall, continue my work.'

On July 25, 1944, the BBC announced that only Germany's total and unconditional surrender would end the war. For Hitler there was no option now but to continue the fight, even to the bitter end. And so, as he recuperated that late July, Hitler began to develop the most audacious military plan of his career – a last, desperate gamble to defeat the Allies in the West.

2. Camp Maxey

Camp Maxey, Texas – July 1944

As Hitler recovered from the assassination attempt, several thousand miles away at Camp Maxey, Texas, another blisteringly hot July day had just begun. The humidity was already oppressive with the sun beating down on the endless rows of two-story white barracks, glinting on their new paint and their green-tiled roofs. Outside a headquarters barracks, Robert Kriz, a tall, twenty-seven-year-old major, walked briskly toward a jeep, limping slightly from a leg wound sustained in North Africa. By his side was sandy-haired, blue-eyed, twenty-year-year-old First Lieutenant Lyle Bouck, one of the youngest commissioned officers in the U.S. Army.

The two officers' shoulder patches were emblazoned with a blue and white checkerboard pattern on a black field, indicating that they belonged to the 99th Division, which had been activated two years earlier and had yet to see combat. Kriz was the senior intelligence officer – S-2 – of the 99th's 394th Infantry Regiment, one of the division's three combat commands.

Major Kriz and Lieutenant Bouck jumped into the jeep and set off through the maze of barracks, passing the notorious obstacle course where many a callow private had been humiliated by sadistic platoon sergeants, a mock German village where street fighting was practiced, and the parade ground where Sergeant Joe Louis, the world boxing champion, had put on an exhibition the previous December.

9

Kriz had selected the baby-faced Bouck to lead a reorganized intelligence and reconnaissance (I&R) platoon of the 394th Infantry Regiment, confident that the precocious young Missourian would shape an excellent team designed to be the regiment's 'eyes and ears' once it reached combat in just a few months' time.

Lieutenant Bouck relished the challenge, eager to excel in his first command. Though he looked like a teenager, he was wise and tough beyond his years, and thankful to the military for providing an alternative to the hopelessness and despair that had characterized much of his childhood. 'We were a really poor Depression family,' recalled Bouck. 'My father was a carpenter but there was no construction work. We moved around a lot when I was a kid and lived in houses without indoor plumbing or electricity. There were five kids and we lived in places with only one bedroom. We didn't always have enough to eat; we picked berries, ate dandelions. We didn't think anything of it. We thought everyone lived that way.'

Major Kriz knew that Bouck was no 'ninety-day wonder,'[3] fresh out of officer training school. He had in fact been in the army for six years, having joined the National Guard in Missouri at age fourteen and gained invaluable experience at Fort Benning – he had graduated so high in his class that he had been kept on as an instructor. He had finally joined the 99th Division that March, at the same time as several hundred disgruntled Advanced Specialized Training Program (ASTP)[4] students whose college training programs had been abruptly canceled. Soaring casualties in the Pacific and the massive buildup to D-Day had meant grabbing every potential infantryman the army could get.

'I'd like you to be the new I&R platoon leader,' Kriz had told Bouck.[5] 'First, go through the records and pick out people who graduated from high school, preferably those who were in college. There's a group of ASTPs who've got high IQs and were on college campuses until recently. They're unhappy but trainable. We're going to get into a training program. I'll give you the schedule. We've got all summer to do it. I think we're going to head for combat by early fall.'

In selecting the twenty-five men for the platoon, Bouck and Kriz had judged athletic ability as crucial. Long, difficult patrols behind enemy lines would require superb stamina and fitness. All the men also had to be experts with the M-1 rifle. And every one must have an IQ of at least 110. The platoon would be an elite unit – Kriz's chief source of information about the enemy's activities. It would comprise the best men from the previously undermanned platoon, outstanding privates from infantry companies, and several ASTPers.

It was around 5:00 A.M. when Platoon Sergeant William Slape – a dark-haired, taciturn, Oklahoman – ordered the reconstituted I&R platoon to form up outside their barracks.

Bouck and Kriz had been impressed by Slape while selecting men to bring the platoon up to full strength. Blunt and fiercely patriotic, he was tough and uncompromising but fair with the men.

Slape, like Bouck, had grown up in a Depression-hit community at the heart of the dust bowl, where a spare dime for a movie was as scarce as a job. Unemployment and poverty had left their marks on Slape. He possessed a brittle temper, a total lack of sentimentality, a readiness to use his fists, and an almost religious belief in the character-defining benefits of hard physical labor, having worked in logging and in the oil fields of Texas before joining the army in 1937. He took immense pride in trying to make any unit he commanded the best in its regiment, cajoling his men with odd-sounding 'Okie' profanities and drawling 'Bullsheeeet' when they flubbed assignments.

Slape reminded several men of a particularly foul-mouthed high school football coach, the kind who commanded respect because of his experience and pride in the team. In the eyes of the most intellectual of the platoon, Private Vernon Leopold, a German-Jewish immigrant, Slape was certainly no 'ranting drill-sergeant' like the kind who greeted the newly arrived ASTPers by handing out checkerboard shoulder patches and shouting, 'Get those fucking pisspots[6] off your shoulders!' He was a man of few words who looked 'just like Gary Cooper.' A stern stare from Slape was more than enough to get Leopold and the other men working the way he wanted things done – by the book, the 99th Division way, or not at all.

That July morning, Major Kriz ordered Slape's men to stand at ease, and then he stepped forward. Up close, he was an imposing figure – six-foot-one-inch, a trim 185 pounds, with alert eyes and a pointed nose.

'You men have been specially picked for this platoon,' he said. 'I have chosen Lieutenant Bouck here to be your leader. This is no ordinary platoon and I expect you to do your very best.'

Kriz saluted Bouck and then hopped in the jeep and sped away.

'In time, we will be a great platoon,' said Bouck. 'If you have any questions, go through Platoon Sergeant Slape and I'll make myself available. We're now going to start by seeing that you are physically capable of what we need to do. We're going to run the obstacle course.'

The men marched over to the camp's notorious course where many a new recruit had broken a limb, received skin-peeling rope burns, or snagged himself badly on tight coils of barbed wire.

The first challenge was to get over an eight-foot-high wall. Beyond that lay several twenty-foot logs – fourteen inches in diameter – that the men would have to walk across. If they fell, they would land in deep mud and water. Having crossed the logs, they would have to swing themselves across another stretch of water by a rope. The trickiest section would be the barbed wire tunnels, slightly larger than a man's body

'Every morning,' Bouck told the men, 'we'll meet here at 6:00 A.M. and I will lead you around the obstacle course. Those who can't handle it will be asked to leave. In fact, those who don't want to follow this type of training can leave – right now.'

None of the men took up the offer.

Private Vernon Leopold formed up with the men before the first obstacle. Of all the platoon members, he was the least athletic – a tall, somewhat clumsy twenty-year-old with curly hair and a dark complexion.[7]

Leopold had arrived in the United States with his family in 1938, having fled persecution in Hitler's Nazi Germany. 'After Hitler came to power in 1933,' recalled Leopold, 'we Jewish kids were barred from schools but I was exempt because of my father's military record. But that didn't stop the harassment. It had gotten so bad that even our gym teacher singled out a Jewish classmate who couldn't jump a hurdle and called him a "lame Jewboy." . . . My family found a way for me to attend school in England through the help of the Jewish Community Council of London. I went to school there until in July 1938 when I joined my parents and younger brother on their escape from Düsseldorf. . . . After our arrival in New York, we again moved – to the

Detroit west side. I wanted to enlist but I couldn't because, technically, I was an alien. Enemy alien or not I eventually managed to get drafted in June 1943 by volunteering for induction.' More than any of the other platoon members, Leopold hated the Nazis and understood that the Axis powers must be defeated. 'I didn't need to watch the indoctrination films like the others. I knew why I was going to war.'

That July morning in Camp Maxey, however, it didn't matter a jot how much Leopold hated the Nazis. Was he also a 'lame Jewboy,' or could he measure up to the other bookish ASTPers who had also joined the 99th Division?

Private Leopold started toward the wall.

Lyle Bouck could see that he was poorly coordinated simply from the way he walked.

Leopold tried to jump up and get over but could not.

'Well, he knows how to speak and read German,' Bouck said to himself. 'That's vital. But, goddam, what am I going to do with him? We sure can't use him physically.'

The others in the platoon followed Leopold.

Soon, it was obvious which men were the jocks who had excelled in sports:

ASTPer Corporal Aubrey 'Schnoz' McGehee, a 230-pound Mississipian with a prominent nose and very tightly curled hair who had played on the defensive line for Lousiana State University's football team.

Private Robert 'Siv' Silvola, a swift-footed basketball player with Scandinavian ancestry and features – green eyes, blond hair, and pale skin.

Corporal Sam Jenkins, an easy-going Texan from El Paso who looked like 'a classic New England WASP'[8] until he opened his mouth, and who had also excelled at high school basketball.

Sergeant George 'Pappy' Redmond, a six-foot-one-inch, sandy-haired 'gentle giant' who was slow and laid back (hence his teammates' nickname for him, short for 'grandpa'), except on his high school football team in Danville, Virginia, where he was voted MVP in 1941.

And then there was another ASTPer, Private First Class Carlos Fernandez, also from El Paso, Texas, a wise-cracking, handsome man whose parents had been born in Mexico and who planned to be a doctor after the war.

The fastest over the course was the clean-cut, fair-haired son of a Serbian immigrant, twenty-three-year-old Private First Class Risto 'Milo' Milosevich – another ASTPer who had joined the 99th Division from Tarleton State College where he had studied basic engineering.

That first morning, Milosevich ran toward the wall, kicked himself up, and climbed over expertly, and then began to pass most of the platoon as he ran the course seemingly without effort. Unlike the jocks, Milosevich had not played on his high school football team. He had not lacked athletic ability – he had been dropped for ripping a guy's jersey. And he was one of the few attached men in the platoon. On November 3, 1943, he had married his sweetheart from Garfield High School in east Los Angeles, where he'd grown up the son of a hard-driving construction contractor. It wasn't until he had reached grade school that he learned to speak English rather than Serbo-Croat.[9]

Each morning that July, the men gathered at 6:00 A.M. Milosevich would be among the last to start the course but would invariably finish first. It wasn't long before the others in the platoon decided to take him down a peg or two. One morning, Milosevich sprinted toward the wall. There were loud peals of laughter as he slammed into it and cried out in pain. 'The bastards had wet that wall down,' Milosevich recalled. 'I ran full speed and hit the board, and my foot slipped – both knees hit the goddamned board. I couldn't run the course after that for five or six days and had to carry all the guys' stuff around.'

A week into the rigorous training schedule, three men were not performing well. Bouck took them aside: 'Look, for your benefit and our benefit, I'm going to ask you to go back to the unit you were in and we'll get three other guys.'

The remaining men understood that Bouck now meant business. 'He told us to quit goofing off,' recalled one of them. 'Our previous officer, a guy called Thomas, was a real cowboy, wore his .45 hung low, had a little black moustache, only worried about himself. One of the guys had forced beer down his throat at his wedding party – that was how much we respected him. We were thinking when we met Lyle, "Who's this ninety-day wonder, this kid?" But he made it very clear we wouldn't be getting away with stuff anymore. He was the kind you felt you could go down the river with. And boy, when it came down to it later, he sure proved it.'

Even though Leopold had made little progress, he was not asked to leave the platoon, much to the irritation of his squad leader, Sergeant George Redmond. Redmond didn't want Platoon Sergeant Slape breathing down his neck because Leopold had difficulties with the obstacle course. But he recognized that Leopold's fluency in German and proficiency with a radio made him irreplaceable.

Yet Leopold soon rose high on Slape's 'shit list' when the platoon sergeant discovered he had tried to get a transfer out of the platoon to a different unit where his natively fluent German and radio skills would be better employed.[10] As Slape saw it, by going to division headquarters to request a transfer, Leopold had disregarded the chain of command, and he would not let him forget it. No man was too good for his platoon, certainly not a gangly, bookish Jew with a thick Kraut accent. It wasn't long before Leopold became the butt of much of the platoon's practical jokes.

Both Slape and Milosevich, the least racially tolerant of the men, took particular delight in short-sheeting Leopold. Another favorite trick was to move the rifle rack that ran down the center of the barracks so that Leopold would stumble over it after lights out, especially after he'd had a few beers. (Officers could drink liquor, while the men were limited to weak, watery beer.) Mops as well as rifles were laid from bunk to bunk, making the few yards to his bunk a veritable obstacle course. Even when he was sat in the back of a jeep with his radio, Leopold was not safe. Slape would rabbit-jump him – start the jeep and rapidly pull away – and laugh out loud as Leopold tumbled onto his backside in the dust and dirt.

Leopold was not cold-shouldered by his fellow ASTPers and others, however, and quickly made friends in the platoon, among them another radio operator, Technician Fourth Class James Fort, a slightly built twenty-one-year-old from Memphis, Tennessee, who had spent much of the Depression working on his grandmother's farm in Mississippi before being drafted in 1942.

James Fort had extraordinarily bright red hair and was a natural soldier. He enjoyed the discipline and structure of army life so much that he would eventually serve twenty-two years. And he had quickly realized, as Bouck had, that Leopold would be vital in decoding and translating German radio transmissions, and like others Fort admired Leopold for good-naturedly putting up with the constant ribbing.

As the weeks passed, Fort also gained a keen respect for his youthful commanding officer, who quickly saw to it that the men got whatever could be provided to keep up their spirits. Unlike other young lieutenants in the division, Bouck did not chew the platoon out for the slightest infraction or assign menial, mind-numbing tasks, such as cleaning the officers' mess with a toothbrush or picking up countless cigarette butts. 'Compared to other officers he was tops,' recalled Fort. 'He thought about people. He saw that we had everything we wanted, within reason – we were housed well, clothed well, had good chow.'

Another of the platoon who was far from a jock was a reserved, methodical, and well-spoken Minnesotan, Technician Fifth Class Robert Lambert, a gifted communications expert who had excelled in academics in his high school in the tight-knit rural town of Renville. 'We were representative of our country's make-up as we came from eighteen different states,' he later recalled of his platoon comrades, 'reflecting the regional differences of the East, West, Midwest, and South. Because a selection criterion had been some understanding of one or more of the various European languages and national customs, the platoon members formed a multi-ethnic group as well.'

It took several weeks, however, for this diverse group to gel. The men were at first divided between those who had been in the original platoon and the newly arrived draftees and ASTPers. Many of the ASTPers felt that their noncom superiors, country boys such as Slape, resented their education and assumed they were soft and lazy. Matters weren't helped by the division's commander, General Walter E. Lauer, who had set the tone when he greeted the ASTPers to the platoon with these words: 'Young men, you are the cream of the crop, but the cream is sour.' This only increased hostility between the noncoms and the new arrivals, 'jerks who thought they were special and looked down on us . . . and who joked that men [like Slape] got their first pair of shoes when they went into the Army.'

Twenty-one-year-old Private Louis Kalil did not look down on the new 'quiz kids' (ASTPers) sharing his barracks. An old-time 99er, who had been with the division since shortly after its activation, he had belonged to the original 394th I&R platoon before it had been reorganized that spring.[11] It was obvious to him that the college boys were just as fit and adaptable to army life as the division's stalwarts who had not qualified for the ASTP program.

A Mishawaka, Indiana, native of Lebanese descent, Kalil shrugged off some of the men's lighthearted jibes that he was a 'camel-jockey' and got on with everyone in the platoon – everyone except Private Victor Adams,[12] 'a scrawny little guy from Buffalo New York.' Adams was one of the platoon's three privates who could speak German. 'I was born in an immigrant neighborhood of German and Irish peoples,' Adams explained. 'I first entered service in 1939 when the Germans invaded Poland. Our people believed service was a debt we owed for being citizens of the Republic.'

Kalil resented Adams for boasting that he had been in the service so long, implying that he was somehow more patriotic and a 'better soldier.' 'Nobody cared for him,' recalled Kalil. 'He used to peeve everybody. He thought he was better than the rest of us because he was regular army.' Kalil also suspected that when the going got tough, Adams would be a goldbricker – the infantry's term for any man who did not pull his weight. Before they had even been posted to a combat zone, Adams was always bitching about something or acting the smart ass.[13]

For his runner, Lieutenant Bouck soon selected an aggressive and eager Greek immigrant, Private Bill 'Tsak' James,[14] a broad-faced, stocky nineteen-year-old who wanted to be a lawyer and had been in the ASTP program at John Tarleton State College in Texas with Private First Class Risto Milosevich. An excellent scout and superb shot, especially proficient with a grease gun (submachine gun), James quickly established an effective relationship with Bouck. 'Bill was an excitable "let me do it" kind of guy,' recalled Bouck. 'He was always wanting to do something. I thought, "Well, that's the kind of guy I need. Because there is probably a lot of things I won't want to do and all I need to do is mention it to him and he'll be ready."'

James was well liked by others in the platoon who came to see him as a kind of ever-eager, macho mascot. 'I just can't wait to get in there and let those bastards have it,' James would say.

'Whenever we'd see James come by,' recalled Louis Kalil, 'we'd always shout out, "Here comes Bouck's dog robber [lackey]!" But James didn't seem to mind. He had a sense of humor. He wasn't the type to be hurt by stuff like that.'

As James and his fellow ASTPers showed their mettle that summer on forced marches in which 'you could walk in the mud and have sand blowing in your face all the time' and seemingly endless night patrols, the platoon started to work as a team. 'They molded themselves into a good organization,' recalled Kriz. 'They developed a love of each other – a respect for each other.'

At first, Platoon Sergeant Slape regarded the I&R platoon's days off after night patrols with disdain, telling Louis Kalil's squad that they were 'doggin' it' – slacking off. Indeed, these rest periods looked awfully like goldbricking to his fellow platoon sergeants in the regular infantry companies from which the platoon had mostly been formed. But when Slape himself experienced the long hours scrambling around the prickly scrub in heat that made the men feel as if 'a hot, wet sponge was being squeezed dry all over us by a malevolent god,' he soon changed his mind. Any doubts about Bouck's capabilities also disappeared, although the older Slape subtly made it clear that he, not Bouck, was the more experienced soldier.

It was also soon obvious to every man in the platoon that Bouck was a protégé of Kriz. They got along uncommonly well, given their differences in rank and experience. In Bouck's eyes, Kriz was something of a father figure even though he was less than a decade older. Bouck's own father had been a dishonest 'loser' unlike Kriz, 'the finest officer, soldier and leader' he had ever seen.

Direct, courteous, and always sympathetic, Kriz was nonetheless not an easy man to get to know. While he did not pull rank, he was rather aloof with most other junior officers, having learned not to get too close to men because their deaths would be all the harder to take. He did not discuss his past, for he had already seen enough of war's injustices and horrors (he had been in the bitter fighting in North Africa) to know that good officers do not brag and the truly brave mostly go unrewarded. He did not even tell Bouck how he had been wounded.[15]

In early August 1944, a new regimental commander, Colonel Donald Riley, arrived at the 394th headquarters. Unlike General Lauer, the regiment's new commanding officer was no 'tooter of his own horn' who gave 'windy speeches on hot days' and spouted platitudes such as 'Do it now, do it right, and do it with a smile' – prompting the men to joke contemptuously that 'it' meant sex. Riley had first seen combat in 1918 and had since served with seven infantry regiments. He was incisive, modest, and soon popular with other experienced veterans such as Major Kriz. Before the year was out, his ability to make decisions calmly under immense pressure would help save the regiment from crushing defeat and capture.

Not long after Riley's arrival, it was announced that the division would soon break camp and head overseas. The platoon members took advantage of their last weekend passes to visit the local town, Paris, eight miles away, or Dallas, around two hours' drive from Camp Maxey. Often the men's first stop would be a mom-and-pop restaurant where they could compensate for the Camp Maxey diet of powdered eggs that looked like yellow glue, black-eyed peas that tasted like boiled hay, and grits that were, to one 99er, no more than a 'tasteless pile of corn discards that even a sow would reject.'

In Paris, Lyle Bouck and a friend from Company C, Lieutenant Matthew Reid, gorged on watermelons that the locals sold from stands hastily erected in their front yards. Although the town of eighteen thousand had more than its fair share of prostitutes as 'pretty as the blue Texas sky,' Bouck did not indulge. The army had consumed most of his teenage years, and he had yet to enjoy many of the other men's rites of passage. He did not drink or smoke, and the only girls he wrote to were classmates from grade school – he had quit high school after his freshman year.

Many of the platoon eagerly forked out five dollars for a bus ticket to Dallas. Original platoon members – Private Louis Kalil and three buddies – rented a hotel room, got drunk, partied with easy girls, and left plenty of wreckage behind.

Platoon Sergeant Bill Slape and Private First Class Risto Milosevich also escaped Camp Maxey together that August.

'Slape had no fear,' Risto recalled. 'No fear – of dying, of anything.' Both liked to drink and rough it up in low-down and dirty honky-tonks, and they trusted each other not to tell tales about their escapades back in the barracks. 'In one bar,' Milosevich also remembered, 'three men jumped Slape and were going to beat the shit out of him. A bunch of us from the platoon got there, and we grabbed them and pounded them against the wall. He never forgot that. "Risto!" he'd say. "You saved my life. Those guys were going to kill me."'

In late August, the entire 99th Division was mustered for a final parade before boarding trains and heading overseas. Many men passed out as they waited several hours beneath the scorching Texas sun for General Lauer to arrive and then make another of his windy speeches. Lauer told the men they were finally 'ready for combat. . . . You are the greatest fighting outfit in the world.' Some of the men broke into smiles, knowing only too well that they were not. But for most, having survived the long summer of training, Lauer's words echoed their own confidence. And the sight of thousands of men marching in lockstep filled many with a newfound sense of pride in the 99th Division.

The last few days in Camp Maxey were spent cleaning and boxing equipment. There were no more dehydrating hikes and mind-numbing drills that made the ASTPers feel like khaki-clad automatons with a serial number rather than a personality. Finally, tensions between the ASTPers and old-guard privates and noncoms had eased. Very few men accepted last-minute offers of transfers to noncombat units: already their squads and platoons had become surrogate families, and to abandon them now would feel like desertion and betrayal.

*

On September 10, 1944, the 394th's I&R platoon members cleared their barracks, shouldered their one hundred-pound duffel bags, and marched out of Camp Maxey. To their surprise, the men boarded trains that were equipped with folding bunks, a distinct improvement over the ancient, ill-ventilated carriages they had ridden in to Camp Maxey. Every man wondered where they were headed. North or west? If they went west, they were bound for the death islands of the South Pacific to fight the merciless Japanese. Many were resigned to going west. Surely the training in the intense heat and humidity had been in preparation for jungle warfare? But to their relief the trains headed north, their destination Camp Miles Standish, Massachusetts, the Boston port of embarkation for the European Theater of Operations (ETO).[16]

'The journey took several days,' recalled one 394th infantryman. 'As we travelled through towns during the day, people would line the tracks to wave. It was good to know that the people of America were rooting for us. In one Ohio town, the people bought us gifts. The whole town lined the tracks, reaching up to clasp our hands; they knew where we were going and in their hearts they knew, as we did, that many on the train would never return.'

Finally, the troop trains pulled into rail yards near Camp Miles Standish, midway between Boston and Rhode Island. The hastily constructed camp, comprising 'tar paper shanties,' was a far cry from Camp Maxey. But the men were kept too busy to complain too much. There were new physicals, injections, and psychological tests to see if they were potential 'neurasthenics' who would fall apart at the sound of the first enemy shell passing overhead. The evenings were less frenzied, and the platoon members talked about going overseas – for all but Private Vernon Leopold it would be their first trip across the Atlantic. And they wrote letters home, though they had to be careful what they said, knowing that from now on Bouck and other junior officers would censor the mail lest they give away any military information. The thirsty would go to the PX for a beer and, if they wanted a second before closing time, immediately rejoin a long line as they drank it.

On Wednesday, September 20, 1944, the men attended a final orientation lecture. The following day, they received instruction on chemical warfare, how to abandon ship, and how to stay clean and build latrines once they reached their final destination in Europe – the American front lines, which had by this time reached as far as the heavily defended German border city of Aachen, north of a mountainous and thickly wooded region called the Ardennes.

Before embarkation, each man received a last pass. Lieutenant Lyle Bouck used his to visit the parents of the friend he had made in Company C – Lieutenant Matthew Reid – before being made the platoon commander. He had dinner with Reid and his parents at their home in Providence, Rhode Island, and savored his last hours in America outside a barracks. Little did Reid and Bouck know, as they ate their last hearty American meal, that in just three months they would be sharing a few hard crumbs of bread as they fought to keep each other alive.

On the evening of September 28, the entire division was again united to listen to a final pep talk from General Lauer. As they again waited for him to make his entry, this time into an outdoor athletic stadium, some men took out their army-issue condoms, inflated them, and then patted them into the air and from line to line. 'The GIs roared with laughter and jumped up to keep the "balloons" moving along,' recalled one 99er. 'Officers ran up and down the stairs bellowing orders that were ignored. And chaplains went down on their knees to pray; also ignored.'

The rubbers, designed to curtail a massive outbreak of venereal disease sweeping troops throughout Europe, sailed out of the stadium and landed on passing cars and were popped by the dozen by people in bus lines and walking close by. Lauer, needless to say, was far from impressed. His men's behavior, he thought, was nothing short of 'childish.'

The next morning, the platoon boarded day coaches and then walked along a pier on the Charles River where their ship, the *Excelsior*, was docked. It was just after dawn when they filed up a long, narrow gangplank with flimsy rope guards to keep them from plunging into the cold waters below. Some were a little shaky as they walked across the last connection between them and America. They literally felt as if they were walking the plank. One 99er was so nervous that he lost his grip, fell overboard, and was quickly fished out by one of the harbor patrols assigned to picking downed 99ers out of the water.

The *Excelsior* was part of a convoy of passenger liners and ex-freighters bound for various British ports. Lieutenant Lyle Bouck went to its relatively spacious and comfortable officers' quarters near the top deck. His men clambered down to the bowels of the ship and into a smoky hold, close to the engine room and crammed with narrow canvas bunks with only eighteen inches separating each man.

Around midnight, the *Excelsior* slipped her moorings and steamed through choppy waters out of Boston harbor. Many of the men, particularly Lyle Bouck, were quickly seasick as the boat entered heavier seas. They would be served just two meals a day, but few would be able to keep them down for more than a few minutes.

There was no ventilation, so the platoon's hold, which

already stank from the throbbing engines' exhaust, also soon reeked of body odor and cigarette smoke. Private Louis Kalil remembered the crossing as an airless nightmare. Men would compete to pull guard duty so that they could go up on deck and fill their lungs with cool ocean breezes. Others tried to make the best of the trip and read *Reader's Digest* paperbacks or gambled.

'We'd see if we could get enough guys to make up a good game,' remembered Kalil. 'We were all gamblers except Leopold. . . . I had to show him how to play poker. And you know what? The cards just fell his way and he took us all for about three hundred dollars.'

Another 99er on the *Excelsior* recalled: 'They should have made a movie, "Misery on the *Excelsior*"! A shower in cold salt water was another "thrill" our "tour guides" failed to warn us about. What a scary thrill to see your relatively large "Liberty ship" at the bottom of a trough, looking up to a mountain range of waves. . . . The old ship did groan and creak some, which wasn't real comforting when swinging in a hammock several decks down.'

In his bunk far above in a converted stateroom, Lieutenant Bouck groaned and moaned with acute seasickness. He tried to continue his duties, having been assigned to teaching the men how to read foreign maps, but wave after wave of nausea interrupted the lessons as he vomited over the ship's side or into latrines awash with other men's retchings. 'It was the only time in my life I wanted to die,' he recalled. 'I was so sick.'

To add to Bouck's discomfort, a few days out from America there was a submarine alert. The *Excelsior* was badly exposed, farthest from the heart of the convoy, and he heard a fellow officer say, 'We're going to be it [the target].'

'Fuck the torpedoes!' groaned Bouck. 'Send them in.'

The submarine alerts went on for several days. One afternoon, as the men gathered for a drill on deck, Private Vernon Leopold saw actual depth charges being dropped and wondered whether the convoy was in fact being attacked. Then the *Excelsior* made her way through the Irish sea toward Liverpool. As the division convoy broke up to make for different ports, Leopold stood glumly at the ship's rail looking out at the gray seas. Like the others in the platoon, he was depressed, exhausted, and worried about soon going into combat.

Private First Class Risto Milosevich joined him at the rail.

'What the hell are you worried about?' asked Milosevich. 'You're on your way home!'

Shortly before they docked in Liverpool, Milosevich learned that he had become a father. The ship's tannoy system announced that he now had a baby girl, Carol-Ann.

Another of the platoon, twenty-four-year-old Private John B. Creger, already had a son. A wiry 165-pound farm boy, he had been drafted in 1942 and was one of the most lighthearted men in the platoon, always ready to play a practical joke. Three of his brothers – he had thirteen siblings – were also in service, but he worried most about his eighteen-year-old Irish wife, pregnant with their second child and living with her parents in Virginia.

The *Excelsior* arrived in Liverpool on October 10, 1944, beneath dirty gray skies. The men lugged their packs and filed onto the docks where scouse – Liverpudlian – dockers cracked jokes about how young this latest batch of Yanks looked. As they boarded a train bound for London, the men were each handed a paper bag containing sandwiches, an apple, and an orange. 'Don't open the windows,' they were ordered, 'and don't make any contact with the kids because they'll find out you've got apples and oranges and they'll be begging you for them.'

As the trains passed through stations, gaggles of emaciated, grubby children would line the platforms begging for food, knowing the green soldiers would take sympathy and hand them whatever they could spare. The apples and oranges had soon disappeared into the children's stomachs. One 99er also took a packet of crackers from his C rations and tossed it out of a window. An angelic-looking girl joined a scuffle and grabbed the prize but then screwed up her face in disgust.

'Give us somethin' else!' she soon cried, throwing the crackers back at the stunned GI. 'These taste fuckin' 'orrible.'

Late on October 10, 1944, the platoon arrived at a company-sized camp near the town of Beaminster on England's south coast. The men marched quietly to their new temporary home – a cold and drafty Quonset hut on the grounds of an ancestral home called Parnham House. If they had any fancy ideas of visiting the local beaches, they were warned, they should think again. Every stretch of sand along the English Channel was heavily mined. They were now the guests of a weary but utterly defiant country that had been under attack since 1939.

3. Wacht am Rhein

The Wolf's Lair – September 16, 1944

On September 16, 1944, Hitler held his usual daily conference with his generals and then called the most senior and trusted of them into a private room: Wilhelm Keitel, Alfred Jodl, Chief of Staff Heinz Guderain, and General Werner Kreipe, who was there on behalf of Reichsmarschall Hermann Göring. Hitler looked tired, his mouth slack, as if he was still suffering from the after-effects of the bomb explosion on July 20, 1944.

Jodl summed up the dire situation: The German army had more than nine million men in arms, but there had been well over a million casualties in the last three months alone, over half of these in the West. And now the Wehrmacht was under fierce pressure in the Ardennes, the mountainous area in Belgium and Luxembourg through which the Germans had successfully attacked in World War I and again in spring 1940.

The mention of the Ardennes appeared to animate Hitler.

'Stop!' he ordered Jodl.

There was a long silence.

'I have made a momentous decision,' Hitler finally declared. 'I am taking the offensive. Here – out of the Ardennes! Across the Meuse and on to Antwerp!'

Hitler banged his fist on a map spread out before him that showed the area in question. The Hitler of old, the utterly confident leader, had suddenly returned.

On September 25, Hitler ordered Jodl to draw up specific plans for an Ardennes offensive. Five panzer divisions were withdrawn from the eastern front as a massive logistical operation was set in motion, one that rivaled D-Day in its complexity and audacity and also, crucially, in its ultra-secret nature. The Germans knew that the Allies were now decoding their telegraph and radio communication because they had broken Ultra, the German code system, and so all German orders were relayed in person by officers sworn to secrecy.

On October 11, Jodl delivered his plan to Hitler. Operation Christrose envisioned the deployment of twelve panzer and eighteen infantry divisions. Two things were vital to success: complete surprise and bad weather so that the Allies could not enjoy their advantage of air superiority. The Meuse would need to be crossed within just forty-eight hours and Antwerp reached within a week. Speed would be of the essence.

An equally daring plan of deception was carried out. Rumors and false reports were spread, and General Keitel issued an order that no offensive action would occur on the Western Front; all armies were to concentrate on defending the Fatherland's borders.

By October 21, 1944, Hitler and Jodl had settled on a code name for the operation: *Wacht am Rhein* (Watch on the Rhine). It was a cunning title. If Allied intelligence came across it in decoded German reports, they would assume that the buildup of men was intended as a defensive maneuver in preparation for a fierce defense of the Rhine River, the last major physical barrier facing the Allies on their intended push into the heart of the Third Reich.

That same day, Otto Skorzeny arrived at the Wolf's Lair to report on his most recent escapade: the successful kidnapping the previous week of the son of the Hungarian dictator

Admiral Horthy and the seizure of the Citadel, Hungary's seat of government.

'Sit down and tell me about it – this Operation "Mickey Mouse."'

Skorzeny went into brief detail about the kidnap. Hitler laughed several times. Skorzeny finished his story and stood to leave.

'Stay, Skorzeny,' said Hitler. 'I am going to charge you with a new mission, perhaps the most important of your life. So far, very few people know that we are preparing in utmost secrecy a mission in which you are to play a principal part. In December, the German Army will launch a great offensive, the issue of which will be decisive to the destiny of our country.'

Hitler elaborated: The Allied leaders, having swept so far and fast across France and Belgium to the very borders of Germany, along the West Wall, were confidently predicting that the war would be over by Christmas. If Allied news reports were to be believed, General Dwight Eisenhower could choose to bury the German 'corpse' whenever he pleased. The enemy were complacent and overconfident; their supply lines were overextended; and they were in denial about a key sector of weakness, the Ardennes, and in particular the Losheim Gap, a nine-mile-wide break in a bitterly cold and inhospitable mountain range called the Schnee Eiffel.

'In Hitler's opinion,' recalled Skorzeny, 'neither the British nor the American people wanted this war any longer. Consequently, if the "German corpse" rose to strike a smashing blow in the west, the Allies, under the pressure of a public opinion made furious by having been hoodwinked, would perhaps be ready to conclude an armistice with this corpse which was so lively. Then we could throw all our divisions, all our armies into battle on the Eastern Front and, in a few months, liquidate the threat that weighed over Europe. Moreover, for almost a thousand years Germany had mounted guard against the Asiatic hordes and she would not fail in this sacred mission.'

Then Hitler explained Skorzeny's mission in detail. He wanted him to handpick the best men he could find and train them to pretend to be Americans. His elite team would operate behind enemy lines, wearing American uniforms, driving American jeeps, seizing key bridges across the vital Meuse River, and giving false orders to the Americans to create widespread chaos and then panic. Skorzeny's mission would be code-named 'Greif' after a mythical German bird.

'Your preparations must be completed by December first,' stressed Hitler. 'I know the time given to you is very short, but I count on you to do the impossible. Of course you yourself will be at the front when the time comes for your troops to go into action. However, I forbid you to venture into enemy lines; we cannot afford to lose you.'

Skorzeny was not pleased by this order. He had never forsaken his men while they carried out his orders. But he kept his counsel, resolving to tell his battalion commanders that he would join them if the situation became critical.

'I'm going to give you unlimited power to set up your brigade,' added Hitler. 'Use it, Colonel!'

Hitler stood up and held out his hand.

'Good-bye, Skorzeny. I expect to hear great things of Operation "Greif."'

The next morning, October 22, 1944, Hitler sent copies of his plan, Wacht am Rhein, to Field Marshal Walter Model, Hitler's choice to command the attack, and Field Marshal Gerd von Rundstedt, commander in chief of all ground forces in the West.

Rundstedt was older and conservative, widely respected by Wehrmacht troops, and viewed the plan as far too ambitious. Model was more daring but also quickly decided that Hitler's plan didn't 'have a leg to stand on.' During a meeting with Hitler, both agreed that more men were needed and the attack should proceed on a narrower front to stand a chance of breaking through the Allied lines effectively and then seizing Antwerp. They outlined alternative plans as Hitler paced impatiently back and forth before them.

'Don't you remember Frederick the Great?' Hitler finally interrupted. 'At Rossbach and Leuten he defeated enemies twice his strength. How? By a bold attack. . . . Why don't you people study history?'

The lesson was simple: Frederick had taken bold action, and then luck had turned his way, rewarding his courage. An alliance between his enemies had ruptured and Frederick had gone on to win the Franco-Prussian War.

'History will repeat itself,' maintained Hitler. 'The Ardennes will be my Rossbach and Leuten. And as a result another unpredictable historical event will take place: the Alliance against the Third Reich will suddenly split apart!'

Model and Rundstedt knew it was useless to argue further. Their best strategy would be to try to ensure the success of Hitler's plan by doing all they could to prepare adequately in the little time – around six weeks – that remained to them. And so, throughout November, they carefully amassed more than two hundred thousand troops and countless tons of supplies.

Twenty-five new divisions were created, comprising navy and Luftwaffe personnel, middle-aged men culled from industrial plants, and tens of thousands of the Hitler Youth, some as young as fifteen. Because Hitler doubted the loyalty of his Wehrmacht generals, he entrusted the make-or-break attack – through the Losheim Gap – to an old Nazi friend, SS General Sepp Dietrich, a burly, hard-drinking former sergeant in World War I, loyal follower since the 1920s, and now commander of the Sixth Panzer Army.

The planned offensive would be an SS victory. All SS units in the West would be withdrawn and would be re-equipped and reinforced for their new mission. In utter secrecy, hundreds of Panzer and Tiger tanks and thousands of self-propelled artillery pieces would then be sent back and placed behind the front lines and camouflaged so that Allied planes could not observe the buildup.

Parnham House, England – October 1944

October 1944 in England was, as usual, cold and rainy. Once Lyle Bouck and his platoon had settled into their new quarters, they began daily hikes into the countryside and practiced reconnaissance patrols. The nearby villages looked to them like scenes from Hollywood movies, with quaint thatched cottages, cobblestone streets, and greens where English boys, wearing shorts despite the chilly conditions, kicked around battered leather soccer balls.

The men knew they would be called to the front any day, so they resolved to make the best of their short stay in England. The nearest major town with a USO,[17] where English 'gals' served tea and biscuits, as the limeys called cookies, was in Beaminster.

In the town's pubs, the platoon sipped apple cider and warm pints of strong ale; ate countless fish and chips (served, to their surprise, in newspaper), steak and kidney puddings, and shepherd's pies; tried to cavort with British Land Army girls; played darts; and scratched their heads over the confusing British currency with its bobs, sixpences, and half-crowns before paying their bar bills.

Bouck had money to spare that fall. An avid baseball fan who had played as a boy in the same St. Louis neighborhood as the legendary Yogi Berra, he had bet a senior officer in the 394th fifty dollars that St. Louis would win the World Series that fall. Both men's bets were deposited with the regimental chaplain. Then *Stars and Stripes*, the overseas news-paper, announced that the St. Louis Cardinals and the St. Louis Browns would compete in the World Series. The officer tried to cancel the bet but the chaplain, siding with Bouck, who had not specified which St. Louis team would win, refused to return the officer's money.

On many nights, platoon members would return drunk to their Quonset hut. The local Brits were slow drinkers, able to nurse a pint for hours on end it seemed. But the youngest men in the platoon, still schoolboys in many respects, chugged back the hoppy brews in a few seconds with predictable results – a pint of British beer was four times the strength of the 'piss-water' they had been issued back at Camp Maxey.

Among the heaviest drinkers was Private James Silvola, who earned extra beer money by becoming the platoon's barber. He almost started a fistfight with Private First Class Carlos Fernandez one night when he urinated in Fernandez's bed, mistaking it for the latrine. 'Hell, if you can't hold your beer,' yelled Private Louis Kalil, 'don't go out at night!'

The high jinks continued each morning before roll call. Sergeant George Redmond would place his penis on the pillow of a sleeping man, wake him, and crack up when he saw the man's horrified reaction. Back in Camp Maxey, Redmond had also entertained the platoon by pulling out a guitar and changing the words to hillbilly songs that he sang with an exaggerated Southern twang: 'I've got a big fat dong, It's big and strong and twelve inches long.'

Inevitably, the high spirits would backfire, especially with locals who had tolerated an 'American occupation' of GIs since late 1943 when millions of 'overpaid, oversexed' Yanks had arrived in Britain in the buildup to D-Day. Fights between drunken 99ers and Brits were common that fall as men relieved their pent-up anxiety and aggression in town-center brawls that were usually quickly broken up by MPs.

Private First Class Risto Milosevich recalled one night when Private Bill James returned to the barracks 'a bloody mess,' having been beaten up by 'Tommies,' as English soldiers were called: 'We climbed in all the jeeps and started looking for them. Finally, we found them and beat the shit out of them. We figured James probably had had it coming to him; he'd probably been trying to steal one of their girls or something. But we didn't care. We just beat the crap out of them.'

Other than Beaminster, the platoon's favorite destination on a weekend pass was London, specifically Leicester Square and Piccadilly Circus, notorious for its 'Piccadilly Commandos' – prostitutes – who roamed the heart of the city's heavily bombed West End.[18]

In late October, Private Vernon Leopold and radio operator Jim Fort buddied up on a three-day pass to London. Leopold had been to school in London in the mid-1930s and was keen to show Fort his old haunts as well as visit his father's cousin.

The pair arrived in London one afternoon by train, wandered through the streets in places piled with fresh rubble caused by V-1 bombs, and took a room at the Regent Palace Hotel in Piccadilly where Leopold's father had stayed on visits to London before the war. They strolled around Soho and then headed for dinner at a fancy restaurant. In the subways beneath them – the London Underground – thousands of families huddled on blankets with cardboard boxes containing their family possessions; the cries of frightened babies and children echoed along the squalid platforms that had for some been their nightly homes since the Blitz began in 1940.

The restaurant's menu was remarkably fine given wartime British rationing. As Leopold and Fort ate, they noticed an elegantly dressed young woman sitting alone at a nearby table. Before long, she was chatting away with the two unworldly 99ers. Then she looked at her watch.

'You know,' said the charming lady, 'I have only about a half an hour.'

'A half an hour to do what?' asked Leopold.

'To find somebody to go to bed with.'

'What's the deal?' asked Fort, the ranking noncom.

'Well,' she replied, 'I'll take a guinea from each of you.'

Leopold and Fort declined the offer and fled to their hotel, where they asked for a wake-up call. The following morning, there was a knock on the door. Leopold opened the door, and a pretty chambermaid entered and walked over to Fort's bed. He was fast asleep. She started to gently shake him awake, whispering, 'Time to wake up.'

Fort opened his eyes.

'I must be in heaven; you are an angel,' he said groggily.

The maid was indeed strikingly attractive. She was the spitting image of Angela Lansbury, who would become a major Hollywood star.

Before leaving London and with Fort in tow, Leopold managed to visit his father's cousin, Siegfried. While Leopold attended school in London, Siegfried, who was director of

Dr. Scholl's Footwear Products, had looked after Leopold. When he heard that Leopold was headed for the front lines, Siegfried made him a farewell present of a can of foot powder. He told him that it might help to prevent blisters and sores in foxholes, a common and debilitating condition for soldiers on the western front.

When Leopold and Fort returned to camp, their platoon buddies eagerly listened to their London 'war stories.' Private John Creger had never heard of the name 'Siegfried' except in connection with the Siegfried Line – Germany's famous western defense bulwark that the division would someday soon attack. He pestered Leopold and Fort endlessly for a close description of this generous 'Uncle Siegfried' who had sent him off to the war with a can of foot powder. He and others roared with laughter at Leopold's description of his father's cousin as a 'well-groomed' Dr. Scholl executive.

'Well-groomed?' As far as they knew, only horses and dogs get groomed, and so 'well-groomed' became a platoon buzzword.

The next day the platoon learned that the 99th Division was again shipping out, this time bound for the front lines. The fun and games were over. On October 24, 1944, just two weeks after arriving in Britain, all men were restricted to camp while MPs combed the area for AWOLs (soldiers absent without leave) who had overstayed their three-day passes in local villages and towns. On November 3, the members of the 394th Regiment boarded trucks and were taken to a deserted train station. It was so cold that some men started a fire with benches to keep warm.

Just after dawn the next day, Lieutenant Lyle Bouck and his men boarded a ferry boat in Southampton. 'I guess I was like most of the guys,' recalled Private Louis Kalil. 'At that point I thought it was maybe fifty-fifty I'd make it home.'

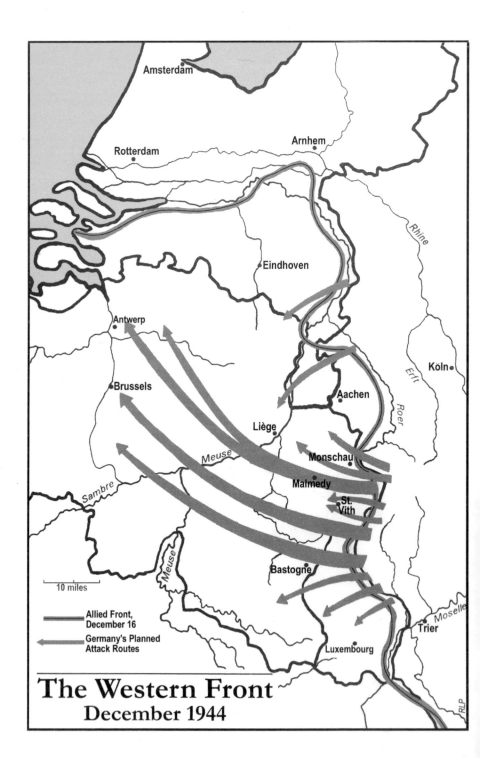

Amsterdam

Rotterdam

Arnhem

Eindhoven

Antwerp

Köln

Brussels

Aachen

Liège

Monschau

Meuse

Malmedy

Sambre

St. Vith

Meuse

Bastogne

Moselle

Trier

10 miles

Luxembourg

Allied Front,
December 16

Germany's Planned
Attack Routes

Rhine

Erft

Roer

The Western Front
December 1944

4. The Ghost Front

The 394th Infantry Regiment crossed the English Channel overnight, arriving in Le Havre on November 5 to be greeted by their first sight of the intense fighting that had left most Norman towns and cities in ruins. Half-sunken ships littered the harbor. Le Havre's docks had been flattened by Allied bombing, and so the men made their way to shore in LCIs (Landing Craft Infantry).

Many infantry companies were ordered to march through Le Havre's shattered streets, but Lieutenant Lyle Bouck and his men sped through the city in jeeps, weaving between burnt-out tanks and vehicles. It was late afternoon when they pulled up in a muddy field just outside the city. Their first task was to clear it of mines before setting up pup tents and digging in for the night. Already there was a bitter chill of winter in the air, and that night temperatures dropped to near freezing.

The next morning, the platoon again piled into jeeps. 'We were given a strip map,' recalled Robert Lambert, 'and [told to lead] the regiment into Belgium.' Unlike the newsreels, there were no cheering crowds full of pretty mademoiselles eager to smother their liberators with kisses and pour wine down their throats. Several weeks had passed since the Yanks had first arrived, and locals were no longer so welcoming as they now struggled to restore essential services and find food. Besides, there was no time to stop and fraternize. The jeeps sped on, without headlamps at night, bouncing along rutted lanes heading toward the Belgian border. In one village, a local held up a bottle of cognac. Private Vernon Leopold gladly accepted it and took a swig, and the jeep moved on before he could hand it back.

It was, according to several accounts of the 99th's trip, a rare incident of generosity. 'Going through the narrow streets of one small town at night,' recalled a fellow 99er from the 395th Regiment, 'we thought it was raining on our heads. But it was the local citizens emptying their chamber pots on us and it wasn't all liquid either.'

The first stop was the Belgian town of Aubel, the 99th's assigned concentration area, just across the French border. Here they would await specific orders before moving up to the heavily fortified Siegfried Line along the German-Belgian border, known to the Germans as the West Wall.

On November 7, 1944, the platoon members again pitched their pup tents and resigned themselves to another miserable night, this time in a muddy field outside Aubel.

Leopold could speak passable French and struck up a conversation with the farmer who owned the field. Before long, the farmer was offering the platoon the use of his barn for shelter. 'Needless to say,' recalled Leopold, 'Lyle Bouck immediately accepted the man's hospitality; not only that, within the hour the entire I&R platoon had hot water for shaving, real fresh milk to drink, and other refreshments. I discovered to my great joy, thus, that speaking the language of the area would prove to be a great asset.'

Leopold's standing with the platoon rose even further when the farmer invited them to eat breakfast in his kitchen the next morning.

As it turned out, Leopold's linguistic ability 'also had its burdens.' Within hours, Colonel Donald Riley, the 394th's commanding officer, got wind of Leopold's diplomatic skills and ordered him to accompany him, three bodyguards, and Major Robert Kriz on visits to other units camped nearby.

Earlier that day, the 394th's companies lined up at the quartermaster station adjacent to regimental headquarters to be issued galoshes and overshoes. Leopold had big feet – size 12D – and the GIs on supply detail were unable to find a pair of overshoes his size. Only later did he learn that Kriz, whose feet were the same size, had already been issued the only galoshes that size that had been on hand. Leopold was left with just his two pairs of ordinary GI-issue leather boots for slogging through the snow and mud of the area.

Throughout the day as he accompanied Colonel Riley, Leopold stood guard shivering outside tents and farm-houses, where officers of the frontline units were quartered, in driving sleet and snow. Soon, the lanes and fields had turned to muddy, freezing slush. When he got back to the platoon, Leopold pulled off his sodden boots and discovered that his toes had gone numb. Without overshoes, it didn't matter now how much of Dr. Scholl's foot powder he used. Unless he could keep his feet dry and warm, the mild frostbite would develop into a serious case of trench foot.

On November 10, 1944, the 394th received Field Order No. 1 from divisional command: 'Regimental Combat Team was to relieve Regimental Combat Team 60 of the 9th Division on 14 November 1944, and prepare plans to act as a counterattack force in the division sector.'

The men once more jumped into their jeeps and headed into the heart of industrial Belgium. Now the locals were more welcoming. There were friendly smiles from dark-haired, olive-skinned women wearing silk stockings, grateful to the Americans who had liberated them just weeks before.

In the countryside, the men saw their first evidence of Hitler's scorched-earth policy for his armies in retreat. In some villages, every building had been gutted, every barn burnt to the ground, every animal killed. Crops had been sprayed with acid, wells had been poisoned, homes had been ransacked, and even mattresses had been slashed with bayonets.

It started to snow heavily as the platoon began the long ascent toward the Losheim Gap where they would set up operations in the hamlet of Hünningen, a grim collection of around twenty-five stone farmhouses and cottages ten miles from the Siegfried Line. The winter issue for GIs in Europe was a shirt, a field jacket, trousers, a wool overcoat and beanie cap, and long underwear. But the clothing had yet to be issued and so, as they climbed into the Ardennes, the biting winds and drifting snow made for a miserable introduction to the fast-approaching winter. It was impossible to keep warm or dry in their midweight combat jackets.

When the convoy stopped the men lit fires, but for security reasons these had to be extinguished after dark, which came surprisingly early at around 5:00 P.M. In sodden sleeping bags, the platoon shivered and swore, damning the weather and this godforsaken corner of Europe.

When the men woke in darkness the next morning, they discovered that ice had formed on the inside of their tents. Outside, a foot of fresh snow had blanketed everything that didn't contain a GI: jeeps, chow trucks, half-tracks, artillery pieces. To one 394th major, the thick frosting looked beautiful set against the backdrop of mature pines planted in perfect rows. But for almost all the dogfaces – ordinary GIs – under his command, the Christmas card vista made them feel utterly miserable as they chewed their partly frozen C rations and chocolate-substitute D-bars.

The platoon members set out once more, now with specific orders to relieve the 9th Division, their jeeps slipping and sliding through a fresh foot of snow that had fallen in just an hour the night before.

'Do you think you'll know anyone still in the 9th Division?' Lieutenant Bouck asked Major Kriz as they began the last leg of the journey.

'I doubt it.'

Indeed, it was extremely unlikely that any of the officers and men in the 9th Division's 60th Regiment, to which Kriz had belonged, would still be with the division. After fighting its way across North Africa and then playing a key role in the invasion of Sicily, the 9th Division – nicknamed the 'Go-Devils' – had fought its way 450 miles across France that summer. Then, on September 13, it had penetrated 6 miles beyond the Siegfried Line into a heavily forested 50-square-mile region just to the north of the Losheim Gap – the Hürtgen Forest, which was bounded by the cities of Monschau, Dueren, and Aachen. Within days, Kriz's former regiment had dubbed the area a 'green hell' where the pine trees were so tightly packed that men wandered lost and dazed for days on end. On October 24, 1944, the 9th Division had been relieved. In six weeks of constant attrition, it had advanced three thousand yards on a 3-mile front at a cost of 3,836 casualties – an American had died or been wounded for every bloody yard. Major Kriz's old regiment, the 60th, had been virtually wiped out, suffering almost a 100 percent turnover in men.

The Ardennes Forest – November 11, 1944

The platoon moved closer and closer to the Siegfried Line. From their jeeps, the men stared sullenly at the passing landscape as they wound toward the Schnee Eiffel – impenetrable forest, like the Hürtgen, skirted by sloping fields where hay bales formed icy patterns and some crops had been left unharvested because of fierce fighting that fall. They were in an area of Belgium that had belonged to Germany before the Versailles Peace Treaty and where five out of every six of the hardy and reserved residents spoke only German.

As they got closer to Hünningen, they passed through the small town of Malmedy, a foreboding-looking place with its soot-stained medieval structures and icy, cobbled streets. Thick mist and hedgerows frosted with ice greeted them as they climbed the last few miles toward Hünningen. Finally, as darkness fell on November 11, the jeeps pulled up outside a stone schoolhouse beside another building that had been set up as the 394th's regimental command post.

Thank God they were not going to spend the night in a tent or foxhole like the 394th's infantry companies. On exploring the new quarters, the platoon members discovered to their delight that the building's cellars were full of potatoes. Someone quickly liberated a block of cooking grease from a mess sergeant, built a fire, made a rudimentary stove, and then started to fry the potatoes. Maybe life on the front lines wasn't going to be so bad after all. As long as the men could warm themselves by the stove each evening, the falling temperatures outside would not yet be unbearable. And any day now, they had been promised, plenty of winter clothing would arrive.

The following morning, the platoon began to explore Hünningen. Although the village was in Belgium, it felt very much German. The signs were all in German. Yellowed remnants of Goebbels's propaganda posters were still plastered to some buildings.

Lieutenant Lyle Bouck saw an old woman dressed in what looked like rags and a few 'trustee' civilians, left behind to tend the many herds of dairy cattle in the area, but the village was otherwise empty of Belgians. In fact, the entire 99th sector, stretching fifteen miles from the village of Monschau at the northern edge of the Losheim Gap to the remote hamlet of Lanzerath to the south, had been evacuated in October – and not simply to protect the civilian population from the ravages of war.

The area was a hotbed of Nazi sympathizers and partisans, so the 99th Division had interned much of the population to safeguard from guerilla attack. But not all of them had been rounded up. The entire region was dotted with potential spies, as Bouck and his men would soon learn.

The local people's loyalty was indeed as murky as the morning fogs that had quickly rusted discarded German equipment. Private Vernon Leopold had visited the area in the early 1930s and knew its history. The eastern area of Belgium, called Eupen-Malmedy, had been German before the 1919 Versailles Peace Treaty and had only been turned over to Belgium as reparation for Kaiser Wilhelm's invasion of the neutral nation in 1914. In 1940, Hitler invaded and reclaimed the region as part of the Third Reich, and its population once more became 'Volksdeutsche' (ethnic Germans).

For the first couple of days in Hünningen, although the platoon was in the front lines, there was little sign of enemy activity. It seemed that the talk of this sector being an inactive Ghost Front was true: the Germans and the Americans were simply facing off, nursing their wounded, and resting up during the winter before the widely anticipated spring offensive that would deal the death blow to Hitler's Reich.

Twenty-year-old Corporal Sam Jenkins, the youngest man in the platoon by six months, recalled that other than the German buzz bombs that flew low and slow on their way to Liege – the platoon was dead in the center of 'buzz bomb alley' – there was at first little to worry about. The ugly rockets, which made a hauntingly loud *putt-putt-putt* sound, flew so close to the ground that some men even fired at them with their M-1s.

Radio operator James Fort was amazed when he saw the damage caused by a buzz bomb that had landed nearby: 'There was a place on one of the roads near our positions where some people said a buzz bomb crashed. I remember that the trees were cut down for about a couple hundred yards, like it might have been if a tornado had hit the woods.'

The weather continued to deteriorate. To platoon members such as Jenkins and others who had grown up in Texas, California, or the South, it appeared that winter was their true enemy. Jenkins – a tall, soft-spoken ASTPer who by now counted fellow Texan Private First Class Carlos Fernandez as his closest buddy in the platoon – had an older brother who was stationed in Hawaii, a heaven-sent posting compared to Belgium.[19] As he and others rubbed their hands together beside the makeshift stove in their billet, they would talk about home and all the things, especially the weather, that they now dearly missed.

By contrast, for several men the weather as well as the terrain were surprisingly familiar and they adapted far better to the marrow-numbing cold. Private James Silvola had hunted since he was a boy in the pine forests around a small Minnesota town called Virginia, near the Canadian border. The Schnee Eiffel reminded him of the rugged border country he had scouted in his childhood: 'I got along better than the majority of the men with the cold and snow. Northern Minnesota had a very similar climate.' In fact, temperatures back in the town of Virginia were often twenty to thirty degrees lower.

Fellow Minnesotan Robert Lambert coped just as well. 'Frostbite and trench foot exposure was a serious problem for all of us and became more serious each day as the weather worsened,' he recalled. 'During those [first] days I often thought about how fortunate I was to be a descendant of northern European ancestors.'

By November 12, the 99th Division had suffered its first two casualties – from frostbite. Most men began to carry a spare pair of winter socks with them at all times. Every evening and morning from now on, they would ritually change into dry socks, examining their feet for the first signs of trench foot: a darkening and swelling of the skin around their toes.

The Siegfried Line – November–December 1944

Soon after the arrival of more winter gear came the platoon's first mission from Major Kriz. Bouck was to take one of his squads to a regimental observation post and then cross over into enemy territory for the first time.

Kriz pointed to a gap of about five miles in the American lines between the 99th Division boundary and that of the 102nd. 'Go out here and see if you can find something out about the enemy. And remember: Don't come back the way you go out. If the enemy spots you going out, then they can react and create an ambush when you come back the same way.'

Bouck returned to the platoon's billet, called Platoon Sergeant Slape over, and asked him to select five men for the patrol. Bouck would lead it.

It was important to be able to move as quietly and quickly as possible, especially in the heavy snow. Bouck wore just his field jacket to keep out the cold and armed himself with a light .30 carbine and a Colt .45. He had modified the carbine by taking two clips and welding them together so that he had sixteen bullets in one, sixteen more in the other, and a round in the chamber. He had also had the sear cut. 'When you pulled the trigger it clicked and you had to pull it again to fire another round,' he later explained. 'If you cut the sear and then pulled on the trigger, the gun would just keep firing. If I needed some firepower, I didn't want to be yanking on the trigger all the time.'

Bouck, Slape, and four others, including Private Vernon Leopold, climbed into two jeeps and drove a mile to a command post. The long months of drilling and endless night exercises boiled down to this – their first penetration of enemy lines. They would have to be aware of every step they took because of German mines and booby traps known to be dotted all along the Siegfried Line: S-mines, the twenty-pound Riegel antitank mine, and perhaps the most fearful, the 'Bouncing Betty' that, once tripped, exploded at waist height and sent hundreds of ball bearings flying at the upper torso and testicles.

'How the hell did you end up with this kind of job?' Bouck asked himself as he led his patrol out into the darkness of no-man's-land – the few hundred yards that separated them from the pillboxes, dragon's teeth, and minefields of the Siegfried Line. Immediately, it became clear that patrolling with visibility down to often zero degrees would be exhausting, nerve-jangling work. It was hard enough to see where one was actually stepping, let alone read a map and judge distances.

The darkness was so ink-black, so consuming, that Bouck and his men could see a distance of no more than a couple of yards in the draws where a soupy mist had settled. The pine forests skirting the mountain pastures were like something out of a Gothic horror story, arousing primeval fears. The trees were so tightly bunched in Germanic, orderly rows that to enter only a hundred yards without a compass was to risk getting lost in an infernal maze.

For Leopold, the thought of capture was particularly terrifying. As a German Jew in an American uniform, he could expect to be shot on the spot. To make matters worse, he had been suffering from a bad cold and 'asthma-type cough,' which had kept some of the platoon awake since arriving in Hünningen and 'had created some concern and controversy as to whether it was safe to have me along, since absolute silence was essential,' remembered Leopold. 'After some debate and soul-wringing, "leadership" decided that my presence was essential. . . . I suspect that they rationalized that I was coughing with a German accent and that these guttural bellows of mine might help to ensnare some lost German trooper for us to bring home as a trophy for POW [Prisoner of War] interrogation.'

Fresh snow blanketed the ground. In some spots, human and wild animal urine had stained the snow bright yellow.

The squad crawled forward toward the German lines. Suddenly, Leopold started to cough. Bouck scrambled back on all fours.

'Damn it,' Bouck hissed. 'Be quiet! Suck on some snow!'

'But not the yellow stuff,' someone wisecracked.

Leopold made sure it was white: 'The mouthful of snow was "manna" from heaven – gone, momentarily, was the pernicious tickle from my throat, the tightness from the chest, and with it the urge to cough. As we wound our way onward, single file through the dense, snow-covered forest, I scooped up fistful after fistful of pure-white fluffy snow and shoved it down my itchy throat just as fast as I could. I kept it up for the entire four hours or so of this patrol – without suffering a single cough.'

Exhausted and relieved, Leopold and the others made their way back to the American lines, gave the return password to an outpost, and headed back to Hünningen for some fried potatoes and much-needed sleep.

The platoon's first patrol had been intensely sobering.[20] The long, hard months of training had not prepared the men for the reality of trying to move silently and unobserved in such harsh conditions and across such difficult terrain. They now knew that they would need every ounce of stamina and strength and as much rest and decent food as they could snatch.

Two men would suffice for the next patrol, so Bouck took along his runner, Private Bill James. A German body had been spotted not far from the front lines. 'See if you can search the body for possibly vital intelligence,' Kriz had ordered: 'Be sure to take some wire along and hook it to a leg; pull it and move it to make sure it's not booby-trapped.'

Bouck and Private James found the body, placed a wire around a leg, and pulled it. There was no explosion. Then they crawled up to the corpse and pulled a small wallet out of the German's jacket. It contained an identity card, their first important piece of gathered intelligence. The corpse belonged to the understrengthed and inexperienced German

347th Infantry Division, which had manned the Siegfried Line since late October.

Not long after Bouck saw his first dead German, he encountered his first live ones: two prisoners captured by the 394th's Company E and then brought back to the regimental headquarters beside the platoon's billet for questioning. Bouck was astonished by their youth – they were mere teenagers.

Bouck then headed out to the command post of Company C; one of his squads was due to make a patrol from its position that night. As the light began to fade, Bouck located Captain James A. Graham Jr., a burly Texan who had been his company commander at Camp Maxey. Bouck and Graham were talking under a tarpaulin near dugouts when gunfire suddenly erupted nearby. A German patrol had slipped through their lines. Bullets spat all around. Bouck returned fire instinctively with his modified carbine. Three Germans were killed. Bouck and Captain Graham were unscathed. 'What struck me about the incident was how quickly it was over,' recalled Bouck. 'There was no time to think, only to act. I'd never imagined actual combat happening so fast.' It was a valuable lesson for such a young officer, who would soon need to make life-and-death decisions in split seconds as events changed with startling speed.

Leopold vividly remembered that night's patrol: 'An all-night excursion to Losheim to stir up some enemy outpost action to fill in the regimental target map or something. With my discovery of snow as an anesthetic superior to cough drops I had now apparently become somewhat of a hero – a mascot, one that could not be done without on a patrol. So again we set off on a night-time stumble through dark, alien forests, seemingly haunted by evil spirits in field-gray uniforms.

'When we finally approached what appeared to be a German dugout or outpost on the edge of a forest bordering a field outside Losheim, Lyle said to me: "Go up there, point your M-1 into their firing slot, and tell them to come out – don't worry, we'll cover you," pointing to six to eight buddies next to him whose rifles and carbines were cocked in my direction and who were as scared as I of who might emerge from that hole at my command. Conditioned to obey on reflex, I tiptoed up to the hole and, imitating the guttural voice of my former Nazi gym coach, shouted "*Raus*," which means "out" in English. When nothing happened, I at first thought that the Germans in that dugout weren't the good obedient soldiers they were cracked up to be, but eventually the hole was found to be deserted.'

A few days later, Bouck learned that his platoon was to receive a replacement, Private Clifford Fansher, a farm boy from Boise, Idaho. Fansher was one of hundreds of thousands of young Americans forced to endure the abominable replacement system that winter, arriving alone and afraid on the front lines, joining platoons such as Bouck's that had been together since training and had little energy and time for 'wet-mouths,' as the raw recruits were called. On first sight, Bouck was not impressed: 'He looked like a little weasel – his face was all dried up. I didn't think he fit in the same category as the rest of the guys. But we made the best of it.'

Private Fansher's arrival coincided with the run-up to Thanksgiving, much anticipated because Eisenhower had ordered that every man in the ETO be given a decent Thanksgiving meal in order to lift morale. The platoon members all hoped that there would be no patrols on Thanksgiving itself – a far better blessing than Eisenhower's meal – but on the day before Thanksgiving Kriz issued orders for a patrol. 'Your squad is going to have to go out tomorrow,' Bouck told Sergeant George Redmond. 'Major Kriz called up. We've got to go out. When you come back, we'll have your meal for you.'

Redmond was none too pleased but set off to inform his men without complaint. The following night, his squad, including Privates Leopold and Louis Kalil, set out in awful conditions; the men were soon soaked to the bone. 'Even the Germans were smart enough to stay inside – wherever they were,' recalled Kalil. 'Even so, we knew every time we went out that none of us might come back. The fear was there – all the time.' Finally, Sergeant Redmond's squad traipsed back to their billet in Hünningen. 'We were miserable – red-faced, cold, and there was no meal!' added Kalil. 'We were all peeved about it. There was a lot of cussing, and I told Bouck to go shove his hot dinner up his ass. As it turned out, we didn't eat anything at all that night. We were so tired we just changed and went to bed.'

The men's nerves were getting ragged. They phlegmatically called their excursions a 'bit of hunting and shooting,' but this was simply to underplay the fact that they were involved in a lethal sport requiring 'steel nerves,' as Major Kriz put it.

Getting enough sleep was crucial if they were to be as alert as possible.

One evening, as the platoon was laying out its 'fart-sacks' – sleeping bags – to snatch a few hours' shut-eye before a midnight patrol, Bouck heard the drunken shouts of a 394th warrant officer named Montgomery. Incensed by his fellow officer's insensitivity and lack of professionalism, he jumped up and went to the head of a flight of stairs leading to the house's ground floor.

'Is that you, Montgomery? . . . Hey, we're trying to get some sleep – we're about to go out on patrol.'

Montgomery swore at Bouck.

'Look, if you don't shut up, I'm going to come down and shut you up.'

'No, I'll come up there,' threatened Montgomery.

'Come up then.'

Bouck began to climb down the stairs. He saw the scrawny figure of Montgomery approach a landing. He was looking down at the steps in the dim light. Bouck hit him square in the jaw, breaking it in two places and knocking him out cold.

'Someone better get this guy out of here,' Bouck ordered.

Montgomery was carted off to a nearby aid station. The men did not get any sleep before heading out that night, but thankfully the rest of the patrol was uneventful.

The stakes were higher than usual for the platoon's next mission. This time, there could be no coughing, not a peep, not a single misstep. Kriz had ordered Bouck to lead a patrol to scout a route that he could then use to launch the 394th's first major raid behind enemy lines. Under a bright moonlit sky, Bouck, Sergeant Slape, Private First Class Milosevich, and Private Fort arrived at an abandoned German outpost near the village of Losheim on the Siegfried Line. The post comprised a couple of log cabins and an observation shelter high in a fir tree. Milosevich looked across a field toward Losheim; bales of wheat lay piled in frozen pyramids. Suddenly, he saw two figures running between the pyramids, around three hundred yards away.

'I saw two figures,' whispered Milosevich.

'Aww, you're seeing things,' someone said.

The 394th's sector had already been dubbed 'Creepy Corner' because so many were being spooked by the slightest movement. But Milosevich wasn't one of them. He had seen two Krauts, all right, and they were no doubt sprinting back to their lines this very second to alert their regiment that the *Amerikaner* were prowling around no-man's-land.

'They'll come back with more men,' Milosevich whispered to Bouck. 'We should get the fuck out of here.'

It was an unnerving return to their positions. 'On this same patrol we had to negotiate a minefield that the Germans had laid,' James Fort explained. 'We moved through the mines in single file, with the man in front pointing out the mines to those behind.'

Bouck was the last man in line. Suddenly, his foot tripped a wire. To his everlasting relief, it did not go off.

Back in Hünningen, once the patrol had safely returned, Private First Class Carlos Fernandez got to work preparing a detailed reconnaissance map based on the patrol's observations. Since their arrival in Hünningen, he had become vital to the platoon and indeed the regiment because of his ability to draw such maps with superb accuracy.

Fernandez had attended the same high school in El Paso as Corporal Sam Jenkins, where he had been popular, as he was now in the platoon, for his wisecracks and infectious optimism. He had planned to go to medical school before the war, but he was also patriotic – he'd had a chance to avoid service but had not taken it. His Mexican-born mother had begged him to cross the Rio Grande after the attack on Pearl Harbor to avoid the draft. Identifying himself as an American, Fernandez had repeatedly refused.

Early on November 18, 1944, Major Kriz set out into the mist with forty men from the 394th's 1st Battalion, using Fernandez's map to make their way to Losheim. That same morning, in another location, the regiment lost its first men killed in action. First Lieutenant Charles M. Allen, S-2 of the 3rd Battalion, was riddled from head to groin by MG-42 machine gun fire. Two more men were killed as they tried to recover Allen's body. By contrast, Kriz's raid was an outstanding success. According to 99th Division records, 'The patrol suffered no casualties and killed two of the enemy. Furthermore, the patrol accomplished its mission by capturing two prisoners from an enemy outpost in a house on the western edge of the village.'

Milosevich saw Kriz return from the raid. What impressed him most was that Kriz had brought all his men back alive.

During interrogation, it emerged that the prisoners belonged to the 3rd Company of the 989th Grenadier Regiment of the 277th Volksgrenadier Division. Just twenty-four hours before, their regiment had arrived in the sector after a long rail journey from Hungary.

The prisoners did not know why they had been moved more than a thousand miles across Europe to the Ardennes with such haste. That was the most closely guarded secret in the Third Reich. It would not be until just hours before they attacked the 99th Division sector that even the senior officers of the 277th would learn why. The men Kriz had captured were, of course, part of the massive buildup of German forces that would shortly begin the greatest battle ever fought by the U.S. Army.

Dueren, Germany – December 3, 1944

While the 394th patrolled the Ghost Front that early December, fifty miles to the north of Hünningen, on the outskirts of the Hürtgen Forest, twenty-eight-year-old SS Lieutenant Colonel Jochen Peiper received an order to move his Kampfgruppe to a small Rhenish town, Dueren, that had been devastated in a daylight bombing raid by the U.S. Eighth Air Force.

Peiper had created more than his fair share of death and horror in over four years of war, but as he ordered his men to help civilians clean up in Dueren he was shocked by the extent of the carnage. The bodies of women and children littered the smoking ruins. 'We had to scrape them off the walls – it was that bad! . . . I could have castrated the swine who did that to those innocent people of Dueren – with a blunt piece of glass.'

By December 1944, Jochen Peiper had become the ultimate poster boy for the Schutz Staffel – the SS. Of medium height with long swept-back hair, bright blue eyes, and a winning smile that revealed polished white teeth, he had joined the Hitler Youth in 1933 and been accepted into the elite cadre of the SS at age nineteen. Having changed his name from Joachim, a biblical name, to Jochen because the SS did not hold the Bible as a sacred text, he had then survived the SS officer training course at Dachau, site of the Third Reich's first concentration camp. To harden the Third Reich's young supermen, instructors placed impact grenades on recruits' heads – if they so much as twitched, the grenade would fall to the ground and explode.

Peiper had then quickly distinguished himself as a highly intelligent, arrogant, and impetuous SS zealot. But he did not join the Nazi Party, arguing later that he did not want party membership but rather his own talents to further his career. He was, however, a fanatical supporter of Adolf Hitler; his most prized possession was a signed copy of *Mein Kampf.*

Chomping on the finest Cuban cigars, Peiper had toured a defeated Poland in early 1940 alongside SS chief Heinrich Himmler. After serving as a loyal adjutant in Hitler's Polish headquarters, he had joined the Führer's praetorian guard – the Leibstandarte Adolf Hitler, of the 1st SS Panzer

Division, and during the spring 1940 invasion of France was awarded a First and a Second Class Iron Cross.

The 1st SS Panzer Division was originally the 'Death Head' unit, responsible for the running of concentration camps, but had been turned into a frontline combat unit after the outbreak of war. And so Peiper and his men's insignia – the Death Head, a silver skull – could not have been more fitting to their role as the most merciless crack troops of the Reich.

It was thanks to his exploits in Russia that Peiper became a favorite of Hitler and famous throughout the Reich for his daring and brutality. Under the command of the 1st SS Panzer Division's Sepp Dietrich, he had saved an entire infantry division through a brilliant and audacious tank maneuver.

As a rule, neither the SS nor the Red Army took prisoners when they battled each other, and the wholesale destruction of villages as the Germans retreated in the summer of 1943 before a massive and relentless Soviet advance had been common practice. 'On various occasions,' recalled one of Peiper's men, 'we burned down whole villages with blowtorches.' Near Kharkov, Peiper had commanded a unit that had orders to 'bump off all inhabitants, including women and children. It was generally known in the unit that Peiper actively participated in the action.'

Having added the Oak Leaves to his Knight's Cross by destroying a tank single-handedly in Russia, Peiper had then moved to Italy to deal with partisan attacks, where he was known to have ordered his men to wipe out resistance in a Piedmont town; thirty-three civilians died in the process. By the end of 1944, there would be plenty more.

But early that December, as his men gathered children's body parts from shell holes, 'Blowtorch Peiper' had no inkling of the pivotal role he was about to play in Hitler's last gamble. Knowing the war could not now be won, he was resigned to die fighting with his beloved Leibstandarte, Adolf Hitler. Any other future was unimaginable. And now, after seeing villagers splattered across walls, he was equally determined to avenge the murder of Dueren's Volksdeutsche by taking as many *Amerikaner* as possible to the grave with him.

5. Shadow Soldiers

It was just after dawn when Major Kriz pulled up in a jeep outside the platoon's billet. 'I've got something important I need you to do,' he told Bouck. 'Come with me.' Bouck got into the jeep and they set off into the nearby hills, following a road that led toward the German border. They passed through deep forest divided by a steep railroad cut, bounced along rutted lanes, and then pulled up near a tree line overlooking a hamlet called Lanzerath, less than a mile from the Siegfried Line.

Lanzerath was little more than fifteen drab wooden houses centered around a small church and a stone building called the Café Scholzen, where the villagers had gathered before the general evacuation of the area by the U.S. First Army in October. But it had a key strategic significance: it lay on a north-south road with a junction that led to the 99th Division's rest area in Honsfeld to the west. If an attacking force took the village, it would have access to an excellent tank-supporting route through a badly undermanned sector of the American front.

Several two-man dugouts, until recently manned by the 2nd Division, had been constructed a few feet back from the tree line. They looked down on an open pasture, about two football fields in size, that sloped down to a dirt road that led to the heart of the hamlet. The pasture was bisected by a barbed wire fence. When the morning fogs burnt off, the position allowed for excellent observation of a road leading from the Siegfried Line into Lanzerath and the nearest village, Losheim, on the German border.

That morning, Major Kriz explained the overall strategic position to his young lieutenant. Four American infantry divisions of about sixty-five thousand men defended the Ghost Front with the 99th Division in the northernmost position. A gap of around five miles existed between the 99th Division and the 2nd Division to the south. This gap was defended solely by Task Force X of the 14th Cavalry Group and, in Lanzerath, by four three-inch-gun crews from the 2nd Platoon of Company A, 820th Tank Destroyer Battalion, which occupied a small farmhouse on the edge of the village.

All along the five-mile gap, Task Force X and the 2nd Platoon in Lanzerath needed infantry support. It was vital that the gap be temporarily reinforced by units such as Bouck's platoon until new regular infantry companies could be brought in to strengthen the line.

To complicate matters, that day the 2nd Division was being relieved – to be employed in an attack on the Roer River dams – by the greenest division in the European Theater of Operations (ETO), the 106th Division. But the 106th, which had just arrived from the States and did not yet have full strength and adequate supplies, would not be occupying the Lanzerath position. '[Lanzerath] is outside of our division boundary, regimental and corps boundary,' added Kriz. 'But we need someone to occupy it temporarily.'

Bouck was not overjoyed by Major Kriz's new orders. I&R platoons were not intended to be frontline riflemen; routinely, they were under explicit orders not to engage the enemy but to stay in the shadows, carrying out unobserved intelligence-gathering patrols. The highly mobile platoon did not have sufficient firepower to hold such a position in the event of a strong German attack. And Bouck knew his men would not be pleased to be reassigned to the duties of a regular infantry platoon after training for so long to perform a very different function. But orders were orders, and besides Major Kriz was a man of his word. It would not be long before the platoon would be back to its normal duties.

'You've got some guys at regimental ops and some at regimental headquarters,' added Kriz. 'Take the rest of your platoon and get them in these holes [at Lanzerath]. It looks like they could be improved.'

The platoon would act temporarily as the eyes and ears of the 99th on its exposed right flank at Lanzerath. Lieutenant Bouck was to stay in continual contact with the 14th Cavalry's Task Force X and the 1st Battalion of its own 394th Regiment based at nearby Losheimergraben.

Bouck and Kriz returned to Hünningen. Bouck located Sergeant Slape and then returned with him to the position above Lanzerath where they then walked from foxhole to foxhole. The 2nd Division, which had been there before, had done a good job. The holes were deep enough for two men to stand up, and there was even a small cabin about a hundred yards to the rear in the forest where the men could get a fire going and huddle together when it got really cold.

'I'm going to look the situation over more,' said Bouck. 'Go back, get the rest of the platoon, vehicles and radios and all the equipment, and then bring it up here.'

Two hours later, the platoon arrived in seven jeeps.

'These are our new addresses,' Bouck told his men, pointing to the foxholes. 'We've got the axes and saws. Cut down some trees and put some covers on these holes.'

The assistant squad leaders, Corporals Sam Jenkins and Aubrey McGehee, got to work with their men, relocating and improving the dugouts, laying rows of ten- to twelve-inch pine logs, in Alpine fashion, over the top of them, and placing some 125 fragmentation grenades, attached to the holes by wires, along the position's perimeter. In the event of a German attack, these grenades would act as a final line of defense.

While the men began to chop down trees, Slape and radio operator James Fort set up telephone and radio communications with the 14th Cavalry in Lanzerath, the 1st Battalion in Losheimergraben, and 394th Regiment headquarters back in Hünningen. Once this vital communication was established, Sergeant Slape and Bouck worked with the platoon's squad leaders in locating the optimum fields of fire.

Bouck was still not satisfied. They had set up an excellent fixed position, but they still lacked adequate firepower if they were going to be able to hold it during a concerted German attack. During the past few weeks, Bouck had been buttering up an officer in ordnance supply back at division headquarters in Mürringen, hoping he might be able to provide extra ammunition and weapons. Bouck knew that the division's 57mm antitank gunners had removed the armored side shields from their guns to make them easier to move around in the atrocious conditions. Some units had seized the opportunity for extra protection and persuaded engineers to weld the shields onto their jeeps, which were then mounted with machine guns. Bouck had tried to procure one of these armored jeeps through regular channels but with no luck.

The ordnance officer was keen to get hold of any German booty – captured German insignia, anything with a swastika or silver SS lightning symbol, and especially German weapons such as the much-prized Luger. By now, the platoon had collected a sizeable cache of identity cards. Bouck gathered the German memorabilia and set off to Mürringen. He found the supply office there and handed it over.

'Come with me,' the officer said with a smile.

They went behind a building. There stood an armor-plated jeep mounted with a .50-caliber machine gun. Bouck jumped in and drove as fast as he could back to the position, not stopping for fear of a more senior officer commandeering it.

'Jesus Christ,' said a delighted Sergeant Slape. 'Where did you get that?'

'Forget about it. Just get it in position, dig a hole around it, and get it camouflaged. Make sure the field of fire is as effective as possible.'

The .50-caliber machine gun, unlike the German MG-42, was bulky and difficult to handle. But it was a formidable weapon: at medium range it could pierce light armor and blow holes the size of a shovel blade in the enemy.

Bouck again examined the position. Only his left side remained exposed if the Germans came through Lanzerath itself rather than in a flanking movement through the surrounding forests. Bouck and Slape walked across the pasture and to their delight found a pile of logs and some stumps in the exposed area. 'Dig a three-man foxhole here so you can see this whole left side,' Bouck had soon ordered Corporal McGehee, Private James Silvola, and Private First Class Jordan 'Pop' Robinson.

It did not take long to dig the new hole with the burly McGehee wielding the shovel – his arms were the width of the logs they had cut to reinforce the other dugouts. Nicknamed 'Schnoz' by his many high school friends because of his prominent nose, McGehee had begun desperately to miss his young wife, Agnes, a cheerleader from his high school in McComb, Mississippi. The couple had married in 1943 after McGehee had won Agnes over by selling an old convertible Model T Ford to buy her a wooden music box that played 'I love you' over and over.

Robinson, Silvola, and McGehee would occupy the newly dug hole forward and left of the position. Sergeant Redmond and Kalil would take the hole behind them, and Sergeant Slape and Milosevich were to their right. Bouck would help man the next hole with James. Radioman Fort, Fansher, Creger, and Adams would take positions along the center of the defensive line, while Jenkins and Preston would share a hole on the right flank. Bouck set up his command post behind the line of foxholes, near the cabin (see map overleaf).

In the event of an attack, Sam Jenkins and Robert Preston, a fair-haired Maryland-born veteran of the original I&R platoon, would operate a .30-caliber Browning automatic rifle, the standard issue light machine gun for infantry platoons. 'Preston was a very quiet guy and really popular with the other men,' recalled Jenkins. 'He had a thick head of hair, which was why his nickname was Mop. It wasn't until we were assigned that foxhole that we got close.'

As he prepared their position, Preston shared the same kind of weary cynicism of most frontline troops that early December, knowing the war was far from over in spite of the predictions by overconfident American generals, none of whom had yet visited a single frontline position in the Ardennes to see how miserable and unforgiving foxhole life in subzero temperatures could be.[21] Some nights, it got so cold that men were afraid even to doze in their holes – they might not wake up again, literally freezing to death in their sleep.

Another of the platoon less than enthused by their new duties was Private Joseph McConnell, a caustic wit when

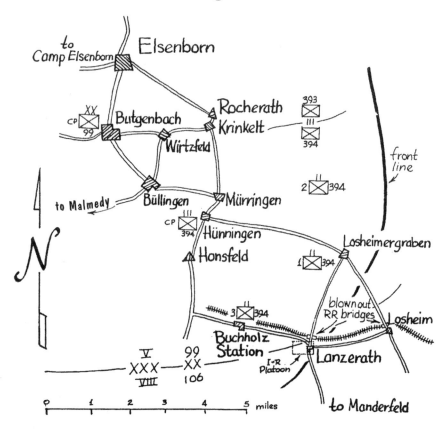

Hand-drawn map of the I&R's area of operations during the Battle of the Bulge. Prepared by Carlos Fernandez in 1981, thirty-seven years after the battle.

Lyle Bouck or Platoon Sergeant Slape were out of earshot. McConnell had grown up on some of Philadelphia's toughest streets. Highly intelligent and quick-footed, he liked very little about army life. There was a job to be done. The quicker it was over, the sooner he could get out of uniform and forget the army. There was no use bellyaching – that just made things worse.

The entire platoon hoped that by New Year they would be back to their formal duties, holing up between patrols in the cellar in Hünningen and eating fried potatoes. Besides, things could be a lot worse – they were in a relatively quiet area, unlike some of the 99th's combat units fighting just five miles north to a bloody stalemate as they tried to pierce the Siegfried Line and reach the Roer River dams.

Ziegenberg Castle – December 11, 1944

As the I&R platoon settled into its new address above Lanzerath, the first of three hundred thousand Germans who would fight in the Battle of the Bulge arrived at their jump-off points only a few miles from the Allied front lines. All trains in Germany operated now in just one direction, toward the Ardennes. By night, using straw on the frozen and rutted roads to muffle their sound, some twenty-eight hundred new armored vehicles, fresh from factories across Germany, had been assembled all along the Ghost Front. To avoid detection from the air, these vehicles and other supplies had been heavily camouflaged with fir branches and parked beneath the tall pines of the Schnee Eiffel.

Allied intelligence had spectacularly failed to detect the scale of the buildup. Complacency, an overreliance on Ultra and signals intelligence rather than on-the-ground eyewitness reports, Wacht am Rhein – Hitler's brilliant campaign of deception – and plain old incompetency had combined to create the most fatal ignorance in the U.S. Army's history. On the eve of the battle, not a single Allied soldier or general knew what the Germans were really up to. Where new German forces had been observed, it was assumed that they were part of a general buildup to counterattack near Aachen or simply to reinforce the Siegfried Line in anticipation of an Allied spring offensive.

Although General Omar Bradley, the commanding general of ground forces in the sector, and General Eisenhower, Allied supreme commander, were concerned about the weakness of their position in the Ardennes, they believed the Germans were too beaten down and lacked sufficient manpower and supplies to launch an effective attack through the region. Yes, Erwin Rommel's Panzers had stormed through the Ardennes in 1940, but they had faced little resistance and benefited from excellent weather and road conditions. Along with the 99th Division, three other divisions – the 106th fresh out of training, and the 4th and 28th badly mauled in the Hürtgen – would suffice until fresh divisions could be assembled for the broad-based spring offensive.

By December 11, 1944, the German buildup was complete. That morning, Adolf Hitler moved to a new headquarters behind the Siegfried Line, near the castle of Ziegenberg, from where he would direct operations. The date for the attack was announced: December 16, 1944. Then Hitler called together his battle commanders. As they entered Hitler's headquarters, they were told to lay down their weapons: Hitler was increasingly paranoid about his personal security. After the bomb plot of July 20, 1944, he distrusted almost all his Wehrmacht senior staff. The arriving generals were also made to swear on their lives that they would keep secret what Hitler was about to tell them.

For an hour, Hitler regaled them with the history of Frederick the Great and the glories of National Socialism. Then he got to the point: at 5:30 A.M. on December 16, 'Null Hour,' three armies would attack through the Ardennes, punch a hole in the Allied lines, and then thunder toward Antwerp. Sepp Dietrich's Sixth Panzer Army was to advance toward the Meuse through the Losheim Gap. South of the Losheim Gap, General von Manteuffel's Fifth Panzer Army would attack the strategically vital towns of St. Vith and Bastogne, where several excellent roads formed junctions, and then advance northwest to protect Dietrich's southern flank. Erich Brandenberger's Seventh Army would probe even farther south and block off any attempt by the Americans to move in reinforcements. If all went according to plan, the Allies would be sent reeling and would soon begin peace negotiations, abandoning their demand of unconditional surrender.

'This battle,' Hitler finally stressed, 'is to decide whether we shall live or die. I want all my soldiers to fight hard and without pity. The battle must be fought with brutality and all resistance must be broken in a wave of terror. In this most serious hour of the Fatherland, I expect every one of my soldiers to be courageous and again courageous. The enemy must be beaten – now or never! Thus lives our Germany!'

Lanzerath, on the Ghost Front – December 13, 1944

Snow fell in large, fluffy flakes, soon blanketing the platoon's dugouts with the perfect camouflage. 'Man, that's great,' thought Lyle Bouck as he watched the position above Lanzerath disappear beneath a thick frosting of white. 'Nobody will be able to find us under this.'

The platoon had now spent three days in its isolated position. 'We all felt that the position we had been put in was a very dangerous one due to the small number of men we had and the terrain,' recalled Corporal Sam Jenkins. 'Also, we did not have too many heavy weapons.'

Fellow Texan Carlos Fernandez had been on guard duty

the night before. 'How dark and eerie those nights were,' he recalled. 'Standing in the cold, snowy night, staring towards all directions at once and hearing artillery reports to our far left [in and around the Hürtgen forest] – getting so "bug-eyed" that I actually saw a tree move over towards another tree and stand there together as if conversing!'

Creepy Corner had begun to spook others, too. 'An extended state of fear existed,' recalled Bouck. 'Your imagination tried to run away with your eyes as you would stare at the form of a tree against the snow during the nights. Every once in a while this tree would seem to move and suddenly "attack you." The days and nights ran together. Only a new replacement could tell you the date or that it was Tuesday or Sunday.'

On moving into the position, Private Vic Adams had placed three grenades on sticks in front of his dugout and then attached pull wires. That night, he suddenly thought he saw Germans crossing the open field; he pulled a wire and instantly woke up the entire platoon.

Another incident left Sergeant Slape and Private Creger on edge. 'We were operating an observation post in the church steeple in Lanzerath,' recalled Jim Fort, the platoon's radio expert. 'Slape and Creger were in the steeple when a German patrol entered the church below. Luckily for the Germans, they didn't check the steeple nor the communications wire running from the church.'

It was by now so cold, Fort also remembered, that he could hear twigs and branches snapping in the forest to their rear from the weight of ice. The winds were so biting that the men had to erect a canvas screen around their latrine – an open-air slit trench. Although they had a bathtub, a very rare luxury on the front lines, it was a brave man indeed who dared wash in it. It was no one's fault, but the training in the heat and humidity of Texas had ill-prepared the men to fight a winter war.

One hope lifted the men's spirits: they might get to see the most famous pair of legs in history, insured for more than a million dollars. On December 17 – Bouck's twenty-first birthday – Marlene Dietrich, the German-born film and cabaret star, was going to perform in a USO show back at the 99th Division rest area in Honsfeld, nicknamed Camp Maxey. One of the men would be selected to attend.

Dietrich's usual shtick was to play a saw with a violin bow, flirt and joke with the troops, and then serenade them, often changing the words of her best-known songs to humor the men: 'When we are marching in the mud and cold, and when my pack seems more than I can hold, My love for you renews my might, I'm warm again, my pack is light.'

Whom would Bouck choose? To avoid accusations of favoritism, he decided they should draw straws, or rather pine needles, that he cut into different lengths. Private First Class Jordan 'Pop' Robinson, at thirty-seven the oldest man in the platoon by a decade, drew the longest straw.

Before the war, Robinson had worked in the mines of far eastern rural Tennessee. 'He could do things with a rifle that none of the others could,' recalled Lyle Bouck. 'The men would throw beer cans up, and he'd shoot them perfectly.' Bouck had selected Robinson because of his 'woods smarts.' 'He was a great outdoorsman. There wasn't anything that was too rugged for him. He was very comfortable in the environment, probably better off perhaps than when he was at home.'

Like every GI shivering in foxholes that December, Robinson had heard Dietrich sing 'Lili Marlene' on the radio. All along the Ghost Front, in German bunkers and stinking dugouts, the words to her signature song were particularly appropriate: 'Resting in a billet just behind the line, Even tho' we're parted your lips are close to mine; You wait where that lantern gently gleams, Your sweet face seems to haunt my dreams, My Lili of the lamplight.'

As the temperature continued to drop well below freezing, Lyle Bouck visited Lanzerath. There he met with men from the 820th Tank Destroyer Battalion who were using the village as their base. Bouck asked if they could give him a warning in the event of an attack. They agreed, and a land line was run from the unit to the platoon position.

The 820th occupied the home of the Schur family. In exchange for cigarettes and chocolate, Frau Schur cooked hot meals. Her daughter, Suzanne, an attractive 25-year-old, waited on the soldiers and joked with them. At night, however, she slept between her parents just in case any of the Yanks got the wrong idea. Suzanne's sixteen-year-old cousin, Adolf, visited most days. Soon, the 820th had adopted him as their mascot, teaching him to swear like a true dogface and sending him on errands. Adolf, with his older brother and parents, lived in a house on the northern fringe of Lanzerath, about four hundred yards from the I&R platoon's position.

Also in Lanzerath was a forward artillery observation group of soldiers from Battery C, 371st Field Artillery. The four-man unit was led by a sharp-witted lieutenant, Warren Springer. As with many of the I&R platoon's ASTPers, he had never imagined he would end up in the front lines, creeping around dragon's teeth, squinting through an observation periscope, retreating after dark to his sandbagged observation post on the second floor of one of Lanzerath's stone farmhouses.

'I was assigned to go to field artillery school, and luckily I ended up working on the faculty for eighteen months,' recalled Springer. 'It was a good living, a nice life. You could leave your shoes outside the door for an orderly to shine. But then I got orders to join the 99th Division. That was a sad day. I heard some fellow say, "Gee, I'd like to get in and see some combat." I thought the opposite: "It's going to take six MPs to get me out of here!"'

Second in command of Springer's unit was Sergeant Peter Gacki, a soft-spoken South Bend, Indiana, native who had gotten married on, of all days, December 7, 1941, as Pearl Harbor was being bombed. When his draft notice arrived, Gacki could have taken a deferment because he worked in an engineering factory that supplied aircraft parts. But he had accepted the draft and joined the 99th Division at Camp Van Dorn just after its activation.

The other members of the field artillery unit were Technician Fourth Grade Willard Wibben and Technician Fifth Grade Billy S. Queen, a pudgy, bespectacled young man who looked as if he belonged behind a clerk's desk in a quartermaster office, certainly not on the front lines, though he was in fact a skilled observer.

The men had observed little activity since moving into Lanzerath. But then, on December 13, Lieutenant Springer spotted a local Belgian acting suspiciously and accosted the man. The man said he was going to pick up some shoes from a relative in town; Springer suspected he was a spy and turned him over to the 3rd Battalion for questioning.

That same day, the I&R platoon suffered its first casualty. In his foxhole that morning, Private Vic Adams pulled off his socks and saw that his feet were turning black. Adams received permission from Lyle Bouck to return to Hünningen and get his foot looked at. He would soon be evacuated from the front,[22] one of more than a thousand men in the 99th Division hospitalized for trench foot, pneumonia, and frostbite before the Battle of the Bulge had even begun.

Not long after Adams's departure, Major Kriz arrived at the platoon's position in a chow jeep driven by Private Sam Oakley, a tall, gangly Virginian, soft-spoken and madly in love with his young wife back home. Kriz was pleased with the reinforced location. An infantry platoon would replace the men just as soon as was possible. That night, radio operator Jim Fort took his turn on guard with another platoon member on the .50-caliber machine gun. There were unusual noises, a distant clanking that the platoon had not heard before and suddenly what sounded like two men walking and breaking through the crust that had frozen on top of the snow. '[Lyle Bouck] or Sergeant Slape gave the order to open fire,' recalled Fort. The .50-caliber machine gun burst into action. The next morning, just after dawn, Fort found the source of the noise: a German scout dog trained to sniff out enemy positions. Fort stared at it, lying riddled in the snow.

As Major Kriz saw it, the scout dog was yet another sign that the Germans were up to something. 'For a period of days prior to the Battle of the Bulge,' he recalled, 'we could see ski tracks through our lines – you'd see snowshoe tracks. On one patrol we saw these Germans trying to bring in dogs. Our Intelligence and Reconnaissance Platoon killed a couple of them for us and I took them up to division but that was the last I heard of it.'

The Germans had resorted to using canines for a specific reason. Fearing the Allies might capture and interrogate any of the storm troopers massing in the Schnee Eiffel, Hitler had ordered that there would be no human patrols in the last days before his all-out attack. For once, he was being overcautious. The American intelligence apparatus was clueless beyond his wildest hopes.

German Front Lines, Schnee Eiffel – December 14, 1944

A light snow fell that Thursday morning ten miles east of Lanzerath. Staff cars pulled up outside a forester's house and out stepped the senior combat officers of the 1st SS Panzer Division – the spearhead of Sepp Dietrich's Sixth Panzer Army. It was just after eleven when they gathered before the division commander, SS Colonel Wilhelm Mohnke. Beneath the surrounding pines, hundreds of tanks and armored vehicles lay silently in wait.

One of Mohnke's officers arrived late that morning, held up by the long lines of trucks that had filled the Schnee Eiffel's narrow mountain roads. Jochen Peiper walked into the forester's home wearing a polo-neck sweater and black leather jacket; his cap, with its faded badge, was worn at a typically jaunty angle. According to Otto Skorzeny, he was 'tense in that cynical way of his, knowing that something big was going to happen – just how big I already knew from the Führer himself but he had sworn me to secrecy – but trying not to show just how eager he was to find out why he had been called to this conference. . . . He was a highly trained, nervous hound begging to be let off the leash.'

Mohnke explained the overall German plan of attack envisioned by Hitler. 'It is, I agree, an operation of extreme daring,' he concluded. 'Anyway, gentlemen, there can be no argument; it's the Führer's orders.'

Mohnke told Peiper that his Kampfgruppe would take an assigned 'Route D' that ran from the border village of Losheim through the Losheim Gap to Honsfeld and then through a series of small villages to a town called Trois Ponts, where it joined Belgian Route Nationale N-23, and then to the Meuse. When Peiper examined a map of the route, he commented acidly that the route was 'not for tanks but bicycles.' But Mohnke would not discuss Peiper's objection. The Führer had ordered that Peiper take the route. And that was final.

Mohnke continued to brief his arrogant but formidably competent young colonel: Peiper's 1st Panzer Regiment would be reinforced with special engineers, Royal Tiger tanks from the 501st Heavy Tank Company, and a battalion of Panzergrenadiere – in all, five thousand men would belong to Kampfgruppe Peiper. Some of Skorzeny's English-speaking commandos would go ahead of the force, spreading chaos and confusion by moving road signs, issuing false orders, and destroying communications.

Peiper had one major concern other than the difficult roads. Where would he find extra supplies of fuel? Nowhere near enough had been assigned to his Kampfgruppe if it was to reach the Meuse within twenty-four hours, as Hitler's plan envisioned.

Mohnke said Peiper would be able to seize extra fuel on the way, specifically from a huge American supply depot at Mürringen, the 99th Division's headquarters, code-named 'Dauntless.'

Mohnke ended the meeting by repeating words from a speech that Hitler had given to his most senior generals: 'The battle will decide whether Germany is to live or die. Your soldiers must fight hard and ruthlessly. There must be no pity. The enemy must be beaten, now or never. Thus will live our Germany! Forward to and over the Meuse!'

Few of the assembled officers were impressed by Hitler's oratory. '[It] was the usual rhetoric, intended more for inspiring the rank and file,' recalled Otto Skorzeny, 'who were mostly young impressionable recruits, than battle-hardened, somewhat cynical commanders. I think, "old hares," as we were, we only half-listened to Mohnke, who had steadily grown red in the face with the effort.'

But Jochen Peiper had heard Mohnke only too well. He would bear the brunt of the responsibility for the Sixth Panzer Army's success or failure. He must do everything in his power to 'provide maximum speed and power.'

In perfect English, Peiper later recalled: 'I decided that my armored half-tracks would proceed as fast as possible until they met resistance and then the tanks would come up to destroy the resistance, following which the half-tracks would again advance. I expected that if all went well I would need only Mark IVs and Panthers to proceed through the mountains and to reach the Meuse River, with one panzer company. Then I could move up the heavy Tiger Tanks later.'

Peiper then briefed his men. There would be no looting and no firing into small groups of American defenders. They couldn't afford to waste a single minute if they were to save the Third Reich.

Lanzerath – December 15, 1944

Radio operator James Fort peered through the narrow forward slit of his dugout. Suddenly, a brave deer ventured near the platoon's positions. 'It came up across the field and Robinson shot at him with an M-1,' recalled Fort. 'He didn't kill him. So he picked up his Browning automatic rifle and shot at him again – this time he just went tumbling. We cleaned the deer up, hung him in the tree, and of course he froze. We were going to start cutting him up and eating him the next day.' The fresh venison would be a welcome change to their rations, especially the chocolate-substitute D-bars, dubbed 'Hitler's Secret Weapon' by many GIs.

The deer incident provided only a temporary distraction. The men were unsettled. The cynical among them didn't like the fact that a liquor ration had been issued the previous night. That was always a signal that something was up. No one was in the mood to talk about fast-approaching Christmas or Lieutenant Lyle Bouck's twenty-first birthday in just two days' time.

As usual, Lyle Bouck examined some of the men's feet that day. It had been more than a month now since Private Leopold had first gotten frostbite, but by constantly changing his socks and staying dry he had managed to get by. But the last few days standing in a dugout had led to a serious deterioration of his condition. Leopold protested that he would be okay, but Bouck was having none of it. 'You're going back on the chow jeep,' he ordered.

The jeep bringing mail and food arrived soon after darkness fell at 4:00 P.M. After the men ate their hot chow, Private First Class Carlos Fernandez accompanied Private Leopold back to Hünningen. 'Apparently, the man who drew the patrol maps for line companies had been taken ill,' recalled Fernandez. 'I was to draw these patrol maps that night and return with the breakfast jeep early the next morning.'

After supper, Bouck told the remaining eighteen members of the platoon that they were to remain awake that night. Major Kriz wanted them to be extra vigilant: there was going to be another 99th Division stab toward the Roer dams. The men were again to be alert to the possibility of some kind of counterattack. Kriz's intelligence indicated that it might be on a serious scale.

Around midnight, a heavy fog moved into the position. Lookouts rotated from dugout to the rear shack and back again. That night's challenge password was 'sunset.' The response was to be 'rain.' Several times, the platoon heard activity in the Losheim area, only this time the noises were far louder than before. They sounded like the clanging and moving of heavy equipment and vehicles.

James Fort radioed back to regimental headquarters in Hünningen to report the unusually loud sounds. At headquarters, Robert Lambert received Fort's message: 'My fellow platoon members reported hearing enemy vehicle noises. They believed the sounds they heard were noises caused by the movement of tracked heavy vehicles, such as tanks, on a highway in enemy territory. It is needless to say that this information was duly recorded and disseminated.'

Down in Lanzerath, members of the artillery observation team also reported the noises to their artillery battery. 'We told them that there were all kinds of lights and noise and stuff going on in Losheim,' recalled Sergeant Peter Gacki, 'but nobody paid any attention to us.'

At the 394th's headquarters in Hünningen, Major Kriz spent a restless night, by now convinced that the Germans were massing for a large-scale attack. 'It was very obvious to me, and to a lot of others, that something was going to happen. You could hear the armored vehicles moving. . . . Everything indicated something was going on and I know that higher headquarters also knew it. I bypassed division several times to see if anyone would listen to me.'

But no one did. And by dawn, it would be too late.

PART TWO
The Battle of Lanzerath

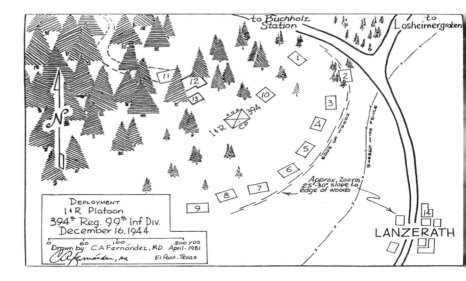

Platoon member Carlos Fernandez's hand-drawn map of the fighting at Lanzerath, prepared years later in 1981.

 1. Redmond and Kalil; visited by Slape.
 2. Robinson, Silvola and McGehee, with bazooka and BAR.
 3. Slape and Milosevich, with .30-caliber machine gun.
 4. Bouck and James; Bouck moved at various times to 4, 7, and 13. He was with James in 13 when they surrendered.
 5. Fansher; moved at various times to 5 and 12.
 6. Baasch and Fort; Fort moved at various times to 11, 13, and 6.
 7. Creger and Adams.
 8. Dustman and McConnell.
 9. Jenkins and Preston.
10. Jeep with mounted .50-caliber machine gun. Slape and James worked machine gun at various times during the attacks.
11. Radio jeep; Fort stayed here and visited 13.
12. Log cabin. Fansher was here and at 5.
13. Entrenchment adjacent to cabin. Bouck, Fort and James were here at various times.
14. Slape and Creger's observation post in Lanzerath.

6. Sturm!

Ardennes Forest — December 16, 1944

In the early hours of December 16, 1944, beneath pines laden with snow, Sergeant Vinz Kuhlbach, a blond-haired twenty-five-year-old German soldier and veteran of Normandy and Monte Cassino, turned on his torchlight. In its bright stare, he could make out the frightened, sallow faces of some eighty men from the 1st Company, 9th Regiment, 3rd Fallschirmjaeger (Paratrooper) Division. Many of the young German paratroops shivered; others stamped their feet to fend off frostbite.

Kuhlbach's company commander had earlier given him a sealed envelope. It contained one of the most important orders in the history of the Third Reich.

Kuhlbach opened the envelope and began to read aloud: 'Regimental Order Number 54, dated 16 December 1944. The Daily Order of the Supreme Commander West. Soldiers, your hour has come! At this moment strong attack armies have started against the Anglo-Americans. I don't need to tell you any more. You feel it yourselves. We gamble everything. You carry within you the holy obligation to give your all, to perform to the utmost, for our Fatherland and our Führer!'

The order was from General Gerd von Runstedt, commander of all German troops in the West.

It was 5:30 A.M. Suddenly, the silence of the deep forest

was broken by enormous explosions. The German paratroopers put their hands to their ears and looked up to see
flashes of light on the horizon. Along an eighty-mile front,
every big gun seemed to be firing nonstop. The sky looked
as bright as day; the shelling was heaviest in the paratroopers'
sector, earmarked for attack by the Sixth Panzer Army under
Sepp Dietrich.

The ghostly quiet of Creepy Corner was no more. 'It had
all been so peaceful as it can only be in the hills where the
fir woods quietly whisper, here and there dropping some of
their mantle of snow,' remembered a German artillery officer. 'A few stars shone out of a black sky; a low cloud layer
hovered in the west. And then ... the mortars sang their
eerie song and sent their cones of fire into the heavens.
Thunder filled the air and the earth shook under the impact
of the blows. At first I was dumb but then I couldn't contain
myself any longer. . . . I shouted and danced and laughed.'

The I&R platoon members dived to the bottom of their
holes, hands over their ears. As shells rained down, most of
them exploded in the treetops, shredding the forest and
sending a hail of lethal wooden shards and hot metal flying
in every direction.

Suddenly, the platoon's command post on the hillside
overlooking Lanzerath received a near-direct hit. Inside,
Bouck crouched down. The barrage sounded as if it was
rolling back and forth along the entire Siegfried Line. If this
preceded a German counterattack, it would, as Kriz had
feared, be no small skirmish.

Bouck tried to keep his nerve. It was easier for him than
others. Alone among the terrified men on the hill, he had
been under heavy artillery fire before. Back at Camp Maxey
during a training exercise, he had been caught out in the

open. He had been convinced that he would die, but some-how he had been able to sprint out of the firing zone uninjured.

Bouck now hoped that the platoon's strengthened dug-outs would be enough to protect them from the lethal tree bursts. Only a direct hit would kill him and his men. But as the minutes stretched into an hour, he and others began to wonder if the hellish shelling would ever cease. 'We thought it would never end,' recalled one of his men. 'There wasn't much of a lull. It totally annihilated the trees in the area.'

Five miles northwest of Lanzerath, at 394th regimental head-quarters in Hünningen, Robert Lambert also waited, hands clasped over his ears, for the concentrated shelling to end. 'It was not long before most of our forward telephone lines had been cut by shrapnel, rendering them inoperative,' he recalled. 'From then on our contact with my fellow platoon members at Lanzerath was by radio.'

As soon as the artillery barrage rolled past, Lambert sprinted up steps leading from a cellar beneath headquarters to the operations room. It was quickly flooded with reports of enemy action against the entire 99th Division's front. The Germans were attacking in strength, opaque figures in snowsuits streaming through the misty woods to take the isolated outposts and line companies by surprise. In the 394th's sector, the situation looked especially grave: Lambert knew the regiment was already thinly spread out, and there was no battalion in reserve to counterattack where the enemy broke through.

The shelling continued for ninety minutes all along the Ghost Front. After an hour, it had become the heaviest continuous barrage suffered by the U.S. Army in Europe.

One German major watched in awe as gunners bracketed sections of the American front and intensified their shelling. 'The earth seemed to break open. A hurricane of iron and fire went down into the enemy positions with a deafening noise. We old soldiers had seen many a heavy barrage, but never before anything like this.'

Such Germans had been assured that the green American defenders – the 99th and 106th – would be left so paralyzed by terror that they would either flee or fling up their hands at the sight of their first German paratroopers. Few would have the nerve to stand and fight. The typical *Amerikaner* in the Ardennes, as described by Nazi propaganda, was a gum-chewing, undisciplined half-breed with no stomach for real war.

In their dugout on the hillside above Lanzerath, Sergeant George Redmond and Private Louis Kalil sweated from fear, no longer feeling the cold. When they dared to glance through the firing slit at the front of the dugout, they could see Lanzerath and the surrounding countryside lit up as if by floodlights. 'We knew it weren't no little thing,' recalled Redmond. 'But I figured if I'd gotten that far, I'd get the rest of the way. You only have to go when your time comes.'

The shells just kept coming. At a 99th Division command post to the platoon's rear, a staff officer who had been told the Germans had just two horse-drawn artillery pieces in the vicinity shouted, 'Christ, they sure are working those two poor horses to death!'

In his observation post in a stone house down in Lanzerath, forward artillery observer Sergeant Peter Gacki heard shells fall in the yard to the rear of the house. But the village suffered little other direct shelling. Gacki reasoned that the

Germans, who had occupied the town since 1940, knew the village would not be hostile to their return and therefore didn't want to 'shoot it up.'

Gacki's commanding officer, Lieutenant Warren Springer, sheltering a few feet away, was now convinced that the local civilian he had handed over a few days before had indeed been a spy. Why had so few shells fallen on Lanzerath, except close to his artillery observation post?

Then there was silence. The barrage was over. It was 7:00 A.M.

Springer climbed the stone steps from the cellar of the observation house and went outside. To his surprise, he saw some of the fifty-five men belonging to the tank destroyer battalion, Task Force X. They were preparing to move out, having received orders to re-form in the nearby town of Manderfeld.

'What's going on?' Springer asked one of the men.

'The Germans are just down the road. You better get out of here in a hurry.'

Without the tank destroyers, Lanzerath would be highly vulnerable to armored attack. Springer returned to his position and told his men that they were also going to leave the village but not the vicinity. They would move to a position where they could better direct fire on advancing Germans. Quickly, his men grabbed their bedrolls and loaded their equipment into a jeep.

One of the last tank destroyers to leave pointed to the I&R platoon's positions above the village. If Springer and his men were going to stay, that would be as good a place as any from which to direct their battery's fire.

Springer already knew about the platoon's position: it was, indeed, an excellent vantage point. He ordered his driver, Technician Fourth Class Willard Wibben, to take a trail leading up through woods toward what might be left of the position after the heavy shelling. The hillside and surrounding forest had been badly hit. The German 155mm guns had gouged holes the size of trucks, and the trees had been smashed to toothpicks. Much of the snow-covered pasture leading down to Lanzerath was black from cordite and the underlying soil that had been showered everywhere by explosions.

Lieutenant Lyle Bouck's first thought as he surveyed the devastation was whether any of his men had been wounded.

'Sergeant Slape!' he shouted.

'Right here, sir,' replied Slape. 'Keep it down, my ear-drums are throbbing!'

Slowly, other men emerged from their dugouts, dazed, pale-faced, cursing the Germans, some rubbing their ears. Slape called for a status report. Men from each hole shouted out. No one was hit; the platoon's positions were intact, as was the jeep-mounted machine gun that had been least protected.

'What now?' asked Slape.

'For now, we're going to stay put,' said Bouck. 'I'll check with headquarters.'

Bouck tried to contact the 1st Battalion by telephone, but the wires had been cut so he called regimental headquarters in Hünningen and got First Lieutenant Edward Buegner, Kriz's assistant, on the line.

'Do we have permission to withdraw?' Bouck asked Buegner. 'We're isolated.'

'The division has drawn strong fire across the whole front,' replied Buegner. 'We don't know what this amounts to.'

'So what are we supposed to do?' asked Bouck.

'Stay right there until we give you orders to do something different.'

Bouck put the telephone down and told Slape they would stay until they received further orders.

A few miles away, Sergeant Vinz Kuhlbach shouted for his men to advance: '*Sturm!*'

Massive searchlights threw light up to the clouds, creating the effect of artificial moonlight. Many of Kuhlbach's men were ex-Luftwaffe conscripts who had been transferred into the infantry with little training. They were armed with the new Schmeisser machine pistol and with rifle grenades, but very few had ever used these weapons in combat.

Kuhlbach and his men started out for Belgium and soon entered the village of Hergesberg. It was deserted. Then they crossed the Siegfried Line, headed toward Lanzerath. Alongside Kuhlbach's company, there were more than five hundred men from the 9th Fallschirmjaeger Regiment, 3rd Fallschirmjaeger Division. Their mission was to clear Lanzerath and other villages of enemy resistance so that Kampfgruppe Peiper could storm through without delay.

Three of Bouck's men, sent back to regimental headquarters in Hünningen before the German attack, were now determined to return to their comrades. Carlos Fernandez, Vic Adams, and Sam Oakley, the platoon's main jeep driver, set off for Lanzerath. As they approached the front lines, they spotted a group of GIs lying prone on the right side of the road with their rifles pointing toward a wooded area on their left side.

'Get that jeep the hell out of here,' shouted one of the GIs. 'There are Jerries across the road.'

Oakley swerved as he turned the jeep around, sending

the hot tins flying, put his foot down, and sped back to regimental headquarters in Hünningen, where Fernandez quickly reported to Colonel Riley. Riley was shocked that Germans had infiltrated so far so fast. 'We hoped this was only a patrol action [by the Germans],' recalled Fernandez. 'I feared very much for my buddies near Lanzerath.'

At the S-2 office, Fernandez found Major Kriz and Robert Lambert frantically trying to assess the scale and extent of the German penetrations. Suddenly, a messenger from a 1st Battalion rifle company ran into the office and handed Lambert a captured German document. Lambert passed it to an expert interrogator of prisoners of war for immediate translation.

The document was Field Marshal von Rundstedt's order of the day – the same order that Vinz Kuhlbach had read to his men before dawn. It was clear that this was no small counterattack but an all-out offensive by the German Army, 'whose objective was to split the Allied forces in two and drive all the way to the sea.'

Lambert briefly wondered whether the document was fake. But it read and looked as if it were authentic. He passed it on to Kriz, who in turn informed Riley.[23]

Riley ordered all strategically placed units, including the I&R platoon, to hold their positions. At all costs, the 394th must try to stall the German advance. It was particularly vital that the crucial Lanzerath road junction be held. If the platoon fell, the 99th's right flank, already badly under-manned, would be in critical danger.

It was shortly before 8:00 A.M. in Lanzerath. Above the village, Lieutenant Lyle Bouck peered through his binoculars to the south, expecting a ground attack. Suddenly there were sounds of explosions and a firefight to the north in

Losheimergraben. Then Bouck heard engines revving. He spotted the tank destroyers of Task Force X speeding north to the road junction just outside the village. He watched as they turned left toward Honsfeld. They were leaving.

Bouck was furious. They had promised to contact him in the event of a German attack, and now it looked as if they were turning tail and abandoning the platoon.

'Gee,' said Private Bill James acidly, 'if they can't sign off on the phone, they might at least wave good-bye as they leave.'

Bouck picked up his radio handset. Major Kriz answered.

'The tank destroyer unit has departed with no explanation,' said Bouck. 'I heard firing to the north near the 1st Battalion. What should I do? Over.'

'Go down into that town and set up an observation post,' ordered Kriz. 'The 1st Battalion is being hit very hard north of you. If something big is happening, we'll need to see south of your position. Out.'

Bouck called for Private James, Platoon Sergeant Slape, and Corporal John Creger. Creger and Slape would set up the observation post in the house abandoned by the tank destroyers. On their way to Lanzerath, they would try to locate where the wires that had connected their position with the house had been cut. Bouck would lead the patrol and then return with James.

Like Slape, Creger was a man of few words and utterly reliable. Bouck had often seen him with a smirk or smile on his face. Now he looked deadly serious as he followed Slape along the fence that cut across the field sloping toward Lanzerath.

The group soon found a break in a wire; they spliced it and then moved on, finding that other wires back to battalion and into Lanzerath had been broken. They were too badly damaged to fix, so the patrol continued down the slope and into Lanzerath.

Back in their position above Lanzerath, the rest of the platoon waited nervously. They too had seen the tank destroyers leave and were concerned now that unless they withdrew they could be quickly overrun by even a small German force with tank support. They had not been trained to fight from a static position. Hopefully, when Bouck got back, he'd get orders to pull out.

Radio operator James Fort hunkered down in his dugout. As soon as the barrage had stopped, he had sprinted over from Bouck's command post and begun to transmit on his SCR-284 radio mounted on a jeep a few yards to the rear of his dugout. With most of the land wires cut, Fort now knew the platoon fate could depend on his effective communication with Lambert and others back at regimental headquarters in Hünningen. For each radio message, he needed to use a special dedication code. Every reply had a matching code to avoid interception by German intelligence. Fort hoped the Germans had not broken the code and were not now reading his messages and sending back false orders. There was no way of being certain with radio communication that the Germans weren't listening in on his every transmission.

Fort turned the radio's dials. The loud blare of German martial music was suddenly on his normal frequency. The Germans were jamming his radio signals. He quickly switched to his smaller 393 radio set and began to tap out Morse code. Outside the dugout, the sky began to brighten. Dawn arrived on December 16 in the Ardennes at just after 8:00 A.M.

*

Down below in Lanzerath, Lieutenant Bouck and his patrol could now see clearly as they ran into the house at the northern edge of the village where the tank destroyers had been based.

Platoon Sergeant Slape prepared to unreel a new land line back to the position.

'I'm gonna check upstairs,' said Private James.

Bouck followed James. In the first room they checked, a heavyset civilian in his late twenties was talking in German on a telephone.

James jumped forward and stuck the barrel of his carbine in the man's stomach.

The man put his hands in the air, shaking with fear.

'Shall I let him have it?' James asked.

'No!' said Bouck.

There was nothing to be gained from shooting the civilian.

Bouck asked him what he was doing. Was he tipping off the Germans? The man had been standing by a window overlooking the town.

The man could not understand English.

'You're right,' said Bouck. 'He's up to no good. But let him go. We don't have room for prisoners.'

He turned to the man. '*Raus mit du!*' (Out with you!).

James stepped back and the man left in a hurry, passing Slape at the bottom of the stairs and then fleeing into the street.

'What was that all about?' Slape called up.

'Nothing, just a spy,' said Bouck.

'A spy. Are you kidding me?'

'Come upstairs. You and Creger put your observation post up here.'

Bouck went over to a window, where the man had been standing, and looked outside. Sure enough, it was an excellent vantage point. The vital road entering Lanzerath from the southeast was clearly visible.

Bouck had perfect eyesight. In the far distance he suddenly saw German troops advancing toward the town.

'Germans!'

The Germans' helmets looked familiar. Bouck remembered seeing them in a training manual – these were paratroopers, among the best combat troops in Germany.

Bouck turned to Slape. 'You and Creger stay here. Call the position and tell me what they're doing. They could stop, keep going, head away from town. Let me know.'

Bouck and James ran down the stairs and hurried back to the position, unraveling a communication wire as they went. Within minutes, word quickly passed from hole to hole that Germans, in the hundreds, were heading straight for them.

On the outskirts of Lanzerath, sixteen-year-old Adolf Schur watched as the Germans advanced. When the shelling had begun, he had taken refuge with his family in their cellar. As soon as it had lifted, he had scurried upstairs, eager to see what might happen. In the early morning light, he had then seen the tank destroyers leave, trailing their artillery guns. Adolf had begun to fear that the Germans were coming. Now his fears were being borne out.

Meanwhile, Private Creger walked over to a window in the house previously occupied by the tank destroyers and looked outside. There was at least a platoon of German paratroopers in the street below. They had their weapons slung – they obviously weren't expecting to come across Americans. But surely they knew Lanzerath had until minutes ago been held by Americans. Had the Belgian spy tipped them off by phone when the tank destroyers abandoned their position?

Slape cranked up the platoon's phone in its heavy leather case.

'The Germans – they're here now.'

'Get the hell out of there!' said Bouck. 'I'll try to get some help down to you.'

Bouck shouted to Robinson, McGehee, and Silvola in the forward-line foxhole: 'Get across the road and see if you can help them.'

The three men rushed down toward Lanzerath, but as they neared the road they saw Germans blocking their entry into the village. More soldiers were moving to their flanks. Soon they would be surrounded. They decided to head toward 1st Battalion headquarters at Losheimergraben, three miles away, and get reinforcements.

The men headed north, their boots crunching through the frozen snow pack. Minnesotan Jim Silvola carried a cumbersome Browning automatic rifle (BAR). Suddenly, they found themselves on the brink of the steep railroad cut that ran east-west to Buchholz Station through the forest surrounding Lanzerath. It was two hundred feet deep, in some places almost vertical. The nearby bridge had been blown up, so the men clambered down and then began to climb up the other side. Just then, they saw German troops down the railroad track. The Germans opened fire. Silvola and his buddies quickly took cover in pine trees growing along the railway cut.

The Germans were from the 27th Fusilier Regiment and were trying to outflank the 1st Battalion at Losheimergraben. Robinson watched as they approached in their camouflaged white ski suits. 'The way they were walking up on us, pretty casual-like, I guess they thought we was dead,' he recalled.

'We was hid pretty well in that pine thicket, playing the old Indian game.'

The Germans opened fire. Robinson fired back with his M-1. Silvola let rip with the BAR, hitting at least one German. Then there was the fierce crackle of Schmeisser machine pistol fire and German light machine guns.

Robinson cried out in pain and fell to the ground. He had been badly hit in the right calf. Blood gushed into the white snow. Silvola blazed away with the BAR. Suddenly, there was searing pain around his shoulder. With a bullet in his upper arm, he continued to fire until he was out of ammunition. Then he dropped the gun, grunting in pain.

Corporal McGehee, the LSU linebacker, ran to his aid. The Germans screamed for them to surrender. McGehee put his hands in the air.

Robinson had eight sulfa tablets, issued to each man to delay infection before he could receive proper medical attention. He knew German soldiers were not issued sulfa: it was one of the first things they took from captured Americans. 'You was supposed to take one a day, and drink a lot of water behind it,' he recalled. 'I knew the Germans would take them from me first thing, so I took all eight tablets. There wasn't no water, so I just ate a lot of snow.'

The Germans approached carefully and then picked up the wounded men. One of the Germans told Robinson that he was American and had lived in Detroit until he was fifteen, when his parents moved back to the Fatherland. 'There were others like him drafted in the German army but they weren't really trusted too much,' recalled Robinson. 'He told me that he wanted to go back to America, and that he was going to surrender as soon as he could get close enough to the American line.'

Silvola, Robinson, and McGehee had been captured by Fusilier Regiment 27 of the 12th Volksgrenadier Division. By nightfall, they would join a column of hundreds of other dazed and wounded Americans from the 99th Division.

Meanwhile, back in Lanzerath, the Germans had begun to search houses in the village. Creger and Slape suddenly heard the sound of a jackboot against wood. The front door was being kicked in. Sergeant Slape ran upstairs to the attic. Creger only just had time to hide behind a door. A German pushed it open; Creger squeezed himself further into the small space between door and wall, took a hand grenade from his field jacket, pulled the pin, and readied his M-1.

'I was thinking if they came in, we would all go to hell together,' recalled Creger.

The door handle pushed into his ribs. Surely, he thought, the Germans could hear his heart thumping like a jackhammer. For agonizing seconds, he listened to the harsh, guttural curses of the Germans as they searched the room.

Bullets came through the attic roof above Slape's head. From their position above the village, other members of the platoon had spotted the Germans entering the building and opened fire. The Germans immediately left the house.

Creger sighed with relief and slipped the pin back into the grenade. He and Slape then followed the Germans downstairs, left by a back door, sprinted to the nearest cover – a cowshed – and ducked down behind several cows.

'I noticed a hay loft above the cows,' recalled Creger. 'I grabbed the loft door and lifted myself enough to look into the loft, and spotted a German soldier searching the loft. I then eased myself down trying not to disturb the cows, then proceeded to crawl across the floor under a cow and left the back door [with Slape] running like hell across a field and after running for several hundred yards, I suddenly realized I was three-quarters of the way through a minefield. I then got out of the minefield and into the woods, paused to catch my breath, and then made a circle through the woods trying to [find] the road.'

Slape and Creger reached the edge of the wooded area. 'We then had to cross a field,' recalled Slape. 'As we did so, we were fired on from our left but the range was either too great or the Germans couldn't shoot because all we got was snow knocked in our faces.'

Creger and Slape made it across the field but then ran into a patrol of Germans at the edge of another woods. Slape and Creger opened fire. '[We] eliminated them with no difficulty,' recalled Slape. 'Three or four Germans with an automatic weapon.'

Slape and Creger crunched on through the snow as fast as they could, getting closer to the road that separated them from their position.

Meanwhile, Lyle Bouck and Private First Class Milosevich also ran toward the road, using thickets of young trees for cover. Suddenly, they spotted Slape and Creger in the woods on the other side of the road.

'Come on over!' called Bouck.

Slape started across. German rifle fire and MG-42 bullets ricocheted all around him, and he fell.

'Christ, he's hit,' thought Bouck.

But Slape got up very fast and made it across. It was Creger's turn. He made it unharmed.

'Ahhh, God,' cried Slape, clutching his chest. 'Didn't get shot – slipped on the ice, fell on my chest.'

Slape had fractured his sternum and one of his ribs. He looked at his boot: the heel had been shot off.

'What the hell are you doing here?' Slape panted.

'Got impatient waiting for you,' replied Bouck. 'I sent Silvola, "Pop" and McGehee to find you. Where are they?'

'Haven't seen 'em. We gotta get outta here.'

'We can ambush them,' said Milosevich. 'I've got grenades.'

'No!' said Slape. 'We'll get killed.'

'Let's get out of here,' ordered Bouck.

He took just a few minutes to get back to the position. Bouck rejoined Private Bill James in the command post. He picked up his binoculars and looked through the slit in the front of the dugout. There were yet more paratroopers in the distance, approaching Lanzerath.

'Where the hell did they jump?' thought Bouck.

He had heard no planes.

'Did they jump sharp [too soon] and land in the wrong place?'

The Germans were soon within range. Bouck picked up his handset and called regimental headquarters again. Germans, perhaps as many as five hundred, were advancing on Lanzerath. He needed artillery support. Right away.

The voice on the other end of the line told Bouck he must be seeing things.

'Damn it!' Bouck shouted. 'Don't tell me what I can't see! I have twenty-twenty vision. Bring down some artillery, all the artillery you can, on the road south of Lanzerath. There's a Kraut column coming up from that direction.'

Bouck waited anxiously, but the whine of 'outgoing mail' – artillery support – never came. He and his men were outside of the 99th Division boundary, outside their own regimental boundary, and outside of the V Corps boundary. Artillery support was by now desperately needed all along the Ghost Front, and it was directed first to assigned areas within boundaries.

Bouck again called regimental headquarters. What was he to do? Stay or go?

'Stay!' Bouck was told. 'You are to hold at all costs.'[24]

From his house on the edge of town, sixteen-year-old Adolf Schur saw a line of German soldiers in mottled uniforms tramp into the village on either side of the road. Suddenly, several dropped out of the column and rushed into Adolf's house, where they found some American rations that had been left by the tank destroyers. Adolf's mother was saving them for Christmas. The Germans grabbed the boxes of rations and ran back to the column.

Back in the platoon's position, Lyle Bouck and his men watched, fingers on triggers, sweat beading on their brows, as the column marched forward. Bouck ordered the platoon to hold fire until he gave a hand signal. He could see at least 250 Germans now moving along the road. A small group passed by, directly in front of him.

'That's got to be their point,' Bouck told James. 'Let them go. I want to get the main body.'

Bouck soon spotted an officer who looked like he was the Germans' commander. Each man in the platoon chose a target. Platoon Sergeant Slape drew a bead on the officer.

Suddenly, a blond teenage girl, perhaps thirteen, came out of one of the houses. Private Bill James quickly had the girl in his sights, finger against the trigger, ready to squeeze, just as he had learned in basic training. But the girl reminded him of his two younger sisters back home in White Plains New York. He relaxed his finger.

Bouck still held up his arm. He saw the girl point toward him. It looked as if she was alerting the Germans to the platoon's presence. Bouck also hesitated – he didn't want to get the girl killed. Then one of the Germans yelled something, and the column of paratroopers dove for the ditches on either side of the road.

'Open fire,' cried Bouck as he dropped his arm.

The platoon managed to hit some of the Germans cowering in the ditches, but it was scant consolation: the chance for an ambush had been lost, and now the Germans knew their position.

Just then, a jeep pulled up behind Bouck's dugout. Lieutenant Warren Springer and his three-man artillery unit jumped out. Could they help Bouck and his platoon? Bouck assigned Springer, Gacki, and Wibben to radio operator James Fort's dugout.

Twigs, broken by German bullets, dropped off trees nearby. Gacki, Wibben, and Springer jumped into Fort's hole. Their fellow artillery observer, Billy Queen, dove into Joseph McConnell's dugout and readied his M-1.

Including Springer's unit, Bouck now had just twenty-two men to fight off an enemy force that looked to be at least twenty times larger. Nothing he had learned at Fort Benning or in the previous weeks on patrol had prepared him to deal with such a hopeless situation. With one swift flanking movement led by experienced squad leaders, so many Germans would surely quickly seize the position and kill or wound most of the men under Bouck's command.

It was around 10:30 A.M.

Milosevich gazed in disbelief as Germans entered the open pasture and then moved toward the fence bisecting it. 'They advanced like they were out for a Sunday stroll,' he recalled. 'I figured we were going to get it, so I was going to take all the Germans with me I could.'

Bouck also watched in amazement as the Germans broke the first rule of combat: Do not attack – and never by walking upright in tight groups – a static position without simultaneous flanking movement and the heaviest possible covering fire.

'When the first guys [Germans] hit the fence,' ordered Bouck, 'I'll give the signal to fire.'

The Germans kept coming, now firing from the hip, and then reached the fence.

'Let them have it,' cried Bouck.

The platoon and the artillery observers opened fire. Bouck did not join in, concentrating instead on what the platoon's next move should be. But a few feet away, Bill James aimed through the dugout's slit and fired with superb accuracy, felling German after German, pausing only to slam another eight-round clip into his M-1.

James then sprinted under fire to the .50-caliber jeep-mounted machine gun and began to sweep the hillside. 'I was only nineteen then and that was the hardest part of it,' he recalled. 'Those kids coming up the hill were eighteen and nineteen, just like me. They charged swaggering, thinking it would be a lark, and suddenly my .50 caliber would tear them up. They were so close I could see their faces, and it was so painful I had to divorce the faces from the action, and fire just at movement.'

In their dugout, two of the artillery observation party – Wibben and Gacki – fed M-1 clips to one of Bouck's men as fast as they could. '[But he] kept running out of ammunition,' recalled Gacki. 'In between what we were trying to do, we were loading clips for him. He emptied those clips as fast as we could load them.'

Meanwhile, Lieutenant Warren Springer tried to direct his artillery battery's fire by calling in coordinates over his jeep-mounted SCR-610 radio. Gingerly, he stuck his head out like a turtle, using the phone extension, and then ducked back in when he came under fire. Some shells landed near the road entering Lanzerath but did not stall the German advance.

Then suddenly the jeep was hit, either by machine gun fire or mortar fragments, and knocked out of action. Springer heard glass breaking: the SCR-610 radio was destroyed. He would not be able to direct any more fire. With all land lines cut, the platoon's only means of communication was now Bouck's and Fort's SCR-300 radios.

Down below, on the outskirts of Lanzerath, German Private First Class Rudi Fruehbeisser, 9th Infantry, 3rd Fallschirmjaeger Division, watched the battle in horror.

'The 2nd Company carried out a storming attack on a small section of wood three hundred meters left of the road,' he recalled. 'During the attack, platoon commander Sergeant Karl Quator and Corporal Fischer, as well as Privates Rench, Roth, and Heube were killed. The platoon commander was wounded.'

Through the slit of his dugout, Private Joseph McConnell suddenly saw one of Fruehbeisser's comrades, armed with a burp gun, appear not far away. He opened up and the German fell. But so did McConnell, hit in the right shoulder.

From their dugout forty yards away, Sergeant Slape and Private First Class Milosevich still fired constantly, only pausing to reload. It was one of the 'most beautiful fields of fire' Slape had ever seen, 'just wide open.' And the Germans were having to cross it to reach him.

Suddenly, a bullet grazed Milosevich's fingernail. He fired again. The Germans seemed crazed if not doped – they were surely out of their minds. Why else would they attack so suicidally? The Germans would dive to the ground as men all around them were picked off. Then an officer or sergeant would scream for them to get up and attack. As soon as they tried to move forward, Slape and Milosevich would cut them down again.

Then everything went quiet.

The platoon tried to catch its breath. The firefight had lasted perhaps thirty seconds. Almost all of the attackers had been killed or wounded.

Lieutenant Lyle Bouck noticed that he was soaked with perspiration, although it was still well below freezing. He felt no tension now that the battle had begun. It was hard to believe that the Germans had not pounded the platoon's position with artillery, mortar, or even machine gun fire. He looked down at the field below, dotted with corpses, body parts, and bloody patches: there was a 'lot of human waste.' The carnage did not disturb him. They had stopped the Germans. They had done their duty and carried out their orders.

'Check your holes and see whether we have any wounded,' Bouck ordered Slape. 'I'm going to take the right side. You take the left.'

They moved along the holes. McConnell was the only casualty. A burp gun bullet was lodged in his upper chest. But he was conscious. He'd fight on. Besides, there were no medics around to patch him up and pull him off the line.

Just before 11:00 A.M., the Germans in Lanzerath prepared to attack again. From their barn, Adolf Schur, his brother Eric, and his father Christolf watched the Germans assemble. Christolf had been a drummer with the Wehrmacht in World War I. 'Now,' he told his sons, 'you can see what war is really like.'

The Schurs watched the Germans attack up the hillside again.

The platoon again opened fire as the Germans got to the fence. This time, it was Private First Class Milosevich who let rip with the .50-caliber jeep-mounted machine gun. The armor-piercing bullets, employed by rear gunners on B-17s to bring down fighters, blew holes a foot wide in the German soldiers. But the .50 caliber's field of fire was too narrow, and the gun was not easy to maneuver from its fixed position in the jeep. Milosevich tried to take it off its stand but burned his hand because it had become so hot. He wrapped a handkerchief over the burn and again picked up the gun so he could better traverse the pasture.

Suddenly, Milosevich saw a German paratrooper to his left only yards from Lyle Bouck's dugout. He fired and the German fell.

The enemy fire suddenly became particularly fierce. Milosevich decided to make for his dugout. A German appeared a few yards away, wielding a 'potato-masher' grenade. Milosevich let rip, cutting the German in two.

Milosevich made it back to his dugout and began to fire again. He screamed for Slape, who dived into the dugout, bruising his ribs.

The Germans kept coming.

Slape took over on the .50-caliber machine gun.

'Shoot in bursts of three!' shouted Milosevich, knowing the gun would overheat and they would be out of ammunition if Slape kept firing away without pausing.

'I can't!' shouted Slape. 'There's too many of them!'

Slape continued to fire, hitting dozens of men with a sweeping arc. Milosevich saw the unwieldly gun start to pour off smoke. When he looked down the hillside, it seemed that they were outnumbered by at least a hundred to one, and the Germans just kept coming.

In their dugout on the extreme right side of the position,

Sam Jenkins and Robert Preston had by now run out of ammunition for their BAR and were using their M-1s. Jenkins couldn't understand why the Germans were attacking again without artillery support. If they brought just one tank into play, they would all be quickly blown off the hill. He fired again and again, knowing it was vital to hit the Germans before they got close enough to throw a grenade through the hole's firing slit.

Nearby, Private Louis Kalil suddenly noticed that some of the Germans were fanning out and trying to infiltrate through the position's flanks. A few feet from Kalil, Sergeant George Redmond was squinting through the sights of his M-1.

To the left of the dugout, a German paratrooper crawled along the rock-hard ground. He got to within thirty yards of Kalil and Redmond and then quickly aimed his rifle, loaded with a grenade, and fired. It was a superb shot. The grenade entered the dugout through its eighteen-inch slit and hit Kalil square in the jaw.

But it did not explode. Instead, it knocked Kalil across the dugout to Redmond's side. Kalil was half-stunned as he lay sprawled on the base of the dugout. Redmond dropped his rifle, grabbed some snow, and rubbed it in Kalil's face. Blood gushed from Kalil's jaw. The force of the impact had forced his lower teeth into the roof of his mouth, where several were now deeply embedded. His jaw was fractured in three places.

Redmond sprinkled sulfa powder on the wound and then pulled gauze out of both their first-aid kits and started to wrap Kalil's face. There was no morphine in the kits to kill the pain. Once the shock wore off, Kalil would be in agony.

'How bad is it?' asked Kalil.

'Oh, it's not too bad, Louis,' said Redmond.

'But I've got blood all over myself. It can't be very nice.'

'It's not too bad.'

'Okay, I'll take your word for it.'

Kalil knew Redmond was trying to make the wound sound a lot less severe than it really was. He could feel the teeth embedded in the roof of his mouth cutting into his tongue.

The battle still raged. Small-arms fire sounded like radio static during an electrical storm, a constant ear-piercing crackle. Redmond's fingers did not shake despite his fear as he wrapped the last of the gauze around Kalil's jaw. He knew the Germans could penetrate their position any moment. If they were to stand a chance, they would need to return to firing as soon as possible.

Redmond tied the last gauze bandage and met Kalil's gaze.

'Don't worry about it,' reassured Redmond.

'If things get to where you can take off, then take off,' Kalil replied.

Redmond looked at Kalil fiercely.

'We're staying here – together.'

'All right.'

Redmond grabbed his M-1 and began to fire. Kalil was now in terrible pain but did the same, aiming with the use of just one eye at the figures that still approached up the bloodied hillside. It was so cold in the dugout that Kalil could feel blood freezing to his face, stemming the flow from the wound. The damned cold had been good for one thing at least. In the desert, he would surely have bled to death.

German Private First Class Rudi Fruehbeisser again watched the battle from the bottom of the hill near a farmhouse. He could see how his fellow paratroopers stood out in their mottled uniforms against the snow as they advanced on Bouck's position and how they were methodically being picked off, one by one. An order was given for the third company of his outfit to attack. As it moved forward, Fruehbeisser saw one of its platoon commanders stumble and then fall to the ground. A paratrooper turned the fallen man over.

'Headshot!'

Nearby, two corporals were hit but not killed.

An M-1 shot cracked out.

Another man grasped his face and fell over, killed instantly.

'Headshot!'

There was another whip of a bullet through the air.

'Headshot!'

Finally, under such intense and accurate fire, the Germans fell back behind several farm buildings.

It was now around midday.

From his dugout, Lieutenant Lyle Bouck suddenly saw a German lift a white flag into the air and walk up the hill. Bouck ordered his men to hold their fire. The German was asking for time to remove wounded from the hillside. Bouck shouted back that he would allow this.

For the next hour, German medics scrambled up the hill and removed their wounded. Meanwhile, more ammunition was distributed to the I&R platoon, and Slape went to each dugout to check on the men and give them encouragement.

Milosevich watched the German medics work on the wounded. The German medics, who wore two armbands and large white body tabards that had a two-foot-square red cross on the front and back, were easily identifiable – more so than American medics, who wore just one armband that often became muddied.

Around 2:00 P.M., the Germans prepared to attack again. Incredibly, it was another full-frontal advance but this time supported by some mortar and machine gun fire. The platoon opened fire again, and the Germans again fell in every direction.

Milosevich saw a medic apparently at work on a German soldier Milosevich knew must be dead because he had just 'shot him full of holes.' The medic was about thirty yards away and kept looking up at Milosevich and Slape's dugout. His lips moved constantly. Mortar fire started to land close to the dugout. Milosevich was sure the medic was directing it. Then the medic turned, and Milosevich spotted a pistol in his belt. Under the Geneva Convention, medics were not allowed to carry weapons.

Milosevich turned to Slape.

'Let me have the rifle. I want to shoot that son of a bitch.'

Slape refused, saying there were too many other Germans in front of them. Milosevich explained about the medic – he was talking into a radio and directing the mortar fire.

'Why, that son of . . .'

Three shots rang out. The medic fell dead.

A while later, during a brief respite in the firing, Milosevich found two bullet holes in his field jacket. Miraculously, he was unharmed. There were more Germans. He returned to firing with his carbine. It was sheer slaughter, as if he was shooting clay ducks back in California at an amusement park.

Slape again scrambled over to the .50-caliber machine gun and began to fire. Quickly, it again overheated and then began to fire rounds even when Slape wasn't pressing the trigger. Suddenly, the gun fell silent. The barrel had finally burned out and was bent in a light arc.

The Germans continued to rush the hill, some firing from the hip. Many received single shots to heart or head, picked off at close range. Not one got past the barbed wire fence. Bodies were soon piled up behind it.

Suddenly, artillery observer Billy Queen, standing beside Joseph McConnell in a dugout, cried out in pain and slumped to the ground. He began to groan, blood seeping from a serious stomach wound. There was nothing McConnell could do for him – he had no medical supplies. Queen began to lose consciousness. Within an hour he would be dead, his body starting to freeze.[25]

The third attack lasted only a few minutes. Then the Germans again fell back.

It was now midafternoon and obvious to all the men that they could not hold out much longer. Most had only a few clips left for their M-1s. Bouck's thoughts turned to how the platoon could abandon the position. He reached for the telephone to his SCR-300 radio and asked again for artillery support and fresh orders.

At regimental headquarters in Hünningen, Fernandez overheard Bouck talking on the radio to Lieutenant Buegner, Kriz's assistant. Bouck said he was surrounded. Then he heard the sound of shooting in the background.

Bouck heard a huge crack beside his ear. A sniper's bullet shot the telephone out of his hand. The radio was also hit. Bouck fell to the ground.

In the dugout beside him, radio operator James Fort heard 'tubes and everything breaking inside the radio.' He looked out of his hole to see Bouck sprawled in the snow beside a jeep.

At the other end of the line in Hünningen, Fernandez heard a hissing sound getting louder, and then 'a sound right out of the movies . . . and suddenly the radio went dead.' Fernandez feared the worst – Bouck and the radio had been blown to pieces.

But Bouck came to after a few seconds. Stunned, he shook himself and got up. Slowly, his hearing returned. The bullet that hit the receiver had exploded only an inch from his ear. He looked at the radio – it was completely destroyed.

Bouck's last line of communication was lost. There would be no more orders. Every decision now would be his alone.

Bouck returned groggily to his dugout, determined to work out a way for the platoon to withdraw under cover of darkness.

But would they be able to hold out that long?

At regimental headquarters in Hünningen, Fernandez immediately reported the loss of communication to Major Kriz. As soon as was possible Kriz tried to organize a relief party, but it quickly became obvious that it would be impossible to reach Bouck and his men, given the scale and speed of the German attack. All along its front, the 394th was fighting desperately to hold similar positions.

Kriz soon had a greater concern than one platoon, a single battalion, or even a regiment. The entire 99th Division, some fifteen thousand men, was under serious threat. This was no spoiling counterattack to hinder the 99th's attempts to penetrate to the Roer dams. Kriz had been right: the Germans had indeed been preparing for a truly massive attack. And now time was running out for the entire Checkerboard division, not just for Lyle Bouck.

*

Five miles to Kriz's east, on the outskirts of the border town of Losheim, Jochen Peiper, the most decorated SS tank commander of the Third Reich, watched his point tank advance. The Panther V suddenly detonated a land mine and was put out of action. Peiper fumed as engineers were called in and began to remove the mines blocking his advance. Ironically, they were not American mines – they had been laid by Germans retreating to the Siegfried Line in October.

Peiper was now hours behind schedule. He began again to advance cautiously. But five hundred meters west of Losheim there was another explosion as a second Panther V drove into another minefield. It was dark by the time the column started up again. Then, southeast of the village of Merlscheid, the column lost its first Panzer, again to a land mine. Driver Werner Sternebeck heard a detonation and then felt the tank jump and come to a standstill. He quickly abandoned it and jumped onto another tank, knowing Peiper would not tolerate a moment's delay.

Again, Peiper learned that the column would have to wait until yet more mines were cleared. If he lost any more time, he would have to consider sacrificing some half-tracks, using them to detonate mines so that the column could push ahead.

Peiper had been ordered to reach the Meuse within twenty-four hours. Yet here he was, ten hours after the barrage had started, only a few miles beyond the Siegfried Line. The 9th Parachute Regiment should have cleared a path to Honsfeld by now. But apparently they were still in Lanzerath. *Was im Himmel* (What in heaven) had held them up all day?

7. The Last Sunset

Lanzerath – December 16, 1944

At 4:03 P.M. precisely, at regimental headquarters in Hünningen, a radio operator received the last transmission from James Fort: 'We are holding our position. Enemy strength 75. They are moving from Lanzerath west to railroad.' The message had been sent at 3:50 P.M.

Above Lanzerath, Lyle Bouck passed the word that the platoon would soon withdraw on a signal of three short whistle blasts. Twenty yards away, Bill James finished removing the distributor cap from the last of the platoon's six jeeps. The Germans would not be able to make use of a single vehicle.

James clambered back into the dugout.

Bouck looked grave.

'What's wrong, sir?' asked James.

'When I blow the whistle, you go with the others. I'll stay.'

'Like hell,' said James, 'you're coming with us or we all stay.'

'Okay, you win,' Bouck finally replied. 'I'll go.'

No one would be left behind. The platoon would leave as they had fought – together. But not until they had the cover of near darkness.

There was perhaps time for one last attempt to get help. Bouck called for Corporal Sam Jenkins and Private First Class Preston. 'Sam,' Bouck told Jenkins. 'You and Bob take off down the Buchholz Station road and go to regiment in Hünningen. See if you can find Major Kriz, get us reinforcements or orders to pull out. We can't hold much longer.'

Jenkins and Preston quickly left their dugout. They had gone fifty yards when they looked back, only to see three mortars land smack on the top of their hole. They hurried on, following a logging trail that led to the position's rear.

Dusk settled quickly.

Down in Lanzerath, villagers could hear an incessant moaning as dozens of wounded paratroopers were laid out in homes converted into aid stations. Behind the Schur farmhouse, fifty yards to the west of the Café Scholzen, Sergeant Vinz Kuhlbach pleaded with 9th Fallschirmjaeger Regiment officers not to send his last few men to their deaths by attacking straight up the hill toward the Americans' foxholes. Surely it was time to outflank the American position? Several officers nodded their agreement.

Kuhlbach and fifty other paratroopers gathered in the backyard of Adolf Schur's house. In the growing darkness they moved into wooded areas leading to the platoon's right flank. There were precisely eight hours and five minutes of daylight that day. Sunset arrived at 4:35 P.M.

Lyle Bouck knew he had only a few minutes before nightfall. The men would benefit greatly from what was left of the light as they retreated through the deep forest to the rear of their position. Bouck prepared to blow his whistle.

At that moment, Germans were crawling into the rear of the position. Slape and Private Milosevich spotted several among the fir trees, their mottled uniforms blurring into the mist and dusk.

The two had resolved to fight to the very end. Slape was as 'scared as hell' but still believed he would somehow live,[26] even with the odds so heavily stacked against him and his men. 'About dark, there were Germans all over the area, inside the perimeter,' he recalled. 'I told Milosevich, "Let's get out of here," and I started out of the bunker by the rear entrance and a German shot a hole in my field jacket (still no blood). He was about twenty yards to the left rear of the bunker. There were three of them. A grenade handled the situation nicely.'

Slape dove back into his dugout where he and Milosevich started to fire their last M-1 rounds. With less than a handful of bullets between them, every shot counted.

'Krauts in the woods to the left!' someone shouted.

Then another of the platoon's last remaining men yelled that the Germans were also infiltrating from the right. Lyle Bouck saw three, perhaps four, figures. He pressed the trigger on his carbine, sprayed the silhouettes, ducked back down, and checked his gun. The two magazines he'd had welded together were empty.

'Did you get anything?' asked James.

'I think so.'

In his dugout at the center of the position, Private John Creger came under machine gun and mortar fire. As he fired back, he heard the *putt-putt-putt* of a V-1 rocket. He looked up to see it pass over and crash into the woods behind him. To his surprise, it did not explode.

There was a lull in the firing. To Creger, it seemed as if the entire war had stopped momentarily. 'I crawled out of the foxhole to see what the hell was going on,' he recalled. 'I spotted this German soldier sneaking up behind us with a hand grenade, and when he saw me, he instinctively threw it at me. The only thing I could do was to hold my head on the ground. Luckily, the grenade was evidently a concussion one and failed to do much damage except for filling my eyes with dirt and rock. I then jumped back into my foxhole.'

In the nearest dugout to Creger's, radio operator James Fort peered into the darkness and saw gray figures infiltrating the position in all directions. 'One of them fired a long burst from a burp gun,' he recalled. 'He hit the radio receiver-transmitter type SCR-284. That took care of destroying it before we surrendered.'

Frantically, Fort removed the bolt from his M-1 and threw it into the snow to prevent the Germans from using it. All he could do now was detonate the grenades he had hung in surrounding trees.

As the Germans closed in, Fort pulled on several wires. The fragmentation grenades exploded all around, but still the Germans kept coming. Then Fort heard a German shout for him to come out of the dugout. It was all over.

Fort slithered out of the front of the dugout with his hands clasped behind his head. A young German paratrooper stood before him, quivering with fear and rage, his finger on the trigger of a burp gun. The German was shaking so much that Fort feared he would fire by accident.

The German stepped forward and stuck the gun's muzzle against Fort's belt buckle.

'*Kamerad?*' he screamed.

'*Kamerad,*' replied Fort.

'*Raus, raus!*' (Out, out!).

The German led Fort away.

In their dugout, Bouck and James could hear sporadic gunfire and Germans yelling.

Suddenly, the muzzle of a burp gun appeared through the rear exit to the dugout. Bouck instinctively pushed the barrel away from him. There was a huge roar. *Brrrrp! Brrrrp! Brrrrp!*

James felt himself 'floating upward and backward' from the force of impact of the burp gun bullets. Then he slumped to the bottom of the dugout, littered with empty M-1 cartridges and shell casings.

'Bill, you're hit!' cried Bouck.

A flashlight lit up the hole.

Bouck briefly saw James's face and winced. It looked like his head had been shot off.

'Mein Gott!' cried the German with the flashlight.

Perhaps ten seconds later, two Germans reached into the dugout, grabbed James's body, and pulled him out.

The Germans then yanked Bouck out. He saw James's body lying in the snow.

James had taken five or six rounds in the face at close range. He had lost an eye and most of his right jaw. Fragments of bone and bullet were lodged in his brain.

'*Wer ist der Commandant?*' (Who's the commander?), shouted Sergeant Vinz Kuhlbach.

Bouck raised his hand.

'I am.'

'Why your men still firing?' asked Kuhlbach.

'They aren't. They must be yours because we're out of ammunition.'

A nearby German officer asked for Bouck's name, but before Bouck could answer a burst of fire hit the officer and then Bouck. They both fell to the ground beside James.

Bouck had been hit clean through his calf. He looked down at his leg. He was bleeding 'like a stuck hog.' He somehow managed to get a tourniquet on the leg.

Meanwhile, the Germans seized hole after hole.

Lieutenant Warren Springer and his two fellow forward artillery observers, Technician Fourth Class Willard Wibben and Sergeant Peter Gacki, had used every last magazine for their carbines. Springer had only a couple of bullets left in his Colt .45.

A German yelled into the back of the dugout: 'Come out, or we throw grenade in!'

Springer climbed out, convinced that the Germans would soon shoot him and his men. But if he was going to go, he'd rather have a bullet in the back of the head than be maimed by a grenade.

To Springer's astonishment, his captors held their fire. 'When I saw they weren't going to shoot I said in English and fractured German: "*Wo ist dein Hauptmann?* (Where is your captain?). We must take care of our wounded." I repeated this several times, and one of the Germans who seemed to be the leader came forward and said in English, "Be quiet – we are taking care of them." He directed Gacki, Wibben, and me to help a wounded German, and at his command the soldiers around us motioned with their rifles and made it clear that we were to get going.'

Private First Class Milosevich and Platoon Sergeant Slape watched as the Germans pulled other men from holes.

'Come out!' other Germans cried. 'Hands up! Come out!'

Milosevich spotted a decorated German officer holding a Mauser pistol. He quickly had him in the sights of his M-1 rifle. There were still a couple of rounds in the magazine.

'I'll get a big medal for shooting this bastard.'

But then something told him not to shoot. He had killed so many young Germans already that day.

Slape picked up his M-1.

'What you doing?' asked Milosevich.

'I'm gonna shoot the Germans!'

Milosevich grabbed the rifle from Slape.

'They'll kill us all. Don't.'

Then the burly figure of a German paratrooper appeared

in front of their dugout and pointed his burp gun at Slape.

'Go ahead and shoot you son-of-a-bitch,' said Slape.

'I won't shoot,' replied the German. 'I'm a soldier.'

Two more Germans pulled Slape out and began to pat him down.

Slape had hidden a hand grenade in his pocket. One of the Germans quickly found it and threw it away.

At the far northern edge of the position, Private Louis Kalil and Sergeant George Redmond were also ordered out of their dugout at gunpoint. The Germans hauled them through the narrow slit at the front, and then Redmond was told to carry Kalil down the hill.

The German captors lined up the able-bodied survivors just inside the tree line and stripped the men of personal valuables and rations. Then several of the Germans raised their burp guns.

This was it. Now they were going to be executed.

Suddenly, a German officer rushed over.

'*Nichts! Nichts!*' he shouted.

The paratroopers lowered their guns a few inches. The platoon had been spared, for now at least.

A German sergeant walked over to where Bouck lay bleeding in the snow beside Bill James.

'Get up!' he shouted.

Bouck staggered to his feet. The German then ordered one of his comrades to help Bouck carry James down the hill.

Bouck went to James's side.

'You'll be all right, Bill,' Bouck soothed. 'I'll get you out of here.'

'*Raus mit du!*' (Get moving!), cried a German.

Bouck and a German paratrooper lifted James to his feet and began to stumble down the field leading to Lanzerath.

It was strewn with so many shell cases and pieces of shrapnel that the metal crunched under foot in the cordite-gray snow.

James briefly regained consciousness.

'Bouck, let's take them,' he whispered, figuring they could use the German propping him up as a hostage. Then James heard the German cry out: *'Ach, meinen Kameraden!'* (Ah, my friends!).

James saw the man's friends littering the hillside.

'My foot dragged over one of the bodies, face up, a blond kid, his eyes staring that blank stare, his lips parted,' recalled James. 'He had no visible mark on him. No blood. But he was dead. My thoughts went to the mothers of these boys and the worry they were enduring at the moment and the anguish they would suffer when they received the news that their sons were dead. Could I but tell these mothers that their boys died brave men – attacking. My heart was crying for these mothers and all humanity when suddenly I thought of my mother.'

If Bouck made it through, he must get in touch with her.

'Bouck, Bouck,' added James, 'tell my mother when you get back that I love her and that I didn't suffer.' Then he lost consciousness.

Bouck noticed a German toting a burp gun following behind. They crossed the fence that bisected the hillside. It had been so badly damaged in the battle that they were able simply to step through a gap. Dead Germans were clumped against it.

'Halt!'

Bouck stopped.

The German with the burp gun stuck its muzzle in Bouck's stomach.

'St. Lo!' the German shouted. 'St. Lo!'

'Nein! Nein!' grunted Bouck.

The German was referring to the fierce month-long battle for the strategically vital Norman town that summer. By July 11, 1944, when St. Lo finally fell, his 3rd Fallschirmjaeger Division had lost more than a third of its seventeen thousand men.

The German suddenly pulled the trigger.

Bouck heard it click.

'It's all over,' he thought. 'I'm dead. I don't even know it. How easy it is to die. It's not too bad.'

Bouck saw the German's face, contorted by rage, a few inches from him and realized he was still alive.

It was now pitch dark. The German was even more incensed because his burp gun had failed. He picked up a rifle and stuck it in Bouck's back.

'Oh, no,' thought Bouck. 'I'm gonna still get it.'

But there was no click.

'*Rausen!*' (Get going!), shouted the German.

Bouck struggled to carry James down the hill, now thinking every step might be his last. Then they exited the field through a gate, walked along a road, and entered the Café Scholzen.

Inside, a single paraffin lantern provided light, casting a flickering shadow over a small bar, a cluster of old wooden chairs and tables, and a cuckoo clock mounted on a wall.

'*Setz dich!*' (Sit down!), ordered a German.

Bouck slumped down, exhausted, on a bench just inside the café, propping James up beside him.

Back at the position, the able-bodied survivors from the platoon were ordered to help carry the German dead and wounded off the hill.

Lieutenant Warren Springer watched as the men began to pick up German bodies.

'Pick up that machine gun,' a nearby German officer commanded.

'*Nein! Ich bin ein Offizier*' (No! I'm an officer), said Springer.

The officer glared and then told one of his own men to pick up the machine gun. Springer would not retrieve weapons for able-bodied Germans but was willing to help with the wounded. 'I had nothing against them once they'd been shot,' he recalled.

Some of the platoon began to use their mackinaws as litters. It was back-breaking work given the quantity of German wounded and the distance – around two hundred yards – that they needed to be carried into the village.

James Fort grabbed one end of a mackinaw. Milosevich held the other end, and they began to lug two of the German wounded down the hill.

Fort was soon so exhausted that he felt close to collapsing.

'Risto, I can't go another step. It's too heavy.'

'On three, drop them,' said Milosevich.

On three, they dropped the makeshift litter and collapsed in the snow.

The wounded Germans screamed.

A German paratrooper rushed over.

'Up!' he ordered.

Milosevich and Fort got to their feet. As soon as the paratrooper had moved away, they dropped the litter again.

When Lieutenant Warren Springer reached the village, he was ordered into a room adjoining the Café Scholzen. A German officer stood waiting to interrogate him.

Springer calmly placed his gloves on a nearby table.

'I'm only going to tell you my name, rank and serial number.'

'I'm not going to press you,' replied the German in English. 'I already know who you are. You're from the 371st Artillery Battalion.'

Springer did not reply.

There was a long silence.

'How long do you think the war's going to last?' the officer finally asked.

'Maybe three or four months.'

The officer looked bored.

'You can go,' he said, motioning for two of his men to take Springer away.

Springer looked over the side-table. His gloves had disappeared.

'Hey! *Meine Handschuhe, meine Handschuhe*!'

The officer snapped at a couple of his men, and Springer's gloves reappeared.

Springer was taken next door into the main café. As he entered, he saw Bill James seated on a bench beside Bouck. James had been patched up by German medics. Only one eye and his nose were visible through brown-paper bandages, which the Germans used instead of gauze. Springer joined his men in one corner.

Sometime later, Lyle Bouck noticed blood seeping through his field jacket. He checked inside – a bullet had grazed his upper body. He looked down at his leg. The wound was not too severe: he had been able to hobble to the café from the position without the pain overwhelming him.

Outside, meanwhile, members of the platoon had been lined up against a wall. 'Even though they [the Germans] were our enemies,' recalled John Creger, 'they showed their respect for our gallant stand against them. One said: "*Amerikaner* is very good soldier." ... A German officer took my cigarettes and offered each of us one and then kept the rest of the pack.'

One by one, Private Creger and his buddies were then brought into the café. Bouck watched as Sergeant George Redmond carried in a wounded man: as with James, only his nose and one eye were visible because of the extensive bandaging.

Bouck suddenly realized it was Private Louis Kalil.

Sergeant Redmond laid him down on the floor. Others from the platoon walked over to check on him, wanting to know how bad the wound was. 'I was just looking out of my right eye and that was it because the rest of my face was covered up,' recalled Kalil. 'They didn't realize how bad it was. Neither did I.'

Kalil had still not been given any morphine. His embedded teeth caused him maddening pain. But he was glad to be alive, amazed that he had not been shot. Thank God their captors were not SS. They were in the hands of the German army. Perhaps that was why they had not been executed.

Then the Germans brought in Private Joseph McConnell. His field jacket had been cut away, and he had a bad gash in the shoulder. He was placed near some wounded German paratroopers. The café now seemed like a strange combination of a command post and an aid station.

Bouck asked a German who looked like he had some authority if James could be allowed to lie down next to Louis Kalil. It was exhausting having to prop up James, whose blood was now soaking Bouck's shoulder, and James would be more comfortable if he was laid down. The German conferred with another officer and then agreed.

Private First Class Milosevich watched as James and the other wounded men from his platoon were placed together.

It filled him with pride to watch his buddies endure their pain so stoically. 'They were really hurt. Boy, they were hurt. James, at least three bullets in his face; Kalil, a grenade in his face; McConnell hit in the shoulders. But they never said a word. There was no crying. Downstairs, they had more German wounded, and they were screaming. The super race was screaming.'

Bill James drifted in and out of consciousness. 'Lying there bleeding all over the place, I thought I was dying. There was this clock hanging there going tick, tick, and every fifteen or thirty minutes the little gong would ring. The clock got into my brain. Whatever was left of my brain, the clock was working at it, trying to keep me focused on life.'

Meanwhile, back at regimental headquarters in Hünningen, Robert Lambert and Lieutenant Edward Buegner, the last man to speak with Bouck before his radio went dead, were still trying to assess the extent of the German penetration in the 394th sector. They now held out little hope that the platoon had survived.

Artillery fire had rained down on the village most of the day. Although the command post was not hit, all the windows had been blown out. 'By nightfall,' recalled Buegner, 'it was highly probable that Hünningen could be overrun by armored columns at any time. . . . Only one or two of us stayed on duty at a time in the S-2 office. Also, even while there we used tables to protect ourselves against shrapnel and falling debris in case our schoolhouse building did receive a direct hit. All others who could took shelter in basements. . . . Our situation was deemed sufficiently precarious to cause us to burn all valuable documents, papers, maps, and anything else which we thought might be of value to the enemy in case we were captured.'

The S-2 office felt colder than a foxhole, with little protection from the gusts of frigid air blowing through the shattered windows. Lambert and Buegner knew that the regiment, and indeed the entire 99th Division, would have to withdraw very soon, perhaps several miles, and then prepare an organized resistance.

Earlier that evening, a battalion of infantry from the 2nd Division, commanded by Lieutenant Colonel John M. Hightower, had been assigned to aid the 394th. Hightower and his men were now fighting valiantly, but their efforts were 'too little and too late.' The initial casualty reports coming into the Hünningen headquarters were appalling – hundreds of men had already been lost. There would be far more. The enemy forces now outnumbered the 394th by five to fifteen at different positions. And they were advancing with a fanatical zeal that the 99th's few veteran officers had never experienced before.

Lyle Bouck looked up at the cuckoo clock on the wall in the Café Scholzen where he was being held, a prisoner of the Reich. At midnight, he would be twenty-one – December 17 was his birthday. One thing was certain now: there would be no celebration.

'Is there some way for us to get out of here?' thought Bouck. 'If there is, should I try to escape?'

It was his duty as an officer to try to escape, but he also had to look after his men. James was still alive, though barely. He could not be abandoned. Bouck didn't know for sure how many others from his platoon were badly injured, but he certainly wasn't going to leave them now.

Platoon Sergeant Bill Slape, facing Bouck, stood beside an unguarded door. Slape nodded toward it. Bouck realized that Slape wanted to make a run for it. Then a couple of

Germans noticed Slape nodding. They quickly took him to another room.

With his hopes of escape dashed, Sergeant Slape thought about the day that was finally coming to a close. 'Every man with us certainly earned an award for bravery and made a gallant contribution to the war,' he would later write. 'I have never seen men fight better or under greater odds than those men did that day.'

Bouck meanwhile settled into a dazed, dreamlike state. Nothing felt quite real. His mind wandered, searching for meaning amongst all the craziness. Finally, it settled on his Aunt Mildred. Just before Bouck had joined the National Guard at age fourteen, she had asked to read his palm.

'If you live past your twenty-first birthday, you're going to have a good life,' his aunt had predicted.

It was almost midnight. Nearby, the pudgy commander of the 9th Fallschirmjaeger Regiment, Helmut von Hoffmann, dozed in a chair.

As midnight approached at the Eagle's Nest, an excited Adolf Hitler discussed that day's advances with General Hermann Balck, in charge of the German lines south of the Ardennes. Hitler told him that Sepp Dietrich had punched through the Losheim Gap. General von Manteuffel was making rapid progress toward Bastogne, and Jochen Peiper was all set to break through to the Meuse. And the weather was holding up perfectly – heavy cloud cover and fog would continue to ground the Allied planes.

'Black! Black!' said Hitler. 'Everything has changed in the West! Success – complete success – is now in our grasp!'

8. The Café Scholzen

Lanzerath – Midnight, December 16–17, 1944

In the Café Scholzen, the hour hand on the cuckoo clock struck twelve at last. Lyle Bouck suddenly felt a kind of release. He was now twenty-one. Maybe his aunt had been right.

Then rage surged inside him.

'Damn them all,' he thought. 'Damn them all.'

For six years, he had risen inexorably through the ranks, becoming one of the youngest commissioned officers in the U.S. military. Then Major Kriz had spotted his potential and nurtured him. Bouck had imagined fighting all the way to Berlin, winning field promotion, confirming Kriz's faith in him. And now? It didn't mean a thing. He'd gotten the best I&R platoon in the division captured and shot up, and he would probably end up being killed. Six years of training and sacrifice – for nothing.

But then Bouck began to realize that the war for him and his platoon was still far from over. He had expected it to be like a lethal boxing match. A guy gets in a round, fights, gets the hell beaten out of him, and then it's all over. But this wasn't like that. It wasn't going to end. And suddenly, it sounded like it was going to get a lot worse.

Bouck heard the rumble of armored vehicles in the distance. A few hundred yards away, SS Lieutenant Colonel Jochen Peiper's half-track entered Lanzerath.

Peiper was furious. He had lost five half-tracks, three tanks, and precious time – he was now at least twelve hours behind schedule. Lanzerath, he was told, had been secured by the 3rd Fallschirmjaeger Division's 9th Regiment. But now Peiper couldn't see any sign of them as he clattered along the cobbled street. No shots rang out. He had the 'disgusted impression that the whole front had gone to bed instead of waging war.'

'They've got their command post over here, sir,' one of his men called out.

Peiper jumped down from his half-track and strode into the Café Scholzen. The room was full of prisoners and German officers, many of them wounded. Unshaven German paratroopers slept in every corner of the café; one of them was even laid out, snoring, on the bar.

'Who is in command?' Peiper shouted.

Colonel Hoffmann identified himself.

'Why have you stopped?'

'The resistance ahead is too strong,' said Hoffmann, reaching for a map. 'I want to wait until daylight. I think there is at least a full American battalion in front of us. They've mined the road.'

Peiper, dressed head to toe in black leather, cut an impressive, menacing figure. His cap had a skull's head and an eagle – the emblems of the SS. At his collar was the Third Reich's second highest combat award, the Knight's Cross of the Iron Cross with Oak Leaves.

Peiper grabbed the map from Hoffmann. There was not enough light on a table to read, so Peiper claimed two parachute daggers and stabbed the map to a wall near the café's sole lantern.

Hoffmann showed Peiper where he thought the Americans were dug in. His men had taken some prisoners but at a heavy cost. The whole area was heavily mined.

'Did you send out patrols to confirm this?' barked Peiper.

'No, it was too dark by then.'

Peiper picked up a telephone and called a major who was dug in on the outskirts of Lanzerath. The major had heard about the 'massive' American presence nearby from one of his company commanders.

No. He had not reconnoitered the hillside himself.

Peiper demanded that the company commander be put on the line.

It was the same story: the company commander had heard about the Americans from one of his junior officers.

No one had actually scouted the area itself.

Peiper slammed the phone down.

'There's nothing out there!' he yelled. 'I want you to give me one of your parachute battalions immediately.'

Hoffmann was reluctant to see another battalion suffer the same fate as his men the previous day, but the famous 'Blowtorch Peiper' was not to be crossed. He agreed, and Peiper ordered the major of Hoffmann's 1st Battalion to attack through the woods and take nearby Buchholz Station at 4:00 A.M.

'If there are truly American mines in the road,' Peiper blustered, 'then I'll just plow right through them!'

Bouck did not understand what Peiper and Hoffmann were discussing, but it was obvious that Peiper had gotten his way. It was perhaps a good thing that the Germans were so distracted. Their attention was no longer focused solely on the prisoners, and they had no idea it was Bouck's eighteen men who had held up the German assault. Bouck started to feel confident that his platoon would come to no harm that night.

Peiper stormed out. He later recalled, 'I went to an adjacent house that had been fixed up as my command post, and issued orders for an attack on Honsfeld. Tanks with mounted infantry (paratroopers) were to use the road, preceded by a half-track company, led by First Lieutenant Preuss. Meanwhile on each side of the road one parachute company was to clear the underbrush and to protect the flanks. This regrouping and preparation consumed much time, as it was extremely dark and the officers had difficulties [trying] to find their men in the houses.'

As Peiper barked orders for the dawn attack, American artillery started to land nearby. After surviving the previous day's firefights, would Bouck and his men now be killed by their own artillery? It was bitterly ironic that the shells now landing so close had not arrived earlier when they were most needed.

'We could hear each shell as it came in,' recalled forward artillery observer Lieutenant Warren Springer. 'The 105s made a high-pitched, whistling noise. There were also some 155s. They made a lower-pitched, "whooshing" sound. As each shell approached you could sense the suspense in the room until the explosion was heard.

'We'd all hold our breath, and nobody wanted to drop off the chair and hit the floor because you didn't want to lose face,' added Springer. 'The shells passed over us because the artillery was firing at a crossroads in Lanzerath.' Springer had given his battery the map coordinates for the crossroads during the fighting the previous day.

As the artillery fire intensified, Risto Milosevich watched the Germans in the café rush to take shelter in the basement: 'Everybody went down there – the guards, everybody. I looked outside and [the street] was clear. Nobody was out there. I was going to take off, with no gun, nothing.'

Milosevich turned toward Bouck.

'I know what you're thinking, Risto,' said Bouck. 'But we can't leave the wounded.'

'Okay,' replied Milosevich.

The artillery fire eventually ceased, and the Germans reappeared from the basement.

Around 3:30 A.M., German paratroopers could be heard gathering outside. They belonged to the 9th Fallschirmjaeger Regiment's 1st Battalion and would be the spearhead of Peiper's advance toward Honsfeld, via Buchholz Station, at 4:00 A.M. There were sounds of tanks revving and then pulling out, their tracks clanking and grinding against cobbles.

The cuckoo clock struck 4:00 A.M.

SS Lieutenant Colonel Jochen Peiper was once again headed for the Meuse.

Private First Class Milosevich heard Peiper and his men pull out. He now felt desperately tired, his adrenaline spent. 'We were as good as dead,' he recalled. 'We were prisoners, sure, but that felt just like being dead.'

Three hours later, around 7:00 A.M., Lyle Bouck was still sitting on the bench at the entrance to the café. He could sense dawn approaching. He looked around. All of the men captured on the hill the previous day, including Lieutenant Springer's artillery unit, were present.

Privates Kalil and James were still laid out on the cold floor.

James was semiconscious. He could feel the warmth of the heated room envelop him and hear the anxious voices of some of his buddies. Through blurred eyes, he saw Kalil, his face pouring 'blood from every pore.'

The sight of Kalil's wound nauseated James. Suddenly, he vomited.

Several wounded Germans lay beside James. They didn't move. He realized they were dead. Lyle Bouck was still close by – he could hear his voice. James knew he was dying now, but he felt no fear.

The Germans made it clear that the prisoners would soon be dispatched to the rear. The able-bodied would have to walk. The critically wounded – Kalil and James – would be separated from the rest of the platoon and taken by truck.

Bouck asked a guard if he could talk to James. The guard agreed, and Bouck knelt at James's side. He knew that James kept a picture of his girlfriend, Chloe, in his wallet, and that James also carried a small Bible. Bouck padded James's blood-soaked chest and asked the guard if he could take something out of the pocket of James's assault jacket. The guard nodded, and Bouck took the photograph of Chloe from James's wallet and placed it and the Bible on James's chest.

'Here's Chloe with your Bible,' said Bouck. 'I'm gonna say a little prayer and you're going to be okay.'

Bouck prayed and then promised James they would see each other again. Everything was going to be okay. They'd meet again when the war was over, back in the States.

'Bill, they're taking me away now. They separate officers from enlisted men.'

'Bouck, Bouck,' mumbled James, 'tell my mother when you get back that I love her and that I didn't suffer. I didn't suffer, Bouck. Tell her.'

Bouck slipped the photograph back into the wallet and placed it with the Bible back in James's field jacket.

'Good-bye.'

James did not respond, but Bouck knew he had heard because he could feel him squeeze his hand.

Bouck stood up. There was no time to say more. A German soldier ordered him outside: '*Raus!*'

Bouck and his men were soon standing in the cold street

outside the café. Bouck thrust his hands deep into his pockets. On one finger, he still had his class ring from officer training school in Fort Benning. It was now a bittersweet memento of all that had so suddenly been lost: the power to serve his country, freedom, and his hope and pride.

The Germans snapped orders. Bouck and his fellow POWs were stood against a wall. Lieutenant Warren Springer thought they were definitely now going to be shot. But the Germans were simply forming them into a group before marching them out of the village.

Bouck saw a gray flatbed truck pull up nearby. The Germans carried Private Bill James and then Louis Kalil out of the café. James was unconscious. Kalil looked distraught.

'Why aren't I going with you?' Kalil asked Bouck.

'They have to separate us. You just keep your stiff upper lip,' said Bouck tearfully. 'You'll get through this. It shouldn't have happened but it did.'

Kalil began to sob. The teeth embedded in the roof of his mouth hurt badly, but not as much as the sudden realization that he was not going to see his platoon again. He had shared his life with some of them for almost three years. How would he manage now to survive on his own?

Sergeant George Redmond walked over and knelt at his foxhole buddy's side. His breath clouded the air as he tried to soothe Kalil.

'It ain't so bad. Things will work out.'

Tears streamed from Kalil's one visible eye.

'We'll see each other again, Lou,' reassured Redmond. 'We will.'

'Okay.'

'Well, you take care of yourself.'

Redmond rejoined the platoon.

Kalil sobbed again as he watched 'Red' and his comrades being marched away.

As the platoon turned a corner, Lyle Bouck looked back one last time and saw Kalil lying on a stretcher. The Germans were placing James on the flatbed truck. 'That's the end of those two,' he thought.

A few minutes later, Bouck and his men left Lanzerath, marching east. Near the vital road junction just outside the village, they passed several corpses of German paratroopers, no doubt killed by the previous night's artillery fire. Like those of their fallen comrades on the pastures above Lanzerath, their teenaged faces were contorted with terror and turning blue. The platoon traipsed on, walking in the opposite direction, following the road Peiper had used the previous evening – the one that wound through the Schnee Eiffel's forests and deep ravines for a couple of miles and then crossed the Siegfried Line, into the Third Reich.

9. Terror

Hünningen – December 17, 1944

On December 17, 1944, as Bouck and his men trudged toward Germany, back in Hünningen at the 394th's S-2 office a sleepless Robert Lambert was making hasty preparations to move out as the Germans advanced. Suddenly a young rifleman came running into the command post. He had been at the American Red Cross rest facility at Honsfeld, less than a mile away, and had just escaped ahead of the Germans.[27] Hünningen, too, would soon be under attack.

Outside, the weather had cleared. Lambert, alongside Private First Class Carlos Fernandez and Lieutenant Edward Buegner, watched as the U.S. Army Air Corps finally went into action: three P-47 fighter-bombers hit road networks to the south of Hünningen and then struck Honsfeld.

Private First Class Rudi Fruehbeisser, one of the paratroopers commandeered by Peiper in Lanzerath, recalled entering Honsfeld and then coming under the devastating air attack: 'There were *Amerikaner* everywhere. We disarmed them at once and broke up their weapons. Just as we were about to mount up again, all hell broke loose. Firing started from windows at the far end of the village. An American mortar opened up on us too. Our tank commander turned his cannon around on an enemy machine-gun nest and scored a direct hit. Suddenly American dive-bombers came falling out of the sky. Almost immediately our mobile flak took up the challenge as they came screaming down. The air was full of flying 20mm shells. All was confusion and sudden death.'

Lieutenant Buegner watched the same air strike in wonder. 'I realized the awesome strength of the German attack when I saw the volume of antiaircraft fire that their advance columns were able to put up against our attacking planes,' he recalled. 'Each bombing run our planes made was like trying to fly through rain without getting wet.'

As the American airplanes swooped down on Peiper's men in Honsfeld, German artillery began to intensify its shelling of Hünningen.

One shell landed in the backyard of the S-2 intelligence office but, to the immense relief of Lambert and Fernandez, the surviving platoon members on duty there, did not explode. As the morning wore on, they watched through their field glasses as German tanks began to encircle Hünningen, silently taking up positions to the west and rear of the town.

As the Germans tied the noose, Lambert was ordered to gather seven or eight men from headquarters company and take a patrol in the direction of Honsfeld.

Visibility was good as Lambert's patrol set out. Suddenly, German tanks near Honsfeld opened fire. Lambert and his patrol had been spotted. They were drawing direct fire and were soon pinned down.

Lambert and his men ran to take cover in the basement of a farmhouse, but then the Germans zeroed in on that too. There was no option but to 'dart and dodge' their way back to Hünningen. It was true, a rattled Lambert reported to Major Kriz: the Germans had taken Honsfeld and were now fast encircling Hünningen itself. They had considerable firepower; Panzers would very soon be rolling into the village.

Lambert had been fired on by the point tanks of Kampf-gruppe Peiper. But Peiper himself had no intention of seizing Hünningen, even though strategically it made sense for him to storm through the village and then head west across the Elsenborn Ridge, which would form a natural line of defense for the Americans if they could manage to retreat in time and regroup there. Such a maneuver – potentially lethal to the entire 99th Division – did not fit with Peiper's far grander design: reaching the Meuse as quickly as possible. And so he pressed on south – not west – toward Stavelot, leaving other units to take care of Hünningen and the Elsenborn Ridge.

Thanks to Lyle Bouck and his platoon, Peiper was seriously behind schedule. But he was now making excellent progress along better roads. Before dawn, he had driven out of Lanzerath without encountering a single American, confirming his suspicion that the inexperienced paratroopers had simply been too scared to reconnoiter the area properly. Knowing that the previous day's delays had badly diminished his petrol supply, Peiper had then stabbed on toward Büllingen, where the 99th Division's headquarters and a fuel dump of fifty thousand gallons were based.[28] Encountering minimal resistance, Peiper had seized the fuel.

It was 11:00 A.M. Now Peiper was rolling toward a vital intersection in the hamlet of Baugnez, a couple of miles outside Malmedy.

Siegfried Line – December 17, 1944

Several miles away, Bouck and his men kept marching toward Germany. Soon, the Siegfried Line's concrete dragon's teeth and pillboxes came into view. It was obvious now to all of the men that the German attack was no spoiling action but rather a major offensive. As far as they could see along the road, there were German Panther and Tiger tanks 'lined up bumper to bumper.'

It began to snow heavily as Bouck and his men were ordered to halt near a line of pillboxes. They stood shivering in the falling flakes, watching the massive column of German armor move slowly west. German soldiers, hitching a ride on a Panzer, shouted obscenities and laughed.

One after another, Bouck's men were marched into a pillbox to be interrogated after being stripped of their dog tags.[29] When Milosevich entered the pillbox he found a German major, in his midthirties, seated at a desk. 'Why did you hit one of our medics?' he asked in perfect English.

'That sounds like something the Germans would do,' Milosevich replied. 'We would never do anything like that.'

Milosevich felt no shame. He was certain the medic in question had been wearing a pistol – perhaps for mercy killings, but nonetheless against the 1929 Geneva Convention that specified that medics should not be armed.

The major jotted something down, looked bored, and then ordered a guard to take Milosevich away and bring another of the *Amerikaner* down from outside.

Lyle Bouck stood outside, watching man after man disappear into the pillbox, growing more and more concerned. Finally, he stood alone, wondering whether his men had been taken somewhere and shot. It was suddenly his turn. Inside the pillbox, he was greeted by the young major, seated behind a desk illuminated by a single bulb.

'Pronounce and then spell your name.'

As Bouck did so, flanked by two guards, he knew it was vital that he not give away information that would help the enemy. Yet perhaps the sole reason he was still alive after his platoon had slaughtered so many Germans was because of the intelligence he might provide. What if he didn't prove useful?

'You're a first lieutenant, right?'

'Yes, sir.'

'What unit were you in?'

The major was determined to discover what kind of force had held up Kamfpgruppe Peiper for so long.

'Just transferred into it – I don't know.'

'What unit were you in before that?'

'I was in some kind of a replacement center.'

'Where was it?'

'I have no idea where it was.'

'How old are you?'

'Twenty-one today.'

'You're what?'

'I'm twenty-one today.'

'Step forward to the desk. . . . Put your hands, palms down, on my desk.'

Bouck did so.

'Where's that ring from?'

'Fort Benning, Georgia.'

The major's stern expression eased. He sat back in his chair.

'Ah ha, so you're a ninety-day wonder. When were you at Fort Benning?'

'1942.'

'I was at Fort Benning in the thirties. It's a beautiful place.'

Bouck was amazed.

'Where were you on the post?' asked the major. 'I remember a place called Harmony Church where a lot of the officer school candidates were.'

'That's where we were.'

'You know, I always wanted a Fort Benning ring. I never did get one. I wonder if I could have yours?'

Bouck slipped off the ring and placed it on the desk.

'I appreciate this. It has been quite a day for me. You can go now.'

Bouck turned to leave.

'You see all those tanks out there?' the major called after Bouck. 'Do you have any idea how your army is going to stop this attack? We have jet airplanes that will knock out your air corps. We have secret weapons which will end the war quickly. We'll be in Paris by Christmas. You'll go home, but not a winner.'

Bouck was led out by a rear exit into the bitter cold. To his relief, he found the rest of the platoon lined up with their backs to the pillbox. German soldiers sitting on tanks a few yards away were 'hollering and yelling' at his men.

One of the Germans ordered Bouck and his men to remove their overshoes and hand them over. Bouck refused. A German soldier jumped down from a Panzer. Bouck protested that he was an officer. It was against the Geneva Convention to take such essential protection from trench foot and frostbite. The German didn't care and began to scream at him.

Sergeant Slape could see things getting very ugly.

'Give him the overshoes, sir. You're not in charge here. We'll all get killed.'

Bouck slipped off one overshoe. Then he pulled at the other until it was at the end of his boot and kicked it away into the snow with contempt.

Another German jumped off the Panzer, rushed at Bouck, and hit him in the neck with a large screwdriver. Bouck lay sprawled in the snow, stunned by the blow.

A few seconds later, Bouck slowly got to his feet. His platoon watched admiringly, taking heart from their leader's defiance. The German soldiers again began to taunt them, obviously waiting for one false move so they could open fire. Bouck controlled his temper. They'd come too far to die because of some dumb gesture of defiance. Then the I&R platoon was lined up with other Americans. Again they began to move east, guarded by SS Shützen – SS privates.

'I don't know why they didn't kill us,' Private Joseph McConnell recalled. 'They had plenty of opportunity to. . . . That day I was sure we were going to get it. Yet all they did was try to get information out of us, but we wouldn't give it to them.'

The column of bedraggled GIs now walked deeper into Germany. As Private First Class Jordan 'Pop' Robinson trudged through the tank-tracked snow with his comrades, he saw a group of Germans who looked like SS officers. They began going through the American ranks.

'They was hunting for Jews,' Robinson recalled. 'At first, I didn't know what was going on. Then this American soldier came over and started to carry me on his back. After a while he told me the Germans was making him do it because he was a Jew. One of them Germans told me that the only thing Jews was good for was to be a horse for an American soldier.[30] Well, I got right off that fellow's back. I told them I didn't want to ride on an American soldier's back.'

Meanwhile, another group of around 250 American prisoners, many of them from the 612th Tank Destroyer Battalion, was also being herded toward captivity. They passed through Lanzerath, following the same route into Germany as Lieutenant Bouck and his men. Two Belgian civilians, suspected of helping the Americans, trudged along at the rear of the column.

The older of the civilians, a middle-aged farmer named Peter Mueller, had fled from the Gestapo with his fifteen-year-old nephew, Johann Brodel. They had been captured by Peiper's men in Honsfeld that morning.

The column stopped outside the Café Scholzen, not far from the Schur family's house. An SS trooper pointed his pistol at Mueller and his nephew: 'Come with me!'

'But we're Belgian,' cried Johann Brodel.

They were taken into the barn. The SS trooper shot Brodel in the back of the head. A second bullet hit Mueller in the neck. He swayed, staggered, and fell to the ground.

Mueller was still alive but pretended to be dead. When the SS soldier left, Mueller sat up and saw his nephew's lifeless body.

Blood pouring from his neck, Mueller made his way to the Schur house. Adolf Schur watched as his mother quickly tended to Mueller's wounds. Suddenly, another SS trooper burst in. He seemed intent on finishing Mueller off. But Adolf's father pleaded with the SS soldier and convinced him to leave.

The killing of Mueller's nephew was the first recorded case of an atrocity committed by one of Peiper's men. Very soon, there would be many more: Kampfgruppe Peiper, as it had done on the eastern front, was again waging Blitzkrieg, sowing more terror and chaos the more it encountered delay and obstruction. Nothing, certainly not the Geneva Convention, was going to stop Peiper and his men as they desperately tried to make up for the delay caused by Lyle Bouck and his platoon.

*

It was now around midday on December 17 in Hünningen. Robert Lambert and Private First Class Carlos Fernandez fed the last of the I&R platoon's records and observation maps into a fire. To escape the imminent German encirclement, they would use their emergency maps, imprinted on silk and sewn into the lining of their combat jackets.

Before pulling out, however, Major Kriz was determined to make one more attempt to locate the platoon. He had not given up hope that they might still be alive. 'With communications out,' he recalled. 'I took out [that morning] towards the I&R position to see if they had evacuated the area, or if not, try to get them out. Because of the infiltration of the Germans and large number of German tanks, I was unable to proceed to the position. . . . Lieutenant Bouck did not have permission to withdraw. I knew that if he decided to leave the position with his skill and the skill of his men, that they might eventually join our outfit at a later date. But if he had followed instructions, his small force would have caused havoc among the Germans, and would go down fighting.'

Malmedy – December 17, 1944

While Major Kriz made his last-ditch attempt to find Lieutenant Bouck and his men, Jochen Peiper and his point tanks stormed through the Baugnez crossroads, headed toward the village of Stavelot where they would need to cross their first major physical obstacle – the Amblève River.

Around the same time, a convoy of some thirty trucks carrying Battery B of the 285th Field Artillery Observation Battalion left the village of Baugnez in the direction of Malmedy.

The leader. First Lieutenant Lyle Bouck Jr., commander of the 99th Division's 394th I&R platoon, speaking at a bond rally, 1945. Courtesy Lyle Bouck Jr.

Adolf Hitler holding his injured arm shortly after surviving the July 20, 1944, assassination attempt. Courtesy National Archives.

Hitler and his favorite commando, SS Major Otto Skorzeny – 'The Most Dangerous Man in Europe.' Courtesy Sueddeutscher Verlag.

German-Jewish refugee Vernon Leopold as a teenager in London, 1930s. Courtesy Vernon Leopold.

Vernon Leopold, *far left*, dressed in Wehrmacht uniform with other German-speaking privates from the 394th Infantry Regiment, Camp Maxey, Texas, 1944. Courtesy Vernon Leopold.

Private Louis Kalil, Camp Maxey, 1944. Courtesy Louis Kalil.

Lyle Bouck, *first row, second from left*, shortly after joining the National Guard in 1938, at age fourteen. Bouck's nineteen-year-old brother, Robert, *first row, fifth from right*, was in the same National Guard unit.

Above: Streetwise Philadelphian Joseph McConnell. Courtesy Joseph McConnell.

Left: Virginian John Creger with infant son, John Jr., 1943. Courtesy John Creger Jr.

'The finest man and leader I have ever seen.' Major Robert Kriz, in Grand Island, Nebraska, September 1942. Courtesy Barbara Anderson.

Above: Corporal Aubrey McGehee, powerful linebacker for Louisiana State University. Picture taken at Camp Maxey, summer 1944. Courtesy Louis Kalil.

Right: Robert Lambert, starting quarterback for Renville High School, Minnesota. Courtesy John Lambert.

Above: 'He would pay the highest price.'
Private Bill James, son of Greek
immigrants, nicknamed 'Tsak.'
Courtesy Anna Tsakanikas.

Right: Private James 'Siv' Silvola, proud
and hardy Minnesotan. Courtesy Jim
Silvola.

Above: El Pasoan Corporal Sam Jenkins, *left*, with his brother. Courtesy Sam Jenkins.

Right: Private First Class Risto Milosevich, son of Serbian immigrants from east Los Angeles. Courtesy Risto Milosevich.

'A True American.' Platoon Sergeant Bill Slape, destined to stay in the army and become master sergeant – the highest rank for a noncommissioned officer in the U.S. Army. Courtesy Mike Slape.

Private First Class Carlos Fernandez, brilliant map-maker, son of Mexican immigrants. Courtesy Delfina Fernandez.

Proud 99er, Lieutenant Lyle Bouck Jr., one of the youngest commissioned officers of World War II. Courtesy Lyle Bouck Jr.

Robert Lambert, one of the platoon's ASTP recruits. Courtesy John Lambert.

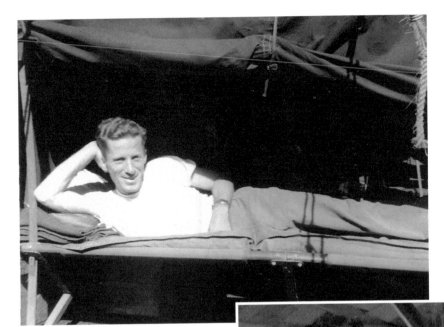

Easygoing, redheaded radio-
operator Jim Fort. Courtesy
Jim Fort.

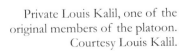

Private Louis Kalil, one of the
original members of the platoon.
Courtesy Louis Kalil.

Checkerboard boys. Several members of the platoon enjoy their last warm weather before heading to the front lines. *Left to right*: Aubrey McGehee, Bill James, Carlos Fernandez, unknown, unknown, Vernon Leopold, and Risto Milosevich.

SS Colonel Peiper, one of Hitler's most fanatical supporters and one of World War II's most brilliant combat commanders. Courtesy Bundesarchiv.

Lili Marlene. Film-star Marlene Dietrich was scheduled to entertain the 99th Division on December 17, 1944 – the day after the Germans attacked. Courtesy U.S. Army.

German soldiers approaching American lines on December 16, 1944. Courtesy Bundesarchiv.

The Battle of Lanzerath. Photo from U.S. Army Military History Institute; legend courtesy of R. H. Byers and *Dauntless*, published by Taylor Publishing Company, 1994.

1. Position of I&R platoon outside the village of Lanzerath
2. Far left fox hole manned by Robinson, Silvola and McGehee
3. Route taken by the German 9th Parachute Regiment
4. House where little girl ran out to warn the Germans
5. Direction of repeated German attacks on the platoon
6. Final flanking attack of the Germans at the end of the day
7. Café Palm
8. Adolph Shur house
9. House used for observation post by field artillery unit
10. and 11. Buildings occupied by tank destroyer battalion before December 16
12. Scholzen house used by I&R platoon as an observation post
13. Café Scholzen
14. Schugen house
15. View of Losheim across the valley
16. Road used by Kampfgruppe Peiper to Buchholz, Honsfeld and Büllingen
17. Road from Losheimergrabben (blown bridge over deep railroad cut)
18. Location where Robinson, Silvola and McGehee were cut off

Suddenly, the convoy was spotted by men in Peiper's point tanks who then quickly opened fire. Shells exploded all around as the Americans abandoned their vehicles and ran for cover. When the firing stopped, they were taken prisoner by a group of Panzergrenadier commanded by a Major Josef Diefenthal, one of Peiper's most trusted officers.

Peiper was several miles past Baugnez when Diefenthal's men herded Company B supply sergeant Bill Merricken and 130 other men into a field about a hundred yards south of the Baugnez road junction. Other than Company B men, the group of POWs comprised several medics from different units and some MPs who had earlier been directing traffic in the village.

Merricken and his compatriots, hands above their heads, were hustled into eight rows about sixty feet from the road. The ground was muddy, with the occasional patch of snow. The Germans were SS, but Merricken and the other Americans were not unduly afraid. They were obviously going to stand in the field until arrangements could be made to remove them to the rear.

Then a German officer, thought to be Major Werner Poetschke, the commander of the 1st SS Panzer Battalion, halted two Mark IV tanks. They were to cover the prisoners with their machine guns.

Suddenly, Poetschke ordered one of the tank commanders to open fire.[31]

Sergeant Bill Merricken saw a German officer aim his pistol at three of his fellow prisoners. The officer fired, killing a jeep driver and then a medic.

An American officer shouted 'Hold fast!' so the Germans would not have an excuse to shoot escaping prisoners. Merricken and the men around him didn't need to be told the obvious. They were already trying their best to stay calm.

The Germans didn't need an excuse.

'*Machen alle kaputt!*' (Kill them all!)

The tanks' machine guns roared.

Men flung themselves to the ground, burying their faces in the mud and under their riddled comrades. There were screams followed by what sounded to one eyewitness like the lowing of slaughtered livestock.

Merricken was shot twice in the back but not killed. The machine gun raked back and forth for around fifteen minutes. Then the tanks pulled away.

There was a haunting silence, broken only by the groans of dying men.

Diefenthal's SS men had moved on. But the nightmare for Merricken was far from over. Suddenly, more vehicles pulled up. Merricken dared not move as he heard engineers of the 3rd SS Pioneer Company enter the field. The engineers began to finish off men whose bodies still twitched. One lay above Merricken.

'The fellow on top of me was completely out of his head,' recalled Merricken almost sixty years later. 'I was trying to keep still, [trying] not to make any noise. But he was in such extreme pain that he started rolling over. I was face down, so I couldn't see what was going on. But he rolled over the back side of my legs, drawing the attention of two German soldiers. They came over. I sensed they were right over us. Then they shot him with a pistol. The bullet went through him into my right knee. He didn't move anymore. I kept perfectly still. I don't know how I did it. But I did. Then I lost all sense of time. I was flat down, my head turned to the left and my left arm covering my eyes and head and face.

'It was so cold that day, just fifteen degrees. If your mouth was exposed, the Germans would see the vapor and they'd know you were alive. So I lay perfectly still. I heard the Germans smashing men's heads with the butts of their guns. They kicked men to see whether or not they were alive or not. They would ask if men needed medical help. Some of the wounded would answer only to be shot.'

For two hours, Merricken lay under his dead compatriot as German tanks and half-tracks in Peiper's ten-mile-long column passed the field. Every now and again, some of the vehicles fired into the field of corpses.

When the rumble of trucks finally ended, Merricken pulled himself free of the dead man above him and then, accompanied by a Company B comrade who had miraculously not been hit, crawled two miles to a farmhouse where an old Belgian woman would hide him in her attic and then help him get back to American lines. Merricken's buddies from Company B would lay frozen stiff, buried beneath deepening snow, for two more months before being discovered.

News of the massacre spread like a frigid gust throughout the Ardennes, brought by a handful of other survivors who reached American lines less than an hour after the mass execution. When President Roosevelt eventually learned of the most notorious massacre of American soldiers of the entire Second World War, he reportedly responded: 'Well now the average GI will hate the Germans just as much as do the Jews.'

Robert Lambert heard about the massacre an hour or so after it happened. 'Somehow during combat news such as that travels throughout the troops with lightning-like speed,' he explained. 'It is believed by some people that the massacre at Malmedy could have resulted from frustrations of SS Lieutenant Colonel Peiper's troops over delays to their timetable caused by the Lanzerath defensive action of the 394th I&R platoon on the prior day.'

Elsenborn Ridge – December 18, 1944

The situation was now grave in Hünningen. By late afternoon that December 17, the entire 394th's positions had been badly overrun; Kriz and his fellow intelligence officers had lost all contact with the regiment's 2nd Battalion. Colonel Riley finally gave the order to pull back with the remnants of the 1st and 3rd Battalions to Mürringen, about a kilometer to the north of Hünningen. From there, what was left of the 99th Division would withdraw along the only road that remained open, through the twin villages of Krinkelt-Rocherath, and then to the higher, windswept slopes of the Elsenborn Ridge. Then every man available, from dishwashers to middle-aged mechanics, would dig in and prepare to hold off several German divisions moving fast in Peiper's wake.

Nothing that could be helpful to the Germans was left behind in Hünningen. Lambert and Fernandez had even destroyed their signal operating instructions. Along with Sam Oakley and Vic Adams, who had not been evacuated to a hospital as Leopold had, they gathered the platoon's bedrolls and duffel bags into an armored jeep. 'Bouck's bedroll was the last piece loaded,' recalled Adams. 'We checked our rifles, ammo and opened a box of grenades. I believe we honestly thought we'd "bought the farm."' Indeed, there seemed little hope of getting out of Hünningen alive.

Adams and his fellow I&R platoon survivors joined a column headed for Mürringen. By nightfall, they had linked up with the 394th's kitchen and supply units there. At around 7:00 P.M., the town came under intense shelling. The men took shelter in cellars.[32]

The next day, Kriz learned that all roads from Mürringen had been sealed off by the Germans except for a narrow lane that led north to Krinkelt. 'We were told to try to make it back to friendly lines via this route,' recalled Kriz's assistant, Lieutenant Buegner.

It was just after 2:00 A.M. when Major Kriz, Lieutenant Buegner, and the survivors of the I&R platoon joined the escape column of around a hundred vehicles, moving bumper to bumper on the narrow lane to Krinkelt. Buegner, Kriz, and Lambert rode in a jeep at the rear of the column. They were barely a mile out of Mürringen when an order passed down the column that they were to abandon all vehicles. Many of the truck drivers quickly ran off. 'However, a number of us saw no immediate reason to run,' recalled Buegner, 'so we stayed and attempted to find out why such an order had been given. . . . Lambert and I volunteered to lead a reconnaissance patrol.'

Within thirty minutes, Lambert and Lieutenant Buegner encountered several 99ers withdrawing from other positions along the lane. Apparently, it was still open all the way to Krinkelt. Anyone who could drive was then ordered to get in the abandoned trucks and continue toward Krinkelt. By 3:30 A.M., the last vehicle in the column had reached Krinkelt and was headed toward Elsenborn.[33] 'Each mile that we [then] traveled toward the west and safer ground,' recalled Buegner, 'made it seem like a heavy burden was being lifted from our backs layer by layer.'

As the road headed into the village of Elsenborn, the column was stopped by men from Company H, 38th Infantry Regiment, 2nd Division. Otto Skorzeny's commandos had been spreading chaos and confusion throughout the region; every jeep coming into Elsenborn had to be halted and its occupants' identity carefully examined.

Vic Adams, Carlos Fernandez, and Sam Oakley proved they were bona fide GIs, and then Oakley drove on into the village of Elsenborn. They could not locate a command post for the 394th, so they decided to find a suitable location for an observation post on the nearest high ground, the windswept area called Elsenborn Ridge. Soon, they came across a gun pit. Oakley parked the jeep a few yards to its rear, and the survivors of the I&R platoon jumped out and began to fortify the position.

Technician Fifth Grade Robert Lambert joined his comrades as they tried to dig holes in the rock-hard earth. In the course of the withdrawal from Hünningen the previous night, all of his belongings, except his rifle and the clothes and ammunition he carried, had been captured by the enemy. Digging in frozen soil was hard work. But it seemed easier after Colonel Riley arrived and informed Lambert that he was promoting him on the spot to staff sergeant. Lambert wondered if the promotion had come about because 'there were many tragic vacancies.'[34] Or had he performed better during a real crisis than he ever thought himself capable of doing?

The men's nerves were worn ragged. Vic Adams watched as a German POW suddenly tried to slip away from a group of fellow prisoners. The 99ers instantly opened up, hitting the German so many times that his body looked like a 'fountain' of blood. Everyone was on edge.

There was not a moment to relax. The men had to fortify the pit and then put up barbed wire concertinas linking it to other hastily dug positions. They had just finished preparing their observation post when the Germans launched a savage attack on Elsenborn Ridge. Thankfully, some two dozen heavy-artillery batteries had just been rushed to Elsenborn, and the Germans were repulsed for the first time. But many attacks would follow, and countless shells would thunder back and forth across Elsenborn Ridge in what was to be the fiercest artillery engagement between Germans and Americans in World War II.[35] Through it all, in arguably the most courageous defensive action in U.S. military history, the 99ers held firm, absorbing the last great blows of the Wehrmacht on the western front.

But it would not have been possible without the stubborn bravery of small units, vastly outnumbered, that had stood and held firm until killed or captured, thereby slowing down the German onslaught of December 16 and buying the 99ers and other divisions critical time in which to withdraw, regroup, and defend re-formed lines. They did not yet know it, but Lieutenant Lyle Bouck and his men's courageous stand at Lanzerath had not been futile – far from it. 'This small group of Americans,' Major Kriz would write, 'had molded together to do something that they did not care to do, under the leadership of Lieutenant Bouck, [and] in giving of themselves gave a vast number of American troops a little more time to change positions, retrench, fight and hold to fight again another day.'

Trois Ponts – December 18, 1944

As the 99th Division dug in on Elsenborn Ridge, Jochen Peiper approached the critical village of Trois Ponts, named for its three bridges across the Ambleve River, two of which could support Peiper's heavy vehicles and tanks. Peiper knew he must pass through the village and cross one of the two bridges if he was to access Belgian route N-23, a fast, wide road that would take him within hours to his final objective, the Meuse.

Peiper's column had come under increasing attack since passing through the Baugnez crossroads, scene of the Malmedy massacre. In the next significant village, Stavelot, yet more time had been lost. Indeed, since leaving Lanzerath, roadblocks, spirited defense from the Americans, heavy shelling, and air strikes had reduced Kampfgruppe Peiper to two-thirds of its initial strength. Crucially, every delay had allowed the Americans to reinforce positions all along Peiper's route.

Around 11:00 A.M., Peiper's point tank, a Panther, rumbled toward the first of Trois Ponts' bridges. Suddenly, it was hit by a 57mm antitank gun. The Panther lost a tread but fired back on the American gunners with its 75mm, killing all four of the crew. Seconds later, however, there was the fateful roar and crash of a bridge being blown up by American engineers. The sound of rubble splashing into the Ambleve had barely passed when the second of Trois Ponts' bridges was also blown up.

The loss of the crossing point was a potentially fatal blow. The nearest bridge now, below a village called La Gleize, at a river crossing called Cheneux, would entail yet another detour Peiper could ill afford, and the bridge might not support his tanks. It was a long shot, but it was all he had.

Peiper quickly ordered his point tanks to re-form and head toward Cheneux. To his delight, around midday, scouts informed him that the bridge there was intact and strong enough to hold his heaviest tanks.

Kampfgruppe Peiper headed in force toward the bridge. By midafternoon, however, it had come under fierce attack from sixteen P-47 Thunderbolts. Ten tanks at the rear of the column were destroyed as the column skidded off roads and took cover. Three of the American planes were shot down.

By late afternoon, the point tanks had made it across the bridge at Cheneux. But the strafing by the Thunderbolts had immobilized several half-tracks and Panthers, blocking the road for the rest of the column.

It was getting dark as Peiper issued orders for the column to proceed past Cheneux. On his map, he could see clearly that he would now need to cross yet another bridge – over the Lienne Creek, at a small hamlet called Habiemont – if he was still going to access the N-23 and then make it to the Meuse. Confidently, he set out once more.

As he did so, American engineers began to wire the bridge over the Lienne.

Darkness had almost fallen when a young American corporal, Fred Chapin of Company A, 291st Engineer Combat Battalion, spotted Peiper's point tank, followed by several other Panthers, as it rounded a bend some two hundred yards from the Lienne bridge.

Chapin had been assigned to turning the detonator key for the charges he and others from Company A had placed on the bridge. A gunner on the point Panther spotted Chapin and opened fire. Chapin hunkered down. A few seconds later, he peered into the twilight. The lieutenant who was to give the signal to turn the key was nowhere to be seen. Chapin searched again. Suddenly, he glimpsed the lieutenant waving at him.

Corporal Chapin turned the key.

There was a flash of blue light and then the thunder of masonry as the bridge collapsed into the Lienne. The last bridge was gone, and with it Peiper's only doorway to the Meuse had closed. According to some of his men, Peiper pounded his knee with frustration. 'The damned engineers,' muttered Peiper. 'The damned engineers!' As Jochen Peiper withdrew his tanks from Habiemont, his strike force – first halted at Lanzerath – was finally blunted.

Junkerath – December 19, 1944

Lyle Bouck's POW column reached Junkerath, a village several miles to the east of the German border. The evening of December 18, the men were marshaled into a large waiting room in the town's train station. Among the scores of prisoners, Bouck recognized the face of Lieutenant Matthew Reid, his old friend from Camp Maxey during his time in Company C of the 394th Infantry Regiment. Bouck's spirits lifted. The two men settled down to try to get some sleep on the station's cold floors.

As the captured members of the platoon dozed fitfully in Junkerath, their comrades Corporal Sam Jenkins and Private First Class Robert Preston scrambled through a deep forest. It was their third night on the run since Bouck had ordered them to withdraw from the position in Lanzerath as dusk had fallen on December 16. Suddenly, they spotted a barn. They had not eaten and were now extremely thirsty. Jenkins could barely move his aching limbs. Swallowing snow had only seemed to make him crave water all the more.

'We need to get some rest,' Jenkins told Preston.

In the early hours of December 19, they crept into the barn and then up into its loft, covered themselves with hay for warmth, and were soon asleep.

Perhaps four hours later, Jenkins was awoken by the sound of German voices. It was light outside the barn.

'Hey, Bob, I think they're coming in here,' whispered Jenkins.

The Germans had spotted the men's tracks. Seconds later, they entered the barn and started to probe the hay with bayonets. One glanced off Jenkins's leg. He sat up, knowing the German would stab him in the chest with the next lunge.

The Germans took Jenkins and Preston down from the hayloft at gunpoint and then stripped them of valuables. Jenkins's high school ring and a watch were seized.

A German captain in his early thirties walked over.

'Did my men take your valuables?' asked the captain in English.

'Yes,' said Jenkins.

The captain called over a sergeant.

'Tell those men to bring those valuables back.'

A few minutes later, Jenkins's watch and ring were returned. The captain hurried away. As soon as he was out of sight, his men took back the watch and ring. Then they marched Jenkins and Preston toward Germany.

Jenkins was stunned by the number of Germans that passed him. At one point, he came across a long column of horse-drawn artillery. 'They'll never beat us,' he thought as he looked in surprise at the horses. 'They're having to pull their artillery with horses. We're going to win this war.'

Jenkins and Preston eventually arrived early on December 19 at the marshaling yard in Junkerath. On the second floor of a nearby building, they were interrogated. The German intelligence officer already knew they belonged to the 99th Division. As Jenkins left the interrogation room, a German guard swung his rifle at him but missed.

Jenkins and Preston then joined the hundreds of American POWs waiting to be shipped away from the front. They were pleased to find among them the rest of the able-bodied members of the platoon: radio operator James Fort, Sergeant Bill Slape, Milosevich, Robinson, Redmond, McGehee, and Creger. Jim Silvola, who had been shot in the upper arm, and Joseph McConnell, with a German slug lodged in his chest, had been separated from the others on the way to Junkerath and sent north toward Frankfurt with other injured POWs.

Slape was delighted to see Jenkins and Preston. 'They told me they had been able to reach Hünningen and the old regimental headquarters building,' recalled Slape. 'But the headquarters had already been evacuated. I was much relieved to see them because they were the only two of my men unaccounted for.'

Allied Command Headquarters, Verdun, France – December 19, 1944

It was also early on December 19, 1944, when General Dwight Eisenhower, Allied supreme commander, gathered his senior generals in Verdun for a crisis meeting. Verdun was a fitting location, being the site of some of the bloodiest carnage and costliest bungling by Allied generals in World War I. The dank, cold atmosphere matched the generals' mood. As they sat sullenly nursing their cups of tepid coffee, several tried to hide their embarrassment and shame, knowing their intelligence had failed spectacularly.

Eisenhower entered the room, took one look at his despondent staff, and announced confidently: 'The present situation is to be regarded as one of opportunity for us and not disaster. There will be only cheerful faces at this conference table.' It was typical of the unflappable Eisenhower, admired as much for his utter belief in victory and infectious optimism as he was for his unequaled diplomatic skills – talents he would soon need in spades as the extent and seriousness of the German attack widened fissures between his most senior generals, who had long been at odds about how best to defeat the Third Reich.

One of the seated generals needed no cheering up: General George S. Patton Jr., commander of the U.S. Third Army. Tall, silver-haired, and immaculately dressed in a specially tailored uniform, Patton was by far the most flamboyant of Eisenhower's commanders, beloved by the American press for his ribald remarks, immense arrogance, and aggression. Since July, his Third Army had rolled with breathtaking speed across Europe, its leader deified all along the way. Month after month, 'PATTON BREAKS THROUGH!' had been splashed across front pages around the world.

Among his own troops, by contrast, Patton was known as 'Old Blood and Guts . . . his guts, our blood!' In their eyes, this pistol-toting, womanizing anti-Semite with ever-growing delusions of grandeur was gutsy, all right, the last American warrior-general. But many suspected that behind all his bluster there was a cold heart. In North Africa he had notoriously slapped a man suffering from extreme combat fatigue, screaming that the man was nothing but a coward, an action for which he was quickly upbraided by an outraged Eisenhower.

A self-described 'widow-maker,' Patton was indeed a compelling and controversial figure, capable of stirring up widely divergent emotions. But everyone agreed that Patton was a master of the art of mobile war. Supported by many highly experienced and tactically brilliant combat commanders, Patton was able to deploy his armored units with

amazing speed, often achieving total surprise, quickly breaking through the German lines, and penetrating sometimes
dozens of miles in a single day.

Having set the pace in the great rush toward the Siegfried
Line, Patton was now eager to get moving again. Like Eisenhower, he saw the counterattack by the Germans in the
Ardennes as a great opportunity, not only to strike a mortal
blow to what remained of the Wehrmacht on the western
front, but also to become yet again the general of the hour,
and then press on toward the mighty Rhine.

Patton believed that Hitler had made a huge mistake in
throwing his best divisions and armor at the Ardennes. At the
salient's northern shoulder, the 99th Division was beginning
to hold the Elsenborn Ridge. If Patton's Third Army could
be quickly unleashed, it could attack the southern shoulder
around Bastogne, cut Hitler's supply lines, surround the
Germans, and then destroy them.

'When will you be able to attack?' Eisenhower asked
Patton.

'The morning of the twenty-first,' replied Patton. 'With
three divisions.'

The other generals laughed.

'Don't be fatuous, George,' said Eisenhower. 'If you go
that early, you won't have all three divisions ready and you'll
go piecemeal. You will start on the twenty-second.'

Patton agreed and the conference broke up, the attendees
filled with renewed confidence.

The Ardennes Front – December 19, 1944

What the others did not know was that Patton had already begun to swing his Third Army, of more than three hundred thousand men, toward the Ardennes. Immediately after the Verdun meeting, he ordered his 26th and 80th Infantry Divisions, and his 4th Armored Division, to get there as fast as possible.

The 4th Armored Division, Patton's favorite outfit, had earned the three-star general his greatest plaudits since landing in Normandy that July. By 11:00 P.M. that evening, it would be on its way to Bastogne from the Saar River on the German-French border to the south. Among its many battle-tested young officers was twenty-four-year-old Captain Abe Baum, a fast-talking Brooklyn-born Jew with the 4th's 10th Armored Infantry Battalion. 'We were in the lead,' recalled Baum, who had picked up two Bronze Stars and a Silver Star in less than three months. 'The roads were frozen over and the metal tracks of the tanks kept sliding badly. But we didn't meet any resistance and we covered 151 miles in nineteen hours.'

Upon arrival in the Ardennes, Baum would be asked to lead a task force of four hundred men and armor into Bastogne, where the 101st Airborne had set up strong defenses but was now coming under fierce siege. Baum's force would reach Bastogne but then be withdrawn just before the town was completely surrounded by the Germans.[36]

Baum would have to wait until spring 1945 to see major frontline action once more. Then he would again command a task force. But its mission would be very different, as Lyle Bouck and the survivors of his I&R platoon would dramatically discover.

Inside the 'Forty and Eights' – December 20–21, 1944

'*Rausen! Rausen!*' shouted the German guards.

Lyle Bouck and hundreds of other POWs were marched out of Junkerath's main train station into the bitterly cold marshaling yard. They were given small portions of a loaf of black bread and some tin cans with hot, bitter coffee and then loaded into boxcars, which had just been used to bring troops to the front. There had not been time to paint white crosses on their roofs to indicate to Allied planes that they contained POWs.

The freight cars were little more than half the size of American boxcars with a small caboose at the end of the train. On the side of some of the cars was the famous French marking, '*40 hommes – 8 chevaux*' (40 men – 8 horses), known from World War I as 'forty and eights.' Seventy POWs would be crammed into each boxcar.

There was no more dangerous time to be traveling on a train into Germany. Once the skies cleared, anything moving on a railway would be viewed as a prime target by Allied flyers. But for now, thankfully, there was a thick cloud cover.

Lieutenant Warren Springer climbed wearily into his box-car. It had been strafed before. He spotted a hole in the boxcar's ceiling and positioned himself below it, reckoning the odds would be very slim that a bullet or shell fragment would enter the car through the same hole.

Some time later, Lieutenant Lyle Bouck heard the clanking and creaking sounds of the train groaning to life. The boxcar shuddered briefly, and slowly they began to move out of the marshaling yard.

The men did not know where they were bound or how long the journey would take. Over the next four days, all they received was two slices of bread each. Four men in Bouck's boxcar died of exposure and their wounds. 'It was good that it was so cold because it kept their bodies from rotting,' recalled Bouck. 'We were full of anger, hatred, cursing, punching one another as people started to die. . . . I'd gotten over my shock at what happened, my personal embarrassment at what seemed like a failure. I thought of how we had such good people and yet this had happened. I had no remorse.'

In some boxcars there was straw on the floor. The men could lie down when their turn for sleep came. Fresh horse droppings in others warmed men's badly frostbitten feet. But there was just hard, frozen wood in Lyle Bouck's car. The only sources of warmth were another man's embrace and a pile of feces getting bigger by the hour in a far corner of the boxcar.

Bouck was soon huddled up next to his friend Matthew Reid, feeling like a starving animal and packed so tightly next to others that he could barely move without someone cursing. The stench from the pile of feces infused every pore, every inch of uniform. By December 21, Bouck's stomach had started cramping. He felt weak, lightheaded. His wounded leg had stiffened and was seeping. Bouck knew the bullet had gone very close to the bone and wondered if it would ever heal.

On the same POW train were several men from an I&R platoon of the 2nd Battalion of the 423rd Regiment of the 106th Division. One of these privates, who had also been thrown into the infantry after the ASTP programs had folded, was a twenty-year-old named Kurt Vonnegut.

Vonnegut and his fellow Americans' ordeal had been worsened by the extent of the Germans' success in breaking through Allied lines. The Germans had not been prepared to deal with so many American POWs in such a short period of time. 'They had a huge hospitality problem,' recalled Vonnegut. 'They had no idea what to do with such a victory.'

Vonnegut would later write the classic *Slaughterhouse Five*, in part based on his experiences as a POW. He and his fellow platoon privates from the 423rd were particularly dispirited as well as bitterly resentful. 'Our regimental commander had surrendered and had sent out an order for us to surrender,' explained Vonnegut. 'It was an illegal order, so we didn't obey it.'

Vonnegut and his comrades had been quickly encircled, as had almost all of the 106th Division. Vonnegut had then tried to evade capture. 'We were on the run for a couple of days not really knowing what the hell was going on; there were about ten of us in my I&R unit. Then the Germans spotted us without us seeing them. They sent in artillery. There was a tree burst, and then they got us. They were mostly old men doing the rounding up. Eventually, we got loaded on that train.'

Many of the captured men had detected signs of increased activity before December 16, 1944. They had reported unusual sounds just hours before the barrage commenced that morning. Now they were paying the price for the complacency of the top brass.

Bouck was just as demoralized and physically exhausted as Vonnegut and the others. But as he fended off the pain of his stomach cramps, he was also increasingly determined to fight back somehow. He had been right that long night in the Café Scholzen in Lanzerath: the war was far from over for him and his platoon. A new battle had begun – a fight for survival. Bouck was not going to lose this one. The German major was wrong. He would return a winner.[37]

But how long would it be before he went home? The

stench of feces, the hunger pangs, the dysentery, the screams of the deranged, the sight of the dead underfoot, the fear – none of it was as bad as not knowing how long the journey deeper into the Third Reich would last.

La Gleize, Belgium – December 21, 1944

Jochen Peiper stood before his commanders in a farmhouse a few miles from the village of La Gleize, which overlooked the Salm River. Strain showed in his pale face.

Significant American relief forces, said Peiper, were attempting to cut off his Kampfgruppe. Paratroopers from the 82nd Airborne were close by, having secured the western banks of the Ambleve River. There was no option but to fall back to La Gleize and await reinforcements. If these did not arrive, Peiper and his men would have to try to break out of the growing American encirclement and get back to their lines. Peiper's exhausted officers nodded their agreement. They had now accepted that the mission to reach the Meuse was over.

Peiper issued fresh orders: German walking wounded and American POWs picked up in the area were to be moved straight away to the cellars of La Gleize.

The town was already under heavy shelling from American batteries. Peiper would nevertheless set up a new command post in the outskirts. The Luftwaffe were promising to air-drop supplies. Peiper had also been told that fuel drums would be floated down the Ambleve to him. By now, he had only enough gas to recharge some of his last tanks' batteries. Unable to press forward or organize a motorized retreat, he was finally stranded, and he knew it. Like Lyle Bouck and his men, all he could do now was hope and wait.

PART THREE

War Behind Wire

German POW Camps

POW Camp Locations of the
I&R Platoon, 1945

10. Guests of the Reich

Inside the Third Reich – December 21, 1944

Dawn was breaking when men aboard Lieutenant Lyle Bouck's POW transport woke to find the roof and metal joints of their boxcar furred with ice like the inside of a refrigerator. A look out of the small air vent in each boxcar revealed that they were standing on a single track in the middle of a forest. The ground and trees were under a thick blanket of snow.

A few guards paced up and down outside the train, their faces creased with the cold. Some men called to the guards, begging them for *Wasser* (water) and food, but to no avail.

Dysentery had by now started to weaken almost half of the men. In every boxcar, there was the continual call for a helmet – 'for Christ's sake, quick!' A helmet was passed down to the afflicted POW and returned to the poor soul whose turn it was to empty it through the vent.

The train gave a lurch and they were off again, passing through silent villages. Finally, they arrived in Koblenz, on the Rhine. For several blocks from the riverfront the city had been repeatedly bombed. Once-beautiful buildings were gutted, a thousand years of civilization reduced to still-smouldering ash. A few remaining church steeples, holed by shell fragments, stood as stark reminders of the Germany that had been a cradle of the Enlightenment and, as recently as the 1920s, a nation of astonishing technological and cultural experimentation.

The train stopped in a rail yard for an hour. Russian slave laborers, housed in derailed cars, worked under guard at repairing tracks and filling in bomb craters.

Then the train jarred to life again, inching toward a bridge that had been badly shot up but still spanned the river. Men wondered whether it would hold. 'Looks like the Ohio at Pittsburgh, except for the color,' one POW said as the train slowly crossed the swirling gray waters of the Rhine. The bridge held, and the train left behind the shattered suburbs of Koblenz. Above, the afternoon skies were clear; the men could see vapor trails from American planes headed home after bombing southern Germany. By evening, the train had pulled into a railway marshaling yard in Limburg am Main, twenty miles due east of Koblenz, almost a hundred miles from Lanzerath.

Bouck and his platoon had traveled on average just twenty miles a day. Now, they expected finally to be allowed off the train. But they were out of luck. The commander of the nearest prison camp, already overflowing with Bulge captives, refused to take them, and so once more they prepared for another horrendous night in their locked boxcars.

Darkness fell. A train approached on another track. Suddenly, its driver jumped down and ran for cover. Then came the distant hum of Allied bombers. Men stood trembling, sweating from terror.

Private Kurt Vonnegut heard the scream of fast approaching Mosquitoes – fifty-two Royal Air Force (RAF) fighter-bombers that specialized in low-level strafing and bombing raids. One of them dropped a flare to illuminate the target area – the rail yards. Men crowded around the vents saw the sky light up, as one recalled, 'like it was Christmas.'

The flare burst about two hundred feet from the ground,

bathing the rail yard in white light as if someone had suddenly turned on a Hollywood studio's arc lights. The flashes from the flare – red, purple, orange, and yellow – were oddly mesmerizing.

A few seconds later, bombs exploded. Men standing in the first carriages were knocked down by shock waves. An engine nearby was blown off a track.

'Crawl out the window!' someone screamed. 'If this damn train ever gets hit and starts burning. . . .'

But the men couldn't get out of any of the vents. They were trapped.

Suddenly, there was a direct hit two boxcars down from Lyle Bouck's. Several officers from Kurt Vonnegut's regiment were killed or wounded.

The impact knocked Lyle Bouck's boxcar on its side. Men tumbled on top of each other, their screams drowned by the roar of the bombers, the bark of heavy machine guns, and explosions. Bouck was unharmed. In another boxcar, a corporal managed to squeeze out. A German guard who lay cowering nearby in a siding saw the corporal and warned him not to try an escape. The corporal ignored the guard and unlocked a boxcar door. Men landed on each other as they leapt the several feet to the icy ground.

Other POWs were soon jumping from open doors all along the train and then running for cover. There was no time to form a human chain and spell the letters 'POW' so the Mosquito pilots could see who they were in fact bombing. Some men were so thirsty that even as bombs rained down they huddled near a ditch, breaking the ice and scooping up dirty water, cupping their numbed hands to their lips. Then the first wave of bombers passed over.

Lieutenant Warren Springer saw German guards run to an air-raid shelter.

'Stay there or we'll shoot you,' another guard warned Springer and others before running off.

Springer and his comrades decided to chance it and were soon sprinting after the guards. But then a second wave of Mosquitoes arrived. Bullets, shrapnel, and wood splinters filled the air. Springer ran to the shelter where he found German guards crouched in a terrified huddle. He noticed a white fleshiness on his sleeve. Fellow POWs looked at him in horror: blood and brains were splattered all over his heavy trench coat. The brains belonged to someone else. Springer had not received so much as a graze.

'The guards then rounded us up and got us back on the train,' recalled Vonnegut. 'Somehow, they put the train together and repaired some tracks.' By one estimate, eight men had been killed in the raid and thirty-six wounded.

The train pulled out again sometime before dawn. But the approach of daylight did not mean they were out of danger. Now that the skies had cleared, much to Hitler's dismay, the Allies were hitting every supply target they could find to the rear of the German front lines. To make matters even worse, the POWs were passing through the Ruhr, targeted that December for massive bombing as the U.S. Eighth Air Force and British Bomber Command stepped up their already three-year-long destruction of its cities and industrial areas.

While Lyle Bouck and the other survivors from his platoon traveled through a devastated Germany, their injured comrades – Privates Vernon Leopold, Louis Kalil, and Bill James – were taken to hospitals.

For the rest of his life, Leopold would reflect on how fortunate he had been to be sent back just hours before the German attack on Lanzerath, thereby narrowly avoiding capture. Labeled a 'frostbite/trenchfoot' casualty, he was taken by train to Paris and eventually flown to a U.S. Army hospital outside Oxford, England. While on the mend there, he received a letter from Sergeant Fernandez at regimental headquarters telling him that his comrades at the Lanzerath outpost had not been heard from since the initial assault and were reported to be missing in action.

It would be more than thirty years before Private Vernon Leopold would discover the fate of his platoon.[38]

Louis Kalil was also on a hospital train, but he was headed in the opposite direction – east, toward the Ruhr Valley – and his fellow travelers were not fortunate GIs but grievously wounded Germans. Kalil was not attended to by medics or doctors inside a carriage. Instead, even though his face wound was life-threatening, he was placed between carriages, out in the open, where he quickly felt as if he was going to freeze to death. He had not been given painkillers. As the hours passed and bitter gusts and snow squalls buffeted the train, he became convinced that only God could save him now.

From his blood-stained combat jacket, Kalil pulled out his standard issue pocket Bible and flipped through the pages until he reached Psalm 23. Blood dripped onto a page as he prayed and then read the psalm out loud so that he could hear its comforting words:

> *The Lord is my shepherd,*
> *I shall not want . . . .*

Kalil read the psalm over and over. It was his only anesthetic. And it worked: he found the strength to keep going through that night's fourteen hours of darkness and the next morning was able to ask one of his captors for a blanket. 'They eventually gave me one,' he recalled. 'But I still had no food and no water. I began to get fevers – the bandage from December 16 had frozen onto my face. I hadn't had it changed. The Germans finally got an interpreter and a German doctor told me I'd gotten gangrene in the wound.'

Kalil knew the Germans would probably not shoot him now. Perhaps they hoped he'd jump off the train and kill himself when the agony of his wounds got to be too much. Another thought obsessed him: How would his parents cope with the inevitable telegram announcing that he was missing in action?[39]

Guards passed where he lay. One kicked him viciously, as if he was a lame dog that should have been put down rather than brought along to block the passageways. 'After a day or two it was so damn cold I was shivering all the time,' Kalil recalled. 'The Germans just kept kicking me. There was nothing I could do. But the worst thing was the teeth embedded in the roof of my mouth. I just couldn't get them out. Finally, they fell out. Then I felt a little relief.'

Eventually, the hospital train ground to halt at a station in the outskirts of a city. Kalil was very weak as he was carried off on a stretcher. He did not have a clue where he was. He was then placed in an ambulance. As it pulled out of the station, Kalil looked through a window.

'Oh my God,' he gasped.

Passing before his eyes were the effects of Allied bombing on a civilian population center: 'Total ruin. There wasn't a building standing. It was just utter destruction.'

Kalil gazed at the remains of rubble and blackened bomb craters where homes had once stood.

'How many people got killed?' he wondered. 'Well, maybe it's fair. They had this coming.'

The city's streets were now narrow alleys block after leveled block. Gaunt German women ferreted about in the ruins with their shoeless children looking for possessions, pulling debris and bricks aside to make passageways into water-filled cellars so they could hide during the next bombing. Others emerged in utter lethargy from the cinder skeletons of their homes, their faces blanched with horror.

By war's end, 131 German towns and cities would suffer the same destruction. More than six hundred thousand civilians would die – twice the number of American combat casualties during all of World War II. Almost eight million Germans would be left homeless. There would be more than thirty cubic meters of rubble for every surviving German in many cities. The extent of such destruction was so vast, so utterly lacking in historical precedent, that to this day its impact has yet to be widely understood in Germany itself.

Kalil's ambulance finally pulled up outside the only building that he could see still standing. The teeth jammed into the top of his mouth had fallen out, but his jaw hurt more than ever as he was carried into the hospital and placed on the fifth floor. He was still not given any painkillers. For two days, he lay alone on a ward before it began to fill with other Allied wounded.

Kalil got to talking with a British private who called himself Robbie and belonged to the British First Airborne. He had been shot in the mouth during British General Bernard Montgomery's Operation Market Garden – a serious setback to the Allies that had culminated in the failure to hold the famous bridge too far across the Lower Rhine at Arnhem on September 18, 1944.

'Where am I?' asked Kalil.

'Hanover,' replied Robbie.

That evening, Kalil heard the wail of air-raid sirens. He wondered why. The city was so utterly destroyed that bombs would have little impact as they fell on an ocean of rubble.

The horror of a mass bombing raid was about to begin, yet again. Or, as the Germans put it, '*Die schwere Leidenszeit beginnt nun abermals*' (The difficult time of suffering now begins again).

Soon, the steady drone of RAF Lancaster bombers could be heard in the distance. Kalil could not yet walk, and because no German offered to help him down to a shelter in the hospital's basement, and Robbie was not allowed to do so, he found himself alone on the ward, waiting for incendiaries and bomb clusters to begin raining down.

From above, Hanover did not look like an ocean of rubble. One BBC reporter, aboard a Lancaster, described the approach to such a German city on a typical night-time raid: 'It's a wall of light with very few breaks and behind that wall is a pool of fiercer light, glowing red and green and blue, and over that pool myriads of flares hanging in the sky. That's the city itself.'

Down below, alone and helpless, the only man left on his ward, Louis Kalil stared through a window. He saw sticks of bombs and incendiaries exploding in phosphorous white patterns across the sea of stones. The hospital suddenly shook as if it had actually been hit. The sky was filled with tracers from antiaircraft guns – white, yellow, green. Some found their target. Mesmerized, Kalil watched a Lancaster twist and turn as it fell to the ground. For what felt like an eternity, he prayed. At last the all-clear siren sounded, and Robbie returned from the basement shelter.

The raids continued almost nightly as Christmas approached. One morning after yet another raid, Kalil was approached by a German interpreter.

'Would you mind if a German family came and talked to you?' he asked.

'I'm not too enthused about it.'

'They just want to come up and see you and talk to you. . . . Do me a favor, will you?'

'Oh, all right.'

The interpreter brought a mother, father, and their young daughter to Kalil's bedside. Their son had been captured in North Africa; they wondered whether he was being treated well as a POW at Camp Taylor in Tennessee.

'Tell them they don't have to worry about him,' said Kalil. 'He's being treated like a king compared to us. Their boy's got an option. If he works, he gets a dollar a day. If he don't want to work, he can just sit in the barracks.'

The family looked surprised and then relieved.

'You tell 'em,' added Kalil angrily, 'he may not want to come back.'

When the family left, Kalil learned that the interpreter, who spoke perfect English, was from Switzerland, a neutral nation.

'How the heck did you end up in this war with the Germans?' asked Kalil.

The interpreter looked embarrassed. 'I didn't know it was going to be like this,' he explained. 'They were paying good money.'

Private Bill James could later recall nothing about his journey to a hospital in Frankfurt. His first memory was of drifting in and out of consciousness as he lay on a stretcher in a 'cold, dark-brown world' where everything seemed unreal. Suddenly, a stretcher carried him from darkness into blinding light. He was in a room crowded with white tables; teams of ghostlike figures clustered around the tables. The smell of ether permeated the air.

James was dimly aware of several white-clad figures murmuring among themselves at the foot of an operating table.

A German doctor leaned close to James and asked his age.
'Nineteen.'

'Well now you'll die!'

The German smiled and held an ether mask close to James's face.

'In fifty years' time.'

James heard the doctor's voice become an echo as the ether took effect: 'in fifty years, in fifty years . . . in fifty years.'

Around the same time that James was operated on, his family back in White Plains, New York, received a telegram. His sister Anna remembered the telegram being opened: 'Oh God, was that a horrible day. We were having company and then we get this message – your son is missing in action. We all cried. We were hysterical.'

Inside the Third Reich – Christmas Eve, 1944

A week after leaving Junkerath, Lyle Bouck and his fellow prisoners were finally given water and fed a small piece of black bread with a smear of bitter-tasting jam. Private Kurt Vonnegut would later describe how the train cars must have seemed to the German guards to take on a human form that night: 'Each car became a single organism which ate and drank and excreted through its ventilators. It talked or sometimes yelled through its ventilators, too. In went water and loaves of black-bread . . . and out came shit and piss and language. . . . The legs of those who stood were like fence posts driven into a warm, squirming, farting, sighing earth. The queer earth was a mosaic of sleepers who nestled like spoons.'

Some of the human spoons were chaplains, such as Father

Paul Cavanaugh of the 422nd Regiment, 106th Division, who would soon provide crucial spiritual support to Lyle Bouck and many other POWs on the transport. Cavanaugh, an indomitable Jesuit priest, had been captured along with thousands of his fellow Golden Lions – so called because of their shoulder patches – from the 106th on December 19, 1944.

The light began to fade.

'They won't bomb on Christmas Eve,' said one officer.

'Hell they won't!' replied another. 'They're out to win this war. Christmas won't be celebrated this year.'

As night fell, Father Cavanaugh heard a low murmur. In one carriage after another, an impromptu carol service began: 'O, Little Town of Bethlehem'; the German guards' favorite, 'Silent Night'; and many others.

Another air-raid siren sounded, ending what little Christmas cheer the men could muster. Again the agonizing wait. But that night Cavanaugh and the men's prayers were answered: the Mosquitoes did not return.

La Gleize, Belgium – Christmas Eve, 1944

The column of defeated SS troopers slogged through the deep snow, desperate to reach friendly lines. At the front, Jochen Peiper was close to collapse, drawing on his last reserves of stamina and adrenaline as he urged his men to hurry up, to push on. Now his mission was to escape the advancing *Amerikaner* with eight hundred of his men – all that was left of Kampfgruppe Peiper's original five thousand.

In La Gleize the previous evening, Peiper had tried to strike an unusual deal with one of his POWs – twenty-eight-year-old Major Hal McCown, a battalion commander who had been captured on reconnaissance on December 22, 1944. Peiper would free around 150 American POWs if Major McCown would guarantee the future release of Peiper's wounded men. McCown had said he could make no such deal but would sign a statement saying that Peiper had attempted to negotiate the safe passage of his wounded. Although Peiper held McCown prisoner, he had little bargaining power – he was almost surrounded, his force effectively defeated. He had agreed that the statement would suffice, and had been in a surprisingly bullish mood even though GIs from three divisions were closing in. 'Oh, I admit many wrongs were committed,' he had told McCown. 'But we think of the great good Hitler is accomplishing. We're eliminating the communist menace, fighting your fight.'

Peiper no longer looked as confident as he and Major McCown, his only American prisoner, traipsed through the deep forest. Since leaving La Gleize, Peiper and his men had paused only for a few minutes to catch their breath.

That evening, they crossed a small bridge. Suddenly, tracer fire from paratroopers of the 82nd Airborne streaked across the sky. 'Mortar fire [then] fell all around, [and] shrapnel cut the trees all around us,' recalled McCown. 'The American machine gun and rifle fire was superior to that of the covering force.'

When the firefight ended, McCown found himself alone, lying face down in the snow. The Germans had left him behind. McCown rose carefully and headed toward American lines. It was almost Christmas Day when he finally reached safety.

Jochen Peiper pressed on. He had been slightly wounded in the firefight with the 82nd Airborne – his first injury in more than four years of fierce combat. At last, his strength deserted him and he collapsed in the snow. From now on, his men would have to carry him.

The last obstacle was a serious one – the Salm River, in full flood. What was left of Kampfgruppe Peiper began to ford the river, the strongest and tallest men standing in the surging waters and helping the wounded across. It was so cold that few could bear more than a minute in the water.

Finally, Kampfgruppe Peiper reached safety in the German-held village of Wanne. Peiper was laid down in an aid station and fell into a deep sleep. He had brought almost eight hundred crack SS troops back with him to fight again. As he slept through that Christmas Day of 1944, his senior officer was already recommending him for the Swords to his Knight's Cross of the Iron Cross with Oak Leaves – the Third Reich's highest honor.

Inside the Third Reich – Christmas Day, 1944

Back on Lyle Bouck's POW transport, the men were so thirsty they were forced to lick the iced bars on the boxcar vents. That Christmas Day, each man took his turn for a few seconds, his breath refrosting the bars for the next man.

Lieutenant Warren Springer watched German civilians dressed in their Sunday best walk that morning through ruins to a church service. It depressed him to think that life was apparently going on normally despite the massive Allied bombing. Perhaps they were making a special effort. Or maybe their fortitude was a sign of something far more ominous: the immense denial of the German people in the face of utter destruction. The Christmas strollers certainly didn't look as if they had given up hope of victory.

Radio operator James Fort was desperate for food. 'We

pulled into a station,' he recalled. 'I have no idea where in Germany. All I knew was that it was Christmas Day. Each one of those boxcars had a small [vent] in the corner – not big enough to crawl out of, but you could get your hand through it.'

It was Fort's turn at the vent. He saw a German civilian, carrying a shopping basket, on the platform.

Fort caught the attention of the German and gestured to his wedding ring.

'Gold! It's gold!' Could he exchange his wedding ring for a loaf of bread?

The German agreed.

Fort ripped the dark, heavy bread apart and then shared it with others from his platoon. It wasn't like the Christmas dinner they had back home, but at least they were able to forget their hunger for a while. And captivity was bonding the platoon members closer to each other than even the events of December 16 and the long months of training.

That afternoon, finally, the men were allowed off the train. It was Christmas present enough for most of them. There was a head count as the POWs stood shivering in the cold. Then, forming a long column of about fifteen hundred men, they were marched away from the rail yards up a hill toward a POW camp called Bad Orb. It was a relief to be out of the boxcars, to be able to stretch their legs and take deep breaths of fresh, cold air.

As the head of the column neared Bad Orb, back along the line men were suddenly ordered to halt. There was crushing news. Bad Orb could only accommodate so many of the POWs. Bouck, his platoon, and hundreds of others were ordered to turn around and march back down toward the train station.

After dark, they found themselves being counted off and

loaded into the same boxcars they had arrived in. Once more, the doors were locked. For the next forty-eight hours, the train stood in the rail yard before it finally groaned to life and moved again. For Bouck and his platoon, the brief respite at Bad Orb had been a mirage, as distant now as their hometowns.

Paris, France – Christmas Day, 1944

At his headquarters in Paris, it was also the worst Christmas Day General Dwight 'Ike' Eisenhower, Allied supreme commander, had experienced. 'General Ike, apologetic because [a] long-awaited Christmas party was impossible, invited some of his intimates to dinner,' recalled Lieutenant Kay Summersby, Ike's British secretary and driver. 'I thought him more depressed than at any time since I'd met him [in May 1942]. He was low, really low.'

It was all Otto Skorzeny's fault. In the first days of the offensive, several of his 'mock Americans' had been captured and then summarily executed. Before being tied to a post and blindfolded, however, they had started a rumor that Skorzeny himself was heading to Paris with a 'suicide squad' of three hundred Germans, intent on killing Eisenhower. 'The story,' recalled Eisenhower, 'was brought to me on 20 December by a very agitated colonel who was certain that he had complete and positive proof of the existence of such a plot. He outlined it in great detail and his conclusions were supported by other members of the Security Staff.'

Kay Summersby was so worried that she couldn't sleep. '[Eisenhower] is just pinned to his office all day; at night he goes upstairs and sleeps,' she wrote in her diary. 'I stay across the way from the office. . . . I lay awake for hours envisioning death and worse at the hands of SS agents. Sleep was impossible – with the tramp, tramp, tramp of heavy-booted guards patrolling our tin roof.'

Ligneuville, Belgium – Christmas Day, 1944

Skorzeny was in fact nowhere near Paris. He was nursing a serious face wound that Christmas Day, in a farmhouse in the small village of Ligneuville. On the evening of December 21, after a failed attempt to take back nearby Malmedy from the Americans, Skorzeny had been hit in the face by shrapnel as he walked toward a command post at the Hotel du Moulin in Ligneuville. Skorzeny had grabbed a glass of cognac left over from an American general, downed it in one gulp, and had then looked at his face in a mirror. 'Carefully I felt my face with my hand,' Skorzeny recalled. 'Above my eye a lump of flesh was missing from my forehead and was hanging down over the eye.'

Skorzeny had refused to take any painkillers, except for more cognac, even as a doctor had sewn his face back together. Patched up, he had then rejoined his men only to learn that a long-awaited battery of heavy guns had arrived but lacked sufficient shells to mount an effective assault on Malmedy.

By New Year's Eve 1944, Hitler's favorite commando would be back at the Führer's headquarters. As soon as Hitler saw his bandaged head, he ordered Skorzeny to be treated by his personal physician, Dr. Stumpfecker. That afternoon, Hitler again met with Skorzeny and appeared ebullient. Skorzeny wondered how Hitler could remain so buoyant in the face of disaster. Perhaps it had something to do with the cocktail of drugs that another doctor had administered that morning to the Führer?

Hanover, Germany – Christmas Day, 1944

Early on Christmas Day 1944 in Hanover, Louis Kalil found himself being carried toward an operating room through wards full of German civilians. Some were dead, a yellow tinge spreading across their corpses. As doctors placed tubes in his neck to drain gangrene poisons, Kalil passed out. He had still not been given any painkillers.

A few hours later, he was shaken awake by Robbie, the British paratrooper.

'Louis, Louis, you okay?' he asked.

'Where am I?' asked Kalil groggily.

'Up on the ward.'

'Oh, okay. What the hell [did] they do?'

'Well, they've got your mouth wired up. And they put a plastic head-strap around your head and rubber bands to hold your jaw up.'

Kalil and Robbie grew closer, talking endlessly about their families and lives before the war. Robbie had been born in Bristol, a British port, the son of greengrocers. He would go back and work there after the war. 'I'd joke with Robbie about his teeth,' recalled Kalil. 'The Germans had given him a set that didn't fit. It was all they had. . . . If it wasn't for Robbie, I'd have gone nuts in that hospital.'

Kalil still could not get down to the shelter during raids. To distract himself from the falling bombs, he read Robbie's only book, a paperback titled *How Green Was My Valley*. And so, as the city was further pulverized, Kalil tried to lose himself in Richard Llewellyn's lyrical classic of a boy's tough childhood in the valleys in Wales. It made for particularly depressing reading. The novel ends with coal burying the boy's father in a fatal mining accident.

Kalil's spirits lifted with the arrival of a fellow American on the ward – a tough 101st Airborne paratrooper named Roy Burke who was brought in on a stretcher one day. Burke had fought with his fellow Screaming Eagles – the 101st Airborne – to hold Bastogne but had been shot through the face and then captured just a few days before Patton's 4th Armored Division had arrived to relieve the town. Many of his buddies had not been so lucky.

Kalil and Burke were quickly inseparable. That night, they slept one above the other in a double bunk. Robbie lay just a few feet from them.

Nuremberg, Germany – December 27, 1944

Meanwhile, Lyle Bouck's POW transport continued its horrific odyssey. The next stop was Nuremberg, venue for the famous Nazi rallies before the war and now a prime target of Allied bombing, which had only intensified as the New Year approached. On December 27, 1944, the train pulled into a rail yard. The men were ordered out of the boxcars, herded into a column, and then marched through the city. Their destination was finally a POW camp, thankfully on the outskirts.

Lyle Bouck and his platoon entered the gates of Stalag XIIID eleven very long days after capture. When the men finally collapsed in flimsy, unheated wooden barracks, they began to pull off their boots. 'I discovered both of my feet were partially frozen,' recalled Sergeant Peter Gacki, one of

the artillery observers captured with the platoon in Lanzerath. 'My galoshes and boots had been taken by a German
soldier, and I'd had to wear [replacement] boots that were
too small. The Germans put several of us with frozen feet
in a small room. They didn't have any medical supplies
except something that looked like axle grease, which we
rubbed on our feet. When my feet began to thaw, I walked
barefoot all night on a cold floor. By morning the pain
eased. On one toe on each foot I found a deep purple spot.
It looked like the beginning of gangrene.'

Sam Jenkins also fought to prevent severe frostbite, which
could quickly lead to gangrene and then inevitable amputa-
tion – a chilling prospect given the medieval medical facilities
in POW camp hospitals. By now, he could barely walk more
than a few yards without collapsing in agony. Thankfully,
he had his buddies to help him around, in particular Aubrey
McGehee, physically the strongest among the captured
platoon.

Barely five days after arriving in the camp, the men again
heard the drone of planes in the distance. More than 500
Allied bombers were nearing Nuremberg. Many of the pilots
from Britain's Bomber Command were intent on avenging
their worst defeat of the entire war. On March 30, 1944,
nine months previously, Bomber Command had sent 795
heavy bombers to obliterate the historic city. In a clear,
moonlit sky, they had been intercepted by a large force of
German night fighters: 170 bombers were destroyed or
written off, and more than 500 aircrew killed in a single
night.

This time, the pilots of Bomber Command would leave
behind something for the people of Nuremberg to remember
for the rest of their lives.

11. The Stalags

Nuremberg – January 2–10, 1945

The RAF Pathfinders came first, dropping flares to guide the five hundred Lancasters toward their targets. Under a rising moon, thousands of tons of incendiary and explosive devices soon followed and the center of Nuremberg was quickly destroyed. The city's famous Rathaus castle, almost all the churches, and about two thousand medieval houses went up in flames. Four hundred and fifteen industrial sites were obliterated. The raid was in fact a 'near-perfect example of area bombing,' as an RAF source would later describe it.

Radio operator James Fort was lying in a bunk in the POW camp on Nuremberg's outskirts when the first bombs landed on the city's center, several miles away. Suddenly, a shock wave threw him clear off the bunk. 'Boy, oh boy,' recalled Fort. 'That was my first introduction to bombing. They did a good job. From what I gathered, they got most of the downtown area.' Some men left their barracks to watch the raid. 'We could hear the shrapnel from the anti-aircraft guns falling around us,' recalled Sergeant Peter Gacki.

The next morning, January 3, 1945, the Germans lined up the POWs outside their barracks and harangued them for allegedly 'showing lights' during the raid. Gacki bridled at the accusation: 'It would have been very dumb to show lights when the city was blacked out.' The men learned that the raid had knocked out the city's water supplies. Gacki's commanding officer, Lieutenant Warren Springer, was soon scraping up snow to quench his thirst.

After roll call, the men were ordered to remove rubble and dig graves. By one estimate, 1,794 Germans and refugees were killed in the January 2 raid, and 29,500 homes had been destroyed. 'Many of us were on work details to [also] clear bodies,' recalled Lyle Bouck. 'At this time I was given a black salve from a German civilian to apply to my wounds – this seemed to heal the tissue in about ten days.'

Cleaning up after Bomber Command had paid a German city a visit was a horrific task that winter. 'Horribly disfigured corpses lay everywhere,' according to W. G. Sebald, one of the few German writers who has described the true impact of terror bombing on his compatriots. 'Bluish little phosphorous flames still flickered around many of them; others had been roasted brown or purple and reduced to a third of their normal size. They lay doubled up in pools of their own melted fat. . . . Other victims had been so badly charred and reduced to ashes by the heat, which had risen to a thousand degrees or more, that the remains of families consisting of several people could be carried away in a single laundry basket.'

A week later, on January 10, 1945, it was announced that the Nuremberg camp was being evacuated. Lyle Bouck and his platoon were ordered to return to the city's rail station, which had been quickly repaired after the raid of January 2. Once again, they were loaded into boxcars and were soon on the move.

The Ardennes Battlefield – January 1945

As Bouck and his men headed toward further uncertainty, the defensive part of the Battle of the Bulge came to an end. The Allies began to push the Germans back to and in some sectors beyond their positions on *Null Tag* (Zero Day) – December 16, 1944. It would take all of January 1945 to regain the initiative on the western front. More young Americans – an estimated twenty thousand men – would die than in any month of the entire war in the ETO. Less than a tenth of the Allied force was British. But one would not have known this from the British press and the utterances of Field Marshal Bernard 'Monty' Montgomery. On January 7, 1945, Montgomery held a press conference that angered every American in Europe, including Eisenhower, Patton, and Bradley. 'As soon as I saw what was happening,' boasted Monty, 'I took certain steps myself to ensure that if the Germans got to the Meuse they would certainly not get over the river.'

The picture Montgomery gave of the battle was of massive American blundering: only when he had been brought in to command the armies holding the northern shoulder had catastrophe been averted. '[The battle was] possibly one of the most interesting and tricky battles I have ever handled,' added Montgomery. 'You must have a well-balanced, tidy show when you are mixed up in a dogfight . . . you can't win the big victory without a tidy show.'

The northern shoulder held not because of Montgomery's leadership but because of the thousands of outnumbered GIs from the 99th and 2nd Divisions who had defended Elsenborn Ridge, enduring night after night of shelling and fierce Panzer attacks in the coldest January in twenty-five years.[40] Indeed, the battle for the Elsenborn Ridge, described by one historian as the 'Little Round Top of the Battle of the Bulge' – was *the* key defensive action that decided success or failure of Wacht am Rhein, Hitler's last gamble.

In claiming credit for saving the day, Montgomery had been grandstanding, capitalizing on the crisis to further his own ambitions. But what most annoyed George Patton was not Montgomery's arrogance but rather his failure to counterattack quickly and aggressively enough. All through that January, Patton echoed in public what he had written in his diary: Had it not been for Montgomery, the Americans could have 'bagged the whole German army. . . . War requires the taking of risks and [Monty] won't take them.'

Newspaper editorials on both sides of the Atlantic inflamed an already strained relationship between Monty and his American colleagues. On December 20, Bradley had threatened to resign when Eisenhower had split command of the battle between him and Montgomery. Then in early January, Monty had sent a directive for Eisenhower to sign that would authorize him alone to command the battle. Eisenhower had refused to sign the directive and, instead, stressed that the war would proceed on a broad front under Bradley's continued command.

If Monty wanted to push for ultimate command, Eisenhower would have to take up the matter with Churchill and Roosevelt. Because American boys were now doing the greater part of the fighting and dying, and because American industrial might and munitions supplied and sustained the British, there would be no question as to who should lead the charge into Germany. Even Monty could understand what would happen if the choice came down to Ike or Monty, or even Monty or Bradley. Sensibly, and with unusual grace, he quickly backed down. 'Very distressed that my [directive] may have upset you and I would ask you to tear it up,' Monty wrote to Eisenhower. 'Your very devoted subordinate, Monty.'

But the damage had been done. Montgomery's comments, and the retorts from deeply irritated American generals, began a private and sometimes public battle between the Allied generals, one that would erupt again and again until the end of the war.

The war of words in the press soon became so heated that Churchill was forced to make a public statement to assuage fears that the fallout over the command of the Battle of the Bulge would not permanently hamper joint efforts in Europe to end the war. In London, Churchill told the House of Commons: 'Care must be taken in telling our proud tale not to claim for the British Army an undue share of what is undoubtedly the greatest American battle of the war and will, I believe, be regarded as an ever-famous American victory.'

Churchill was right. The Battle of the Bulge, as it had now been named, was the greatest that American armies had waged in their entire history – the greatest in number of troops engaged and casualties sustained.[41] Six hundred thousand Americans, from twenty-nine infantry divisions and six armored cavalry units, fought in the Battle of the Bulge. Eighty-one thousand became casualties. Fifty-five thousand British soldiers fought in the Ardennes, with just two hundred killed.

Half a million Germans fought in the Bulge. A fifth of these men became casualties. On both sides, the loss in equipment and supplies was enormous, and for the Germans catastrophic: more than a thousand planes and as many tanks. As one American intelligence expert put it, 'The Battle of the Bulge was [also] perhaps the greatest in its effects on the course of history.' For the German people, let alone Adolf Hitler, the battle was the beginning of the end. It had indeed been Hitler's last, desperate gamble and, in losing it, he had sacrificed his people to what, after the Jews, he detested most – communism.

On January 12, 1945, seeking to exploit the severely weakened German situation on the eastern front – several of the best panzer divisions had been diverted to the Ardennes – Stalin launched an all-out attack. Within four months, the whole of Eastern Europe and much of Germany would be in repressive Soviet hands. Hitler and the German people's greatest nightmare – conquest by the Slavic 'hordes' – would become a grotesque reality as the Red Army raped, pillaged, and killed as indiscriminately as Jochen Peiper's men during its lightning advance closer and closer toward Germany's borders and then, by early spring, into the Fatherland itself.

Stalag XIB, Fallingbostel, Germany – January 1945

Mid-January 1945 also found Private Louis Kalil and his buddies, Roy Burke and Robbie, on the move. They were taken from Hanover by hospital train to Stalag XIB at Fallingbostel, a hundred miles to the north, the most squalid of all camps that held American POWs in Germany during the war.

Kalil was greeted by captured British medics and taken to a ward in the camp's infirmary. His fellow Midwesterner, Private James Silvola, had left the ward only days before, having been successfully treated for diphtheria by a Belgian doctor. 'I then spent most of my time in the barracks because it was so cold,' recalled Silvola. 'The Germans didn't want you outside trying to signal to Allied airplanes. The wound in my left arm healed slowly on its own. I didn't get medical treatment for it.'

The POW doctors, as Kalil soon discovered, could do very little for most men. They worked only with medical supplies they had upon capture along with odds and ends gathered from imprisoned medics – if by great fortune the medics had been allowed to keep their sulfa pills, morphine spikes, and bandages. Operations were performed without anesthetic using smuggled-in razor blades. Wounds were cauterized using heated metal objects. Men had to rely on their inner resources rather than medicine to make it through. Every week that winter at least a dozen POWs died in Fallingbostel, mostly from typhus, diphtheria, influenza, and other diseases accelerated by malnutrition.

It was a lucky man who did not at some point succumb to dysentery, which left sufferers severely dehydrated and caused often fatal weight loss because the men could not keep what little food they were given down or digest it adequately. In most barracks and wards, there were just two latrine pails left by the Germans each night. Both were always overflowing each morning.

Fallingbostel, like every other German POW camp, was a giant petri dish of infection: 'You'd rub your face with your filthy hands and then lick your lips and you'd had it,' recalled one POW. 'With dysentery, a man loses all his self-respect. Nothing embarrasses him any more. If you need a bowel movement, you just drop your trousers and let fly. I felt just like an animal. We were being [treated] like cattle, and we were acting like cattle.'

Pyorrhea, a form of scurvy caused by lack of vitamins, affected every man to some extent. The most chronic cases suffered liver and kidney failure. Most men endured bleeding and swollen gums. Some lost their teeth. Hepatitis and

The enemy. An SS Grenadier takes a break from fierce fighting during the German
breakthrough in the Ardennes. Captured German photograph. Courtesy U.S. Army.

The platoon's headquarters in a schoolhouse in Hünningen, Belgium. Courtesy John Lambert.

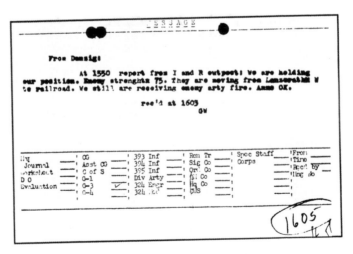

The last recorded communication with the platoon on December 16, 1944. Courtesy National Archives.

Captured GIs are marched through the village of Lanzerath on December 17, 1944, just hours after the I&R platoon was also taken captive. Courtesy National Archives.

Officers from Kampfgruppe Peiper – the same unit that advanced through Lanzerath – scout out the German advance on December 17, 1944. Captured German photograph. Courtesy U.S. Army.

Typical command post near Elsenborn Ridge, December–January 1944–45. Photograph taken by Major Robert Kriz. Courtesy Barbara Anderson.

The top brass confer among the ruins of Bastogne, January 1945. *Left to right*: Generals Omar Bradley, Dwight Eisenhower, and George S. Patton. Courtesy Library of Congress.

The dreaded telegram. Received by Lyle Bouck's mother in January 1945. Courtesy Lyle Bouck Jr.

'He's alive.' Telegram informing Lyle Bouck's mother that he is a prisoner of war. Received four months after his capture. Courtesy Lyle Bouck Jr.

STALAG XIII D - NUERNBERG, GERMANY

BUNK ARRANGEMENT AT STALAG XIII-D NUERNBERG GERMANY

Sketches of a typical Stalag POW camp. Drawings by Robert Neary, Lehigh Acres, Florida. Courtesy *Dauntless*, published by Taylor Publishing Company.

Above: Lieutenant Colonel Robert Kriz, *second left*, stands to attention after 99th Division commanding General Walter Lauer, *far left*, has awarded him the DSC, March 1945. Courtesy Barbara Anderson.

Below: Muster of 394th Infantry Regiment, spring 1945. Courtesy Barbara Anderson.

'We killed a lot of women and children.' Lieutenant Colonel Robert Kriz, with telephone, directs fire while clearing out Ruhr Pocket, April 8, 1945. Courtesy of Earl B. Smart and *Dauntless*, published by Taylor Publishing Company.

The last surrender. Last German resistance in Ruhr Pocket formally surrenders to Lieutenant Colonel Robert Kriz, Iserlohn, Germany, April 16, 1945. Courtesy Barbara Anderson.

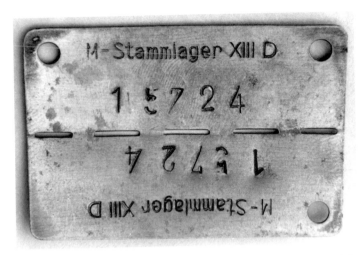

Just a number. Lyle Bouck Jr.'s POW dog-tag. Courtesy Lyle Bouck Jr.

Final destination. Private Vernon Leopold visits Hitler's Bavarian headquarters at Berchtesgaden, summer 1945. Courtesy Vernon Leopold.

Left: Major Abe Baum, commander of Task Force Baum. Courtesy Abe Baum.

Below: Carlos Fernandez, standing beside armor-plated jeep, one of the lucky few from the platoon to escape capture. Courtesy Delfina Fernandez.

First night back in America. Louis Kalil, *left*, and close friend Roy Burke, a fellow POW, enjoy their first drink on American soil, New York, 1945. Both men, severely wounded in the face, are showing their good profiles. Courtesy Louis Kalil.

The road to recovery. Louis Kalil, *center* without shirt, recovering from plastic surgery, Cleveland, summer 1945. Courtesy Louis Kalil.

The pain only got worse. Private Bill James with author John S. D. Eisenhower and Dr. Lyle Bouck, Gettysburg, September 1968. Courtesy Lyle Bouck Jr.

Private John Creger, happy to be alive, 1945. Courtesy John Creger Jr.

Lucky to be alive. Jim Silvola a few weeks after release from POW camp, April 1945. Courtesy Jim Silvola.

'I don't want a damn thing for myself.' Dr. Lyle Bouck signing recommendations for platoon members' awards, St. Louis, late 1970s. Courtesy Lyle Bouck Jr.

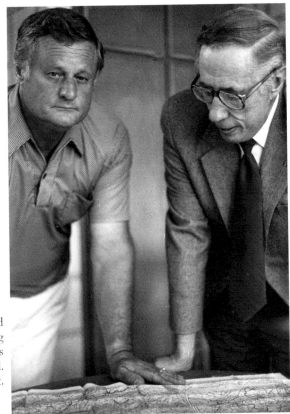

Risto Milosevich, *left*, and Robert Lambert examining map of Ardennes thirty years after they were separated. Courtesy John Lambert.

Back together again. The platoon reunited for the first time on the first day of baseball season, Yankee Stadium, New York, April 5, 1979. *Left to right*: Jim Silvola, Aubrey McGehee, Vernon Leopold, Robert Lambert, Louis Kalil, Sam Jenkins, Carlos Fernandez, John Creger, Lyle Bouck Jr. (Robert Adams not seen). Courtesy Lyle Bouck Jr.

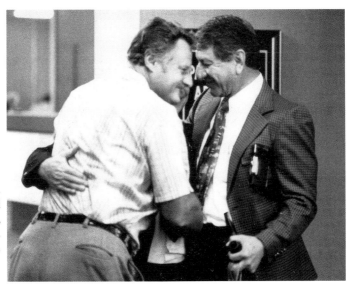

Old buddies reunited. Risto Milosevich and Carlos Fernandez, New York, 1979. Courtesy Lyle Bouck Jr.

Finally recognized. The platoon survivors the night they received their belated awards, Maryland, 1981. Courtesy Lyle Bouck Jr.

anemia – other diseases caused by malnutrition – took longer to take effect. When they were finally diagnosed, it was often too late to do anything.[42]

At least Kalil and Silvola received some treatment. For other wounded men such as Joseph McConnell, who had also ended up in Fallingbostel, there was no help. 'Germany wouldn't give us any medical treatment at all,' he later claimed. But he did see a German doctor who told him in perfect English that he had practiced medicine in Chicago before the war. 'He also told me that my arm was *kaputt*. They would have to cut it off.' Fortunately, the doctor did not amputate; the arm would eventually heal on its own.

McConnell and others in his barracks were forced to sleep on straw mattresses with no blankets to protect them from the cold. They were not allowed showers, and the only liquid they drank was day-old coffee. When Red Cross packages would come, the Germans would open them first and take what they wanted. The leftovers were then given to the prisoners.

Then McConnell got a lucky break. He was transferred to a wood-cutting camp in Weisman, near the Baltic.[43] 'Up there it wasn't bad at all,' he recalled. 'The Germans used to call us American gangsters but that was about the worst of it. We had to cook for ourselves, so at least we knew it was edible. The guy who headed us up there was a Polish guy who was forced into the German Army. He was good to us and sympathized with us.'

McConnell was indeed fortunate. For the rest of his platoon, the nightmare of captivity had barely begun.

Stalag XIIIC, Hammelburg, Germany –
January–February 1945

On January 18, 1945, a week after leaving Nuremberg, Lieutenant Lyle Bouck and most of his platoon arrived at a railroad station near a camp called Stalag XIIIC, outside the town of Hammelburg, about seventy miles due east of Frankfurt. Hammelburg, with a population of six thousand, was the central town of the Ruhr valley, which stretched south into Bavaria. The nearest city was Würtzburg, famous for its ball-bearing factories and medieval buildings.

Bouck and his fellow 'Kriegies' – short for their official German title, *Kriegsgefangene* (Prisoners of War) – were marched up a long hill and into a base called the Hammelburg Lager, comprising a military training area for antitank units and two POW camps at its northern perimeter.

One of the two camps was a massive Stammlager, holding thousands of Allied enlisted men. The noncoms in the I&R platoon – all the able-bodied survivors – were marched into the Stammlager:[44] Corporal Jenkins, radio operator Fort, Private First Class Milosevich, Corporal McGehee, Private First Class Preston, Platoon Sergeant Slape, and Private First Class Robinson. 'It was an insane asylum they had turned into a prison camp,' recalled Robinson. 'There wasn't no heat, and it must've been ten degrees below zero in there. But I got a little bit of treatment for my leg wound.'

As officers, Lieutenants Lyle Bouck and his friend Matthew Reid were herded with around three hundred others toward the *Offizierlager* (Officers' Camp), which already housed some fifty-five hundred Kriegies. In a bedraggled column, they walked through heavily wired gates and were then ordered to form up. The gates were closed and locked. The men were counted as they stood in ankle-deep snow and then taken in groups into an indoor equestrian arena. In front of a dozen Wehrmacht officers, the first batch of Bulge captives to arrive at Hammelburg was then divided into groups of one hundred and marched out of the arena into a compound of ten barracks that had been used to house SS Panzer units in the late 1930s.[45]

Bouck and Reid were issued POW dog tags. Bouck's read: 'M-Stammlager XIIID – 15732.' There was no name. From now on, he would be just a number in the vast German POW system, which stretched from Poland to Bavaria and would house some 250,000 American and British Kriegies by spring 1945.

Then Bouck and Reid were taken to yet another processing area, which had been the camp's beer hall in its Nazi heyday – when Jochen Peiper and his fellow SS elite had undergone officer training there in the mid-1930s. Life-sized murals, depicting drinking parties and German folk heroes, covered the walls. Finally, Bouck and Reid were taken to a barracks. At one end were two small rooms on either side of a narrow corridor. Four larger rooms were full of wooden bunks.

Their new 'address,' just fifty square feet, would also be home to forty other men. Bunk beds lined both walls. In the open space between the bunks were a couple of rickety tables, a brick chimney, and a few benches. Two fifteen-watt bulbs bathed the room in an eerie twilight as gray as the men's faces. And there was just one stove. Keeping the barracks warm was impossible – only forty-eight small coal briquettes were issued for three days. Yet the average temperature that winter was well below freezing: 20 degrees Fahrenheit. Men would soon be scavenging everywhere for wood.

Each man then selected his bunk. Reid and Bouck chose to sleep one above the other. But it was quickly obvious that they would have to improvise sleeping arrangements to combat the cold – there were not enough blankets. And so Reid, Bouck, and others pushed two tiers of bunks together, making a sort of double bed so that they could share blankets and body heat.

That first night, as searchlights constantly played across the compound, there was a brief gathering around the stove. The prisoners rubbed their hands to keep warm, introduced themselves, and shared stories. Then they huddled together in the bunks, fully dressed, and fell into a deep sleep.

The next morning, as soon as it was light enough to see, Bouck and his barracks were awakened by German guards shouting '*Rausen!*'

Bouck and Reid climbed wearily out of their bunk, put on their boots, and shuffled out into the cold.

Outside on the Herman Goering Strasse – the compound's central divide – guards shouted: '*Machen Funf!*' (Make fives!). The Kriegies were to line up in rows of five for counting. The mostly middle-aged German guards wore woolen uniforms and long trench coats. The Kriegies wore what they were captured in, often just tattered assault jackets. Most had lost their trench coats, gloves, and hats or they had been stolen in an enemy breach of the Geneva Convention.[46]

That first morning, the American compound's German commandant, Colonel Fuchs, stood before Bouck and the other new arrivals and laid down the law. In the event of an air raid, the camp sirens would sound three times. Then the Kriegies would have exactly three minutes to return to their barracks. 'Anyone outside their barracks will then be shot,' Bouck and the others were warned. 'Don't come outside to go to the latrine or do anything – just don't come outside. The all clear will be marked by a constant siren.'

It was also pointed out that four thousand Serbian prisoners were in a camp just beyond a barbed wire fence. They had been captured in 1941 during the Nazi invasion of Serbia and included most of the aristocratic Serbian General Staff. On no condition were Bouck and his fellow prisoners to have any contact with the Serbs.[47]

As soon as Bouck and his fellow Kriegies returned to their barracks, the ranking officer assigned them numbers. Two men went to the camp kitchen and returned with a big container of 'tea' – a thin vegetable soup. Then each man was issued a cup, a spoon, and a bowl, often made from discarded ration cans or odd pieces of metal or wood. 'We had very strict rules to make sure no one got more than their fair share, and they worked,' recalled Bouck. 'Numbers one and two got the food; number three would be first in line for it, and then the next day number three and four would get the food and number one and two would go to the back of the food line. Sometimes the "tea" was actually hot, but that was a fortunate day.' To spread on small sawdust loaves of so-called bread, the men were given a red, beet-based jelly. 'That's what we had in the morning with the "tea." There was nothing at noon. In the evening we would get a soup of some kind.'

As Bouck and most of the platoon resigned themselves to a bitter winter in Hammelburg, Robert Kriz, newly promoted to colonel, led an attack to regain a position previously held by the 99th Division close to Lanzerath.[48] 'It was very obvious that [the I&R platoon] had been destroyed or captured,' he recalled. 'The ground area showed that there had been fierce combat, and I remember seeing some crosses, how many I do not know, in this area.' How many of the platoon, he wondered, had been buried where they had obviously fought to the bitter end?

As with all Allied POWs, Lyle Bouck and his platoon members were allowed to send three Red Cross postcards to the States not long after they arrived in Hammelburg. Bouck sent one to an old classmate, Beulah Mae Heutel, back in St. Louis. He did not have her address, but he knew her father owned the local Ford dealership so he addressed the postcard to 'Beulah Mae Heutel at Sunset Ford.' He sent a second card to an old friend from his National Guard days, Eugene Overhoff, who had gone into the air corps. The third was addressed to his mother and father. It was never received. But the one to Beulah Mae was, and she quickly informed his parents that their son was alive in a POW camp.

Bouck's mother, Magdelene, was immensely relieved – she had already received a Western Union telegram on January 5, 1945: 'The secretary of war desires me to express his deep regret that your son First Lieutenant Lyle J. Bouck Jr. has been reported missing in action since eighteen December in Belgium. If further details or other information are received you will be promptly notified.'

Radio operator James Fort's mother would have to wait until the war was over to find out what had happened to her son. 'The Germans gave me a postcard to send back,' recalled Fort. 'I wrote home but the postcard took months to get to her.' When other Kriegies complained bitterly that they never received replies to their mail, the guards snapped back that it had nothing to do with them. The Allied bombers were to blame.

Private First Class Risto Milosevich's family in Los Angeles was particularly hard hit by the news that their eldest son was missing in action and presumed dead. They had lost another son, when he was just seven, because of an incorrectly administered vaccination. Doctors had told the Milosevich family that they could sue the government for compensation. 'I'd choke on every dollar,' Risto's father had retorted. The death had left Risto's mother heartbroken. 'She cried every day until she was seventy-one, when she died – cried every day about that kid.' Now another son was missing.

Risto's father was so devastated by the news that he stopped working and instead sat in front of the radio night and day in the hope that he might hear something about his son's fate.

Corporal Aubrey McGehee's young wife, Agnes, was working as a secretary for the Illinois Central Railroad in McComb, Mississippi, when an MIA telegram arrived at her office that January. Her superintendent called her mother. Then her mother and the superintendent broke the news. 'I was very upset, but I remember I had a lot of faith in President Roosevelt,' recalled Agnes. 'I just knew that he was going to make it all right. I felt Roosevelt could get my husband home if anybody could.'

It was around the same time that forward artillery observer Sergeant Peter Gacki's wife received the dreaded telegram. Gacki had also filled out a Red Cross postcard, but it took too long to arrive – the MIA telegram came first, as was the case with all of Bouck's platoon and Warren Springer's artillery unit. A notice soon appeared in Gacki's local paper that he was missing in action. 'My father had died in 1937; my mother was very upset because I was the only one from the family that had gone into the service.'

In the small Virginia hamlet of Wythville, Private John

Creger's eighteen-year-old wife was beside herself when she read her MIA telegram. She was heavily pregnant with their second child. Their first, John Creger Jr., had been born the year before his father shipped overseas. The night that Creger had been taken prisoner, a picture had fallen off a wall and landed on John Jr.'s head. Immediately, she had known something terrible had happened. How would she bring up two small children alone? 'I used to lie all night listening to the Red Cross broadcasts to see if they would mention his name,' said Mrs. Creger. Her nervous system would never recover from the worry.

Within a fortnight of arriving in Hammelburg, Lyle Bouck realized that his survival would depend on adequate nourishment but also on the 'mutual cooperation and forbearance' of his fellow inmates. To his surprise, he discovered that none of the Kriegies in his barracks swore. It seemed that every man was subconsciously trying to lift himself in language at least above the primitive conditions.

A remarkable intimacy developed between many Kriegies. 'Reid and I were so close to each other that we could read each other's minds,' recalled Bouck. 'We had an advantage over the other men: we had known each other before combat, done a lot of things together, and been in the same company together.' In the noncoms' camp, Risto Milosevich shared a bunk with Sergeant George Redmond. If they needed to turn over or change position, they did so together, sometimes in their sleep, as if they were telepathically linked.

But while some men formed the closest bonds of their lives, in other barracks dissent and discord were the norm. Some men were afraid to fall asleep if they had managed to scavenge or bribe a guard for extra food, in case a fellow Kriegie stole the stash. Soldiers grew their beards and refused to salute senior officers – they had failed so badly during combat, they no longer deserved respect. Many officers had surrendered, under orders from their senior commanders, without firing so much as a shot. The men's bitterness was intense, their unit pride shattered. Many felt that POW life necessitated a new code of behavior: every man for himself, and to hell with the brass.

In Hammelburg, the focus of many of these men's anger was a 106th Division senior officer, Colonel Charles C. Cavender, officially in command of the American POWs in Hammelburg.[49] In early January, while being held at Bad Orb, Cavender had agreed to a German order to provide a list of Jewish POWs from the 106th Division, only to have his own officers refuse to cooperate. Cavender would never recover the respect of his men.

In his first days in Hammelburg, Cavender also infuriated the camp commandant, an aging Prussian, General Gunther von Goeckel, who had lost a lung in 1916 during World War I. Tall, straight-backed, and softly spoken because of his wound, von Goeckel was a reasonable man who knew Germany had lost the war and was intent on abiding by the Geneva Convention, at least as he saw it. And yet one of Cavender's first actions was to declare that von Goeckel would be tried as a war criminal as soon as the camp was liberated.

Von Goeckel responded by making life far worse for all the officers in Hammelburg. He ordered countless roll calls no matter the weather, sometimes during air raids, and withheld life-sustaining Red Cross parcels.

Unlike Cavender and his officers, at least Lyle Bouck and others from different divisions had fought to the bitter end. 'We were captured,' stressed Bouck. 'We had not surrendered.'

The act of surrender deeply affected many men, eating away at already fragile psyches. Private Joseph Crone, one of Kurt Vonnegut's fellow POWs from the 106th Division, was one of many who gave up hope and plunged into apathy and then lethal lassitude. Vonnegut's fictional hero in *Slaughterhouse Five*, Billy Pilgrim, was based on Crone, who allowed himself to starve to death. 'He simply sat down on the floor with his back to the wall,' recalled Vonnegut. 'He wouldn't talk, wouldn't eat, wouldn't do anything, and then died.'

On January 22, 1945, the platoon's spirits rose with the arrival of Red Cross officials; they were told of the severe shortages in food and medical supplies and promised to improve the situation. But when neither embargoed parcels nor medical supplies were handed over, tensions in the camp soared. It was clear to the men that they were being slowly starved to death.

Three days later on the night of January 25, during an air-raid alert, a young lieutenant named George Varion tried to run from one barracks to another across the main camp street – Herman Goering Strasse. Father Cavanaugh, the priest who had been aboard Lyle Bouck's transport when it had been bombed, saw what happened next: 'In the nearest tower was a guard blind in one eye and classified unfit for frontline duty because of his poor eyesight in the other. The clatter of feet on pavement attracted his attention. He fired into the darkness. Varion was hit in the lung and died the next morning.' Relations between Kriegies and guards reached a new low.

Ten days later, the food situation had not improved. Major Albert Louis Berndt, an American doctor in charge of the compound's infirmary, watched with concern as the prisoners got into their *Funfs* (groups of five) at roll call. 'The American fat [had] disappeared from the bodies in my charges, but there was nothing to be done about it. There was not enough edible food to maintain weight.'

The daily ration for the men was officially supposed to be 1,700 calories – below the normal amount needed for men to work and sleep properly, but enough to subsist on if men stayed in bed all day, which many did. But by February 1945, as food became very scarce throughout Germany, the ration was down to just 1,070 calories. One young captain in Bouck's compound, who had played football at West Point, now looked like a skeleton, weighing just 100 pounds. Three months before, upon capture, he had tipped the scales at 220. Bouck himself was down to around 140 pounds, having lost 40 pounds since December 16, 1944.

A listlessness had settled over the whole camp; the only group activity was attendance at Father Cavanaugh's Sunday church service. There were no sports, not even a program of physical fitness. The men were too exhausted to muster the will, let alone the strength. When the Germans provided a few musical instruments, they were hardly touched. No one felt like playing.

It was crucial that men keep their minds occupied rather than dwell on their predicament. Realizing this, Lyle Bouck and others resolved to distract themselves any way they could from the hunger pangs and cold. One day, a man in his barracks found a scrap of flat wood and a piece of wire and used them to make a cribbage board. Soon, cribbage had become a passion. The grimy, dog-eared playing cards came courtesy of the Serbs.

Bouck also joined the Oflag XIIIB 'Toastmasters' Club' and under the leadership of Lieutenant Robert King, a Los Angeles native, practiced public speaking. Meeting twice a week, he and his fellow toastmasters took turns giving impromptu and prepared talks. Another officer had Bouck's entire barracks follow an advanced spelling course. Still another was an expert on geography. Bouck was soon able to name every state in the United States and every capital of every state.

The same conditions prevailed in the noncoms' camp. One man counted the barbs on a section of fence and then estimated the total number of barbs around the encampment. When he announced this number, his fellow Kriegies formed teams to check him out with a barb-by-barb count.

Boredom and fear gnawed at every man, officer or private. Relations between the noncoms and their captors were, however, better than in the officers' camp. And punishment was often less severe. One day, some noncoms were caught breaking camp rules. Their names were taken. Retribution would be doled out at the next morning's roll call.

At roll call, Private First Class Risto Milosevich and others in the platoon watched as a German officer began to read out the names of the offenders: 'George Washington, Abraham Lincoln, . . .' Finally, the German officer himself started laughing 'like hell' and excused the offenders.

Increasingly desperate for food, more and more Kriegies throughout Hammelburg flouted von Goeckel's rules, most often risking their lives to visit the Serbian camp that, unlike the American compounds, regularly received Red Cross food parcels.

One day, Milosevich slipped under the wire and made his way into a Serb barracks. The son of a Serb immigrant, able to speak Serbo-Croat fluently, Milosevich was soon being treated like a long-lost brother. He also quickly discovered that some of the Serbs went on work details into the town of Hammelburg. 'When they were in the town, they would screw the local women and pick up eggs and food. They gave some to me.'

Back in his own barracks, Milosevich shared the food with just one man: his bunk-mate, Sergeant George Redmond. While Milosevich and Redmond ate their secret supply, others sat for hours, scribbling fantasy recipes on scraps of paper and cardboard. 'They were very hungry. Food – that's the only thing that interested them. Most of the time, you get GIs together and they start talking about girls and ass and screwing, but the only thing they were doing was taking recipes down. In hindsight, it was really comical.'[50]

Then, on February 13, 1945, a hundred miles away, everything changed. The Allies so destroyed the German city of Dresden and killed so many civilians and refugees that for the rest of the war the Kriegies' fate would depend on the whim of an increasingly desperate Hitler and his SS adjutants. Should a Kriegie be shot for every civilian killed in the terror bombings? Should camps simply be liquidated as revenge? Or should the POWs be kept alive and used as hostages in a final showdown in the Bavarian Alps? It was anyone's guess.

12. The River

Dresden – February 13, 1945

Since fall 1944, the Air Ministry in London had debated the merits of massive area raids on select German cities to try to break the German war machine and the civilian population's spirit, thereby hastening the end of the war. They decided that a strategy of terror bombing, code-named Operation Thunderclap, would be put into effect when Germany became most vulnerable.

In February 1945, this critical point arrived. The Russians were storming across the eastern frontiers of Germany, and the Americans and British were closing on the Rhine. RAF Bomber Command and the American Air Force drew up a list of prospective targets: Dresden, Leipzig, Berlin, and Chemnitz – all critical supply centers close to the German front lines on the eastern front. Unfortunately, they were also crammed with refugees and wounded who had fled 'Ivan' – as terrified Germans called the vengeful Russians. By obliterating such targets, the Allies hoped to hinder the supply of reinforcements to the eastern front, thereby speeding the Russian advance.

On February 4, at the Yalta Conference, the Russians urged the Western Allies to launch Operation Thunderclap, and soon Bomber Command was directed to prepare huge raids on Chemnitz, Leipzig, and Dresden. The U.S. Eighth Air Force would also be involved, primarily in delivering incendiary bombs during daylight before Bomber Command attacked at night.

Operation Thunderclap started on February 13 with a massive attack on Dresden. A first raid involved 244 Lancasters dropping more than 800 tons of bombs. Because of cloud cover, it was only partially successful. A second raid just three hours later, with clear skies aiding the bombardiers, involved 529 Lancasters. More than 1,800 tons of bombs were dropped with horrendous effect. A firestorm that sucked oxygen from the streets, asphyxiating thousands and turning every organic object in its path to cinder, swept across the city. Countless civilians exploded into flames in the airless inferno. Those who dove into rivers, or pools and lakes in the city's parks, were boiled alive.

No one will ever know exactly how many people died, but the most conservative estimate is at least 40,000 and some have reckoned the total at as much as 135,000. The RAF lost nine aircraft. The hell continued on February 14 and 15 with 311 American B-17s dropping 771 tons of bombs on the already devastated city.[51]

In Berlin, Hitler listened to the reports on the unprecedented devastation in grim silence, his fist clenched. As he did so, propaganda chief Joseph Goebbels called for an Allied POW to be killed for every victim of the Dresden raid. That sounded more than reasonable to Hitler. If Allied POWs were executed, the Americans and British would begin to mistreat German POWs, making it less likely that soldiers would surrender to them without putting up a fight. It would help prevent the mass desertions crippling some Wehrmacht divisions on the eastern front. But Hitler's senior staff did not agree. Probably considering how they might soon have to save their own necks, Jodl, Keitel,

Donitz, and Ribbentrop insisted that such killing of POWs would be counterproductive. Finally, they managed to get Hitler to ignore Goebbels's suggestion.

But the question had been raised. What should Hitler now do with the 250,000 American and British POWs under his control? He had written in *Mein Kampf* that his fate would be either to see Germany dominate the world or crash in total ruin. It was obvious to the Nazi elite that Hitler's scorched-earth policies in the east – destroying everything in the wake of the Wehrmacht's retreat – would now apply to Germany itself: Hitler intended to take the Fatherland down with him.

And if a few hundred thousand POWs were to be buried with millions of others in the rubble? So be it.

Ückerath, the Rhineland – Early March 1945

The first signs of spring had arrived on the western front. The snow melted, rivers had soon reached full flood, and many roads had become quagmires. In key areas, nevertheless, the thaw allowed the Allies to proceed once again. They had pierced the Siegfried Line in vital sectors and were now advancing swiftly once more, just as they had the previous fall, toward the heart of the Third Reich. The Germans put up bitter resistance but could only delay the advance for a few days in a few sectors.

As the Allies swept across the Rhineland, Major Kriz and his 2nd Battalion of the 394th Infantry Regiment were once more in the thick of the fighting.[52]

On March 1, 1945, General Lauer had issued Field Order No. 8, placing the 99th Division at the front of the advance with the objective of seizing a section of the Cologne

Plain, which connected the Erft Canal to the Rhine itself.

After darkness on March 4, 1945, near the small town of Ückerath, a couple of miles from the Rhine, Kriz and his 2nd Battalion ran into serious resistance. Kriz organized his men and inspired them to fight and hold as the Germans launched a desperate counterattack. His leadership was later rewarded with the U.S. Army's second highest military award, the Distinguished Service Cross, for 'extraordinary heroism in connection with military operations against an armed enemy.'

The next day, the 99th Division reached the western banks of the Rhine near Cologne. In just six days, led by officers such as Kriz, the Checkerboard Division had successfully completed Field Order No. 8. The division had in fact moved so quickly that it had been impossible to provide adequate artillery support for the advance. Fighting from house to house and street to street, Kriz and his fellow 99ers had seized 75 towns and villages and taken 1,372 POWs, including men from five panzer divisions. It had been a heady, exhilarating charge after the bitter January spent fighting and dying in foxholes on the windswept Elsenborn Ridge.

Now, three armies were poised to strike across the Rhine. From the north stretching south to Düsseldorf was Montgomery's Twenty-first Army Group. In the center was Bradley's Twelfth Army Group, which included the 99th Division, and Patton's Third Army. To the south, reaching to the Swiss border, was Lieutenant General Jacob L. Devers's Sixth Army Group. But where would the Allies be able to cross in sufficient force and number to create an effective bridgehead? The retreating Germans had blown bridges from north to south, often as the Allies were within sight. The best crossing places for pontoon bridges were heavily defended by the remnants of the Wehrmacht and SS.

In the 99th Division's sector, south of Cologne, there were just a couple of places where the river could possibly be crossed, but then there stretched heavy forest and difficult terrain for fifty miles beyond the Rhine to the west – a potential 'death factory' like the Hürtgen Forest. How many more men would have to die before the Allies got across the Rhine?

Hammelburg – March 8, 1945

They formed a pitiful spectacle: eight hundred POWs who had spent forty-five days being shuffled across Germany from camp to camp during the coldest winter in living memory. They carried rough wool Wehrmacht blankets rolled around their emaciated bodies, backpacks made from old Hessian sacks, homemade portable stoves, and each other as they hobbled into the American compound at Hammelburg.

Lyle Bouck stood and watched the column of eight hundred enter. 'Who the hell are they?' he wondered.

They were veteran Kriegies from Oflag 64 in Szubin, Poland, who had walked more than three hundred miles to reach Hammelburg. They were led by Colonel Paul 'Pop' Goode, a tough West Pointer in his early forties who been captured in July 1944 in Normandy while serving with the 29th Division – the famous 'Blue and Grays' who had landed and been decimated within minutes on Omaha Beach on June 6, 1944, D-Day.

Goode suddenly snapped a command. The eight hundred men came to attention. Then in single file they marched through the entrance gate and down Hermann Goering Strasse, Goode at their lead, his head held high. Beside

Goode was another West Pointer, thirty-nine-year-old Lieutenant Colonel John Waters, just as resolved as Goode to maintain his and his men's self-pride. Waters had been captured on Valentine's Day 1943 near the Kasserine Pass in North Africa, where Colonel Robert Kriz had been wounded around the same time. Since then, Waters had learned the quiet patience and iron will to survive that all long-term POWs acquired. He had another reason for keeping his resolve – his father-in-law would expect nothing less. In 1933, he had married Bea Patton, General George S. Patton's daughter.

Goode quickly asserted himself, replacing Cavender in charge of the camp. He then began with Waters's help to run the American Oflag as if it were a regular U.S. Army base, insisting that men shave, address other ranks correctly, and maintain clean barracks. Goode also eased tensions with von Goeckel. Communion wine and wafers were provided to the camp's Catholic chaplain, Father Paul Cavanaugh. Junior officers began to salute their seniors. More briquettes of coal were issued, and the trigger-happy guards were kept under a seemingly tighter rein.

But Goode had one failing, according to several veterans: he had privately given up hope of making it out of the Oflag system alive. Back at Szubin, after Hitler had ordered the execution of sixty British escapees from another camp – immortalized in the film *The Great Escape* – Goode had lost his nerve and ordered the filling-in of an escape tunnel, much to the dismay of many of his junior officers. Whatever happened during their imprisonment, Goode now believed, the men were likely to be killed by the SS in a final act of brutality at the war's end.

Goode nevertheless made a crucial difference to morale. For Kriegies such as Lyle Bouck, however, it was their faith that now sustained them. Even agnostics and lapsed Catholics had started to appear at Father Cavanaugh's communions. The Depression had tested Bouck's parents' faith too much, and they had stopped taking him to church. But now he went to every Sunday's nondenominational religious service held by Father Cavanaugh. 'I got a real lift from the services,' he recalled. 'I never missed one. They made me feel better.'

For Bouck, like so many of his compatriots, imprisonment would be perhaps the greatest spiritual transformation of his life. Every one of the men would leave the camp profoundly changed. 'I learned to be patient, to always think positive, to always look forward, to plan and prepare,' recalled Bouck. 'And I swore that I would never let something like this ever happen again.'

In the noncoms' compound, James Fort also vowed that he would never be taken prisoner again. He would rather fight to the end than endure another POW camp. By now, he and his platoon buddies were starting to weaken seriously as the cold and starvation took its inevitable toll. Jenkins's frostbitten feet had worsened; Fort and others did their best to find whatever rags they could to bind around them for warmth. McGehee was a different man, having lost much of his strength. Like the others, his muscles had started to atrophy. Milosevich was as grimly stoic as ever but suffering from the first symptoms of hepatitis: stomach cramps and often debilitating lethargy.

'From BBC reports, we knew where the Allied front line was all the time,' recalled their leader, Lieutenant Bouck. 'The knowledge that the Allies were getting closer and closer buoyed us up. One day, we heard that they had reached the Rhine, and that really lifted us. Our own troops were now only a hundred miles or so away. That's when we really found some extra strength.'

Remagen – March 10, 1945

It was an hour or so before midnight when Colonel Kriz ordered his 2nd Battalion to move out. Their mission was to move as fast as possible across the Lundendorff bridge at Remagen as the first 99th Division unit to cross the Rhine. The bridge carried two railroad tracks with a footpath on either side. Twin stone towers stood at either end. In 1939, the Germans had set up an elaborate network of explosives so that they could blow the bridge just ahead of any Allied advance.[53]

Colonel Kriz and his executive officer, Boyd McCune, approached the bridge on foot through Remagen. They each led a single file of men hugging either side of a blacked-out street. Suddenly shells landed, killing and injuring several men and causing panic. Kriz rallied the men as medics tended the wounded. Then the advance toward the bridge began again.

'We led the 2nd Battalion, 394th Infantry, across the bridge under sporadic and intermittent artillery fire,' recalled McCune. 'The shells that hit the superstructure had about the same effect as proximity-fuse air bursts. Needless to say, the soldiers could see this as they approached and it took great courage to make the crossing.'

The men suddenly understood how air crews felt when they came under heavy flak over a target. The air was full of flying shrapnel and artillery bursts. When they looked down through the many holes, they could see the Rhine swirling in dark, three-meter-deep eddies, red-hued from the reflections of exploding shells. MPs shone flashlights onto planks hastily spread across the widest gaps and calmly directed jeep drivers across. Upstream, massive searchlights swept back and forth across the river looking for German frogmen – some of Otto Skorzeny's men had been ordered to destroy the bridge – and boats. Bodies littered the damaged span.

Around ten minutes into the crossing, artillery fire eased as Kriz and his men moved into the lee of a cliff on the eastern side. Finally, they passed the twin towers on the far side. Kriz was summoned to a meeting with the 394th's commanding officer, Colonel John R. Jeter, who had replaced Colonel Don Riley on February 15. As Checkerboard men continued to cross throughout the night, Kriz and Jeter planned a daylight attack to expand the bridgehead.

Meanwhile, McCune stayed on the bridge trying to get as many 99ers across as possible without being hit by artillery fire. The Germans were throwing everything they had at the bridge. McCune detected a pattern to the shelling and quickly instructed units to time their crossings to coincide with brief lulls in the German fire.

Eventually, McCune spent five hours under artillery fire that night and had shrapnel holes in his uniform but was not injured. For this heroic leadership, McCune received the Distinguished Service Cross. Largely because of his unflagging determination to get his unit across as complete as possible, the battalion's planned morning attack went ahead.

By the afternoon of March 11, 1945, Kriz had led the 2nd Battalion an additional three thousand yards and, alongside other elements of the 394th, had captured the towns of Leubsdorf and Arlendorf. By nightfall, the 99th Division had earned the great honor of being the first entire U.S.

infantry division across the Rhine. For the next fortnight, it would fight a bitter, unrelenting battle to hold off German counterattacks and secure the first Allied bridgehead east of the river.

Hammelburg – March 16, 1945

It began as a low whine, and then the Kriegies heard the familiar hum and drone of bombers passing overhead. 'At about 2300 hours, a large number of planes passed overhead near the camp, headed south,' recalled Hammelburg's American surgeon, Major Albert Berndt. 'Bright flashes of light and a loud thunder of heavy bombs sounded soon afterward. The only city in that vicinity was Würzburg.'[54]

The bombing gave Lyle Bouck and his fellow Kriegies a jolt of hope – the front lines were ever closer. Many of the POWs ran out of their barracks and jumped for glee. Men began to shape knives and clubs in preparation for a battle to liberate the camp.

But even as relief got closer, some men could no longer hold out. Illness finally defeated them. Two men in Bouck's barracks died from complications of flu and pneumonia. Others simply gave up. Risto Milosevich watched a fellow GI from Los Angeles, married with a child, as he chain-smoked himself to death. Though he had a family to live for, the GI wasted away as he traded all his food for nicotine. One morning, Milosevich saw his emaciated body carried out of the barracks by the Germans.

Lyle Bouck now knew that unless the Americans arrived soon, he too would waste away. He weighed less than 120 pounds, his skin was jaundiced, and his stomach was cramping again. He had yet to realize that he, like Milosevich, was suffering the first symptoms of acute hepatitis. He wondered whether he would now make it through the spring if he didn't get adequate food and medical aid.

Radio operator James Fort now dreamed every night of eating bacon and eggs. But then, just as he was about to tuck in, he would wake up. Even the simplest of meals had become a culinary masterpiece that starred in every man's nightly fantasies of sustenance.

In spite of his frostbitten feet, Corporal Sam Jenkins now spent the daylight hours as part of an *Arbeit Kommando* (work detail) chopping wood in a forest close to Hammelburg. 'It was by far the longest winter I ever experienced,' recalled Jenkins. At first he had been grateful for the short winter days when the sun sank about 4:30 in the afternoons, but now the days had lengthened with the approach of spring. Jenkins and the other prisoners in his work detail were, however, encouraged when they saw that their guards also had little to eat.

The Third Reich was clearly on the verge of collapse.

Oppenheim – March 24, 1945

It was a beautiful sunny morning as General George S. Patton walked, head held high, onto a pontoon bridge across the Rhine. Two days earlier, his Third Army had successfully crossed in force, beating Montgomery to the post by a matter of hours. He then sauntered with his senior aides, among them a tough World War I veteran named Major Alexander Stiller, toward the middle of the river.

'Time out for a short halt,' said Patton.

The party stopped, exactly midway across the Rhine.

Patton grinned as he strolled to the edge of the pontoon

bridge, undid his fly, and urinated into the river. He turned toward his aides, doing up his fly, and said: 'I have been looking forward to this for a long time.'

Once across the river, Patton ordered the 4th Armored Division, commanded by General William Hoge, to advance. By late afternoon, it had reached the Main River, twenty-five miles to the east. That evening, one of Patton's most senior officers, Major General Manton Eddy, commander of the Third Army's XII Corps, called Hoge with astonishing news.

Patton wanted a task force sent seventy-odd miles behind enemy lines to liberate 'nine hundred American prisoners' in a camp at Hammelburg.

Not long after, Patton himself telephoned Hoge. 'This is going to make MacArthur's raid on Cabanatuan[55] peanuts!'

'We'd be encroaching on the Seventh Army zone,' replied Hoge.

'Bill,' said Patton, 'I want you to put a little task force together. Now get on with it.'

Hoge again objected.

'I've cleared this with Bradley,' replied Patton.

'My people are exhausted. The division is only at half strength as it is.'

'Bill, I promise I'll replace anything you lose – every man, every tank, every half-track. I promise.'

As a new division commander, Hoge was in no position to argue further.

'I'll get Abrams of Combat Command B right on it, sir.'

Hoge put down the telephone and looked at Patton's aide, Major Alexander Stiller, who had listened to the conversation. Stiller hesitated and then explained that there was a reason the 'Old Man' was so determined to send a task force: John Waters, Patton's son-in-law, was one of the POWs.

In early February, three officers from Oflag 64 had escaped and ended up in Moscow. There they had reported to Major General John Deane that Waters and their fellow Kriegies were being force-marched to the west, away from the Russians. Deane had passed on the information to General Eisenhower, who had in turn informed Patton.

How Patton had then concluded that Waters was in Hammelburg remains a mystery. The most likely source of information was the Swiss Red Cross in Geneva, where the POWs' names were registered on their arrival in the camps.

Reluctantly, Hoge contacted thirty-year-old Creighton Abrams, perhaps the most brilliant of Patton's many talented cavalrymen, who had set the pace as the 4th Armored Division raced toward the Rhine.

Hoge knew that Abrams would be even less enthused by Patton's order.

'Fifty miles is a long way,' said Abrams when Hoge had briefed him on the mission. 'If we have to go that far, I want my whole command [around four thousand men] to go.'

'No, it has to be a small force,' insisted Hoge. 'And Army says it has to go tonight.'

'I'd like to talk to Army, sir.'

'Don't worry, you'll get your chance. Patton is planning to come down to your command post.'

Hammelburg – March 25, 1945

The Allies' escalating raids on Würtzburg and other German cities throughout Bavaria incensed many of Hammelburg's guards whose families lived in the region. Some could barely control their rage toward the *Amerikaner* under their guard. Around midday on March 25, 1945, an air-raid siren sounded. Some minutes later, an American lieutenant named John Weeks ran for the latrine, desperate to relieve himself. As he was leaving his barracks, a rifle shot cracked out and Weeks fell. Colonel Goode, General von Goeckel, and Major Berndt, who had just finished a routine inspection of the infirmary, were about a hundred yards away.

'The lieutenant had been shot by a guard who was invisible to me,' recalled Berndt. 'I hoped the guard could see the Red Cross brassards on my arms although they gave me no more right to be out during an airraid than any other prisoner. I knelt beside the lieutenant and turned him over. He was dead. General von Goeckel and Colonel Goode slowly joined me.'

Colonel Goode was furious with von Goeckel. 'I will see to it that the proper reports are made to the American authorities and steps taken to punish those who are guilty as soon as this camp is liberated.'[56]

General von Goeckel apologized and then ordered the guard to be brought to him. According to some reports, the general, no doubt aware that he might soon face a war crimes investigation, then had the man reassigned to an infantry company on the eastern front – punishment enough for any German that spring of 1945.

4th Armored Division's Command Post, Aschaffenburg, Germany – March 25, 1945

At 10:00 A.M. on March 25, 1945, General Patton arrived at Abrams's command post, flanked by General Hoge and Major Stiller.

Patton asked who would be in command of the force to liberate Hammelburg. Abrams replied that he would command it himself. Patton said that was out of the question – it had to be a small force. Abrams suggested Lieutenant Cohen of the 10th Armored Infantry. But Cohen might not be up to it – he had a bad case of piles. Patton, accompanied by Hoge, Abrams, and Stiller, set off to Cohen's command post, where Patton watched as a doctor inspected Cohen's backside.

'This is some sorry ass,' said Patton. 'Terrible.'

Cohen would not go. But among the officers at his command post was the 10th Armored's S-2: tall, red-haired Abraham Baum, the twenty-four-year-old Bronx-reared Jew who had spearheaded the 4th Armored Division's initial drive to Bastogne on December 19, 1944. Before the war, Baum had been a pattern-cutter for women's blouses.

Patton took Baum aside. 'Listen, Abe – it is Abe, isn't it?'

Baum nodded.

'I thought so. You pull this off and I'll see to it that you get the Congressional Medal of Honor.'

'I have my orders, sir. You don't have to bribe me.'

Patton and his entourage left, with the exception of Stiller and Cohen. Stiller explained that he would accompany Baum's task force of some three hundred men because Patton had ordered him to gain a taste of combat. Baum looked at the thin-faced, wiry, middle-aged officer, one of Patton's most trusted aides, and felt uneasy.

Stiller had tasted more combat than almost all of Patton's most experienced commanders already. Only later would Baum discover Stiller's true reason for tagging along: once Baum got to Hammelburg, it would be Stiller's job to find and identify Waters and help bring him safely back to the American front lines.

At 5:00 P.M., Baum gathered his force and briefed his unit commanders. The force of 293 men, with 54 vehicles – 10 medium Sherman tanks, 6 light tanks, 3 assault guns, 27 half-tracks, and 8 jeeps – would break through the German lines at 10:30 P.M. with covering artillery fire. The task force would then take the most direct route toward Hammelburg. It was scheduled to arrive at the camp early on the afternoon of March 27 and return that night.

There would be no division support. Air cover had been promised but could not be guaranteed. There were only fifteen marked maps for the task force – there was not enough time to prepare more. The exact location of the prison camp was not known – the force would have to elicit this information from a German along the route. And there would be just enough fuel, if all went well, to get to Hammelburg and then hightail it back.

Baum's men were exhausted, having slept one night in the last four as the 4th Armored had stormed across the Rhine. But as soon as Baum had briefed them, they shrugged off their fatigue and got to work. Little did they know that they were about to embark on one of the most controversial missions of the entire war.

Hammelburg – March 26, 1945

Lieutenant Lyle Bouck and his fellow Kriegies formed a funeral cortege along Herman Göring Strasse and watched as Lieutenant Weeks's flag-draped casket was carried past them and out of the Oflag's main gate to a nearby cemetery.

A bugler from the Serbian camp played 'Taps' as Weeks's casket passed by. His senseless killing had shocked and enraged the men more than any other loss. 'It was such a waste,' recalled Bouck. 'He wasn't doing anything to hurt anyone. He was from my barracks. Came from Jolliet,

Illinois. His death haunted me for a long time. The Germans buried him beside the two other men I knew from my barracks who had died of flu and pneumonia.'

In the noncoms' camp, Risto Milosevich was now determined to escape. He had collected enough scraps of food from his Serbian friends to last him the several days he reckoned it would take to make it to the Allied lines. From other prisoners' failed escape attempts, he had learned that without several days' supply of food it was impossible to get far. 'Guys who escaped would go to farms to try to steal food, and the local farmers would grab a rifle and bring them back, and they'd be put in solitary confinement. But I had enough food for two guys for ten days. So I chose this young kid who spoke German fluently to go with me. I figured he'd be able to talk us out of trouble. We had a radio in camp, and I knew exactly where the front line was. But then I got sick. It was as if I had an iron ball in my stomach. I got hepatitis like you wouldn't believe. So that killed that. But I know I would have made it, traveling at night, sleeping during the day. I know I would.'

Sometime during that evening of March 26, 1945, a rumor began to spread through the Hammelburg Oflag: an American armored force was heading toward the camp. The story might have been started by a guard or perhaps a Kriegie listening to local German radio traffic. Whatever its origin, the impact on those who heard it was electrifying: their fellow Americans were at hand. Surely, it was now a matter of hours, not weeks, before salvation arrived in the form of General Patton's Sherman tanks.

13. Task Force Baum

Hammelburg – March 27–29, 1945

It was a sunny day. The earthy smell of spring was in the air. The frost-singed grass skirting the Herman Goering Strasse in the American Oflag at Hammelburg was starting to turn green. And Lieutenant Lyle Bouck was for once in good spirits. It was his mother Magdalene's forty-sixth birthday, and he was full of thoughts of the woman who had worked so hard and without complaint to feed and clothe him through the Depression. Thinking about her made him feel better. It took his mind off his empty stomach for a while.

At his headquarters, General Patton wrote his wife: 'Last night, I sent a column to a place forty miles east of Frankfurt where John and some 900 prisoners are said to be. I have been nervous as a cat . . . as everyone but me thought it too great a risk. I hope it works. Al Stiller went along. If I lose that column, it will possibly be a new incident, but I won't lose it.'

At 3:50 P.M. in the Hammelburg Oflag, there were four short blasts on the camp's air-raid siren.

'All men stay in the barracks where you are!'

Ten minutes later, men in Bouck's barracks noticed frenzied activity among the German guards and then heard gunfire. Someone shouted that the Americans were close by, about to liberate them.

Throughout Hammelburg, POWs celebrated in their

barracks as bullets and artillery rounds whistled through the air. Some cried with relief. Others sat in silence, praying. Most hugged their bunk buddies, whooped with joy, and then hunkered down and watched through their barracks windows as Task Force Baum battled for control of Hammelburg, ducking for cover whenever bullets came close. In the infirmary, Major Berndt and his medical aides laid the sick on the floor for protection. A group of around one hundred Kriegies sitting with Father Cavanaugh prayed for final salvation and thanked God for their great fortune.

Several heavy machine gun rounds ricocheted close by, followed by a shell that exploded somewhere in the camp. Cavanaugh and his congregation dropped to the floor. The priest crawled under the table he used as an altar. A few seconds later, he calmed himself and stood up. The men remained kneeling.

Small-arms fire now crackled in the distance.

His hands trembling, Father Cavanaugh made the sign of the cross.

At Colonel Goode's office in the Oflag, it was decided that a senior officer should try to contact Task Force Baum and tell it to stop firing on the Serbian compound that was receiving most of the American fire, no doubt because the Serbs in their gray uniforms looked like Germans from a distance.

Patton's son-in-law Colonel John Waters volunteered. Accompanied by three American officers and a German representative, Colonel Fuchs, he set out through the main gate. The men carried a white flag and the Stars and Stripes. Suddenly, a German soldier appeared from behind a building in the distance. 'He looked over and saw us coming down the road,' recalled Waters. 'I think he must have thought that the German [Fuchs] had surrendered to us. So, he put his gun through the fence at the second rail, and pulled the trigger.'

Waters collapsed. He had been hit below the right hip. The bullet had chipped his coccyx and then exited his left buttock. It was an agonizing wound, but, as was later revealed, he had escaped being paralyzed for life by just a few millimeters.

'It felt like somebody hit me with a telegraph pole,' recalled Waters. 'There was no pain. There was no pain because I was numb from the waist down.'

The German soldier cautiously approached Waters, who lay sprawled in the road.

'You son of a bitch,' cried Waters, 'you've ruined my fishing.'

Fuchs managed to explain their mission to the guard, who then ordered them to return to Hammelburg. The two officers carried Waters in a blanket back to the camp.

Father Cavanaugh had just finished giving Holy Communion when there was a huge shout of jubilation from a barracks across the Herman Goering Strasse.

'What happened?' asked Cavanaugh.

'Father, we're free! We're liberated!'

'The German General [von Goeckel] has surrendered to Colonel Goode.'

'The Stars and Stripes are flying from this building.'

'You're not a Kriegie any longer.'

Lyle Bouck huddled close to Matthew Reid.

'The guards have all taken off,' someone said.

Bouck picked himself up from the barrack floor and looked out into the compound. Two officers were carrying

Waters toward the Serbian infirmary. Bouck figured Waters would not live long because he was bleeding so badly.[57]

It was after 5:00 P.M. as several barracks emptied and men formed a column of fives, carrying packs and rolled-up blankets like bandoliers. They then marched triumphantly past the cheering Serbs, through a hole in the fence, and toward the main body of Task Force Baum, lit up in the gathering dusk by a burning haystack.

As the Kriegies approached Baum's force, they could contain their excitement no more; many broke ranks and rushed the half-tracks and tanks, hugging the crews and gleefully accepting cigarettes and rations from Baum's exhausted men.

Throughout the Oflag compound, other POWs were soon pouring into the open.

'The Serbs are taking off,' said an officer.

Tanks had knocked down some of the perimeter fencing around the Serbian compound. Lyle Bouck saw hundreds of Serbs streaming out of the enclosure, free at last after four years of incarceration.

In the noncoms' camp, a few miles away, others from Bouck's platoon – Corporal Jenkins, Sergeant Redmond, Corporal McGehee, radio operator James Fort, Platoon Sergeant Slape, and Private First Class Milosevich – were overjoyed. They could not see what was going on, but they guessed that the Americans had arrived because of the sounds of battle.

Corporal Sam Jenkins heard the senior noncom in his barracks announce that they were being liberated. The man left to find out what they should do next. As in Bouck's barracks, men hugged each other and made ready to leave. Then the barracks leader returned, looking glum.

'We are not being liberated,' he said. 'They've come for the officers.'

Men cursed and gasped with disbelief.

'Look, if you want to go then go – the guards have left.'

'Go where?' someone asked acidly.

'Well, just go out in the country. Or you can wait until tomorrow and the rest of the American forces will be here.'

Having survived this long, few men wanted to be killed so close to the end of the war.

'If I wait, I'll get some food,' thought Jenkins. 'I might not get any out there.' His fellow platoon members agreed.

Abe Baum stopped his tank on a hillside above Hammelburg.

'I was elated by the fact that I got there,' Baum recalled sixty years later. 'It was a miracle in itself. But I had understood that there was supposed to be three hundred POWs. And out run fifteen hundred. That overwhelmed me. It was unbelievable. I could have thrown up when I saw them. I was frustrated and exhausted, and we hadn't had any rest for two days. It was sickening to see the condition of some of the POWs – skeletons of men. Colonel Goode really couldn't control them. It was doubly sickening because I knew damn well I couldn't take those men back, and even if I did take some with me I wasn't certain whether we were going to make it.'

Baum had been injured by shrapnel the previous day when a round from a Panzerfaust – the German equivalent of a bazooka – had exploded on a cobbled street not far from where he and one of his tank commanders, Lieutenant William Nutto, had been standing. Nutto had been hit in the neck, chest, arms, and legs, Baum in the knee and right hand. Both had been quickly patched up, but now, some twenty-four hours later, their wounds and exhaustion had brought both to the limits of their endurance.

Baum had pulled off one of the great combat feats of World War II. He had stormed fifty miles through heavily defended German territory and arrived at his objective as planned. But the promised air cover had yet to arrive, and only half of Baum's original force was now fit to continue. The dead and seriously wounded had been left beside the road as the force had pushed on, meeting fiercer and increasingly organized resistance – German spotter planes had tracked them and alerted the ground forces along their route.

Task Force Baum's mission was far from over. Getting to Hammelburg had been one thing; returning with the Allied POWs to American lines would be quite another.

Yet more POWs spilled out of the camp, leaping joyfully across the downed perimeter wire.

Lieutenants Lyle Bouck and Matthew Reid headed across open pasture toward a group of tanks from Task Force Baum.

'Let's go with these guys,' said Bouck.

A few minutes later, Baum stood on a half-track and addressed the men. His task force was not the spearhead of the Allied advance. The front lines were many miles away. The task force could only take so many men with it as it tried to fight its way back to American lines.

'If you want to go back into the camp, go back into the camp,' added Baum. 'If you want to take off on foot and try to get back, do so. But I can't possibly take more than fifty or sixty of you.'

There were astonished gasps. Joy began to turn to rage.

Someone announced that only field-grade officers could join the task force on its return. Bouck turned to Reid. He was as angry and bewildered as the other POWs. Sending so few men had been crazy. But at last he had a choice.

'You're now a major,' said Bouck.

Reid looked confused.

'They're saying only field-grade officers can go with them,' explained Bouck. 'Now you promote me to major. Go on.'

'Okay, you're now a major.'

'Let's go.'

Bouck and Reid crawled onto a tank. The crew gave them each an M-3 grease gun. Bouck felt better with a weapon in his hands. Now he was back in the fight. But for what seemed like an eternity, they waited on the tank. 'Dusk was upon us and rapidly early darkness added to the confusion,' recalled Bouck. 'While all this was taking place, there was a considerable amount of hollering and cursing. Much disagreement was in the air.'

They were losing precious time, thought Bouck. Time enough for the German forces around Hammelburg to re-group and try to cut off the task force's possible escape routes.

Then it was night.

Baum was still trying to thin the ranks of POWs clinging to his last remaining half-tracks and tanks. 'Too many got on a tank, and we couldn't rotate the weapon,' he recalled. 'So we had to tell them to get off.'

Nearby, Lieutenant William Nutto looked at the excited Kriegies and felt only exhaustion and despair. He knew the task force was in serious trouble. They didn't even have enough fuel now for all the vehicles to get back.

Another command went out. Men who could not fit onto the vehicles were to form groups and make their way west or return to the camp.

As Baum made his final preparations, Major Stiller suddenly appeared out of the darkness.

'Colonel Waters was wounded during the attack on the camp,' he told Baum. 'They just operated on him. He's going to be okay, but he can't be moved now. We'll have to go without him.'

Baum barely acknowledged the news. He had more important things to worry about than Colonel Waters's condition. Somehow, he had to return alive with his task force to friendly lines.

'We're getting out of here,' someone said at last.

It was around 8:00 P.M. The tanks and armored vehicles, carrying some two hundred Kriegies, revved up and pulled away, leaving thousands of bitterly disappointed POWs behind in Hammelburg.

Task Force Baum crept forward through the inky darkness. Among the Kriegies clinging desperately to the cold metal of the tanks were Lieutenants Lyle Bouck and Matthew Reid. 'As we crossed the field and [moved] onto a road,' recalled Bouck, 'Reid and I realized that we were on the second tank from the front of the column. Reid poked fun about always wanting to lead the way.'

Their tank was part of a probe sent by Baum to find a way out of a growing German encirclement. The probe was commanded by Lieutenant William Nutto who, though severely injured, was the only experienced officer Baum could now rely on to lead such a force.

The probe followed a twisting, narrow trail. Every fifty yards or so, Nutto stopped his Sherman, jumped out, and scouted the road ahead.

It was a maddening pace: the probe inched forward for a few minutes, stopped while Nutto went ahead, and then crawled forward again.

As the hours passed, Bouck and Reid struggled to cling to their tank. When the probe had started out, Bouck and his fellow Kriegies had hoped they stood at least a fair chance of getting away from Hammelburg and back to American lines. But now they were increasingly anxious.

Once more, the probe halted. But this time the tankers turned off the massive engines; the steady rumble and vibration stopped. Men farther along the column hissed for others to be quiet. From around a hundred yards away came the sound of German soldiers singing.

The Kriegies, hoping they would not be heard, waited for the Germans to pass. The seconds ticked by slowly. Then, finally, the singing became more and more distant.

The Shermans began to inch forward, the steady rumble of engines filling the ink-black night once more. Finally, the probe reached the outskirts of a village called Hundsfeld – several houses at a road junction. The homes were dark. Not a lantern flickered.

Nutto spotted logs piled across a road – a German roadblock. He would have to try a different escape route.

Bouck and Reid watched in silence as Nutto's Sherman turned about. Their tank did likewise and then followed Nutto north.

Ahead of Nutto's probe, men moved forward in the last remaining reconnaissance jeep, scouting out the road. Suddenly, there was the sound of gunshots.

Every man now had the same fear, that this escape route would also be blocked.

Nutto stopped and radioed Baum: the reconnaissance jeep had run into trouble.

'Okay, turn off. There's a trail on the map heading west and will probably take you to the main highway at Hollrich.'

Nutto ordered his driver in the lead Sherman, just ahead of Bouck and Reid, to move forward.

The new trail cut through forest, providing better cover. Bouck and Reid clung to their tank as the probe built up speed. The temperature was plunging as the night drew on. The forest blocked the moonlight above. It was hard to see anything in the undergrowth.

Soon, the probe came to a fork in the road. There were houses nearby. Nutto decided to turn right. The probe crawled forward again, passing more houses and then clanging down actual streets. The town was silent. German civilians were huddled in their basements.

Bouck watched as Nutto's Sherman reached the outskirts of Hollrich. The highway lay ahead.

Nutto ordered his driver to move forward. As the Sherman swung onto the highway, Lyle Bouck saw a flash of light streak through the sky. A German Tiger suddenly fired its 88mm gun.

A Panzerfaust round exploded a few feet from where Nutto stood, almost stunning him. 'It was pitch black, no moon, blacker than crap,' he recalled. 'Then I saw the flare from the Panzerfaust and the goddamned thing hit the turret right where I was standing.'

Nutto felt one of his men pushing him from below. He was forced up and out of his seat and then fell off the tank.

Lyle Bouck saw a machine gun open up on the column, hitting several men. Tracer fire stabbed through the darkness. He and Reid leaped off their tank and took cover in some undergrowth at the side of the road.

Nutto could see his tanks trying to back up and pull away. He was in agony as he crawled over a dead body and away from his Sherman. The second Sherman, which Bouck and Reid had just jumped off, was now a target for the Tiger. Nutto saw it receive a direct hit. The Kriegies who had not jumped off were flung into the air from the impact. Then the Sherman burst into flames.

Bouck and Reid made it to a ditch and lay there, hearts

pounding, clutching their grease guns. Their anxiety and weakness were gone, replaced by surging adrenaline.

The flames from the burning tank lit up the sky.

A few seconds later, Bouck spotted a Panzerfaust crew.

'Let's go get them,' said Reid.

The two men crawled through some weeds and saplings. They soon had the Germans in clear view. Both let rip, bullets felling the dark figures.

Reid and Bouck then scrambled back to the column.

Nutto, meanwhile, lay in the road beside his tank. He heard Germans approach and then climb inside the Sherman. They started the engine. Anger surged inside him. The Germans were playing with his tank. 'I was lying there in the road, and bullets were ricocheting around me. Every time a bullet came close it kind of jolted me. Then this German officer comes up and sticks a [Luger] in my face and asks: "Are you Negro?" I almost said something stupid, but I hadn't shaved in a week and was covered in grease. They were all filled with that propaganda crap.'

Nutto tried to pull up his sleeve so he could show his white skin.

'No, I'm not.'

The officer walked on by.

'I guess he'd have shot my ass if I was,' Nutto recalled.

Nutto would later be picked up and taken to a German hospital in Würtzburg.

Meanwhile, his surviving tanks and half-tracks were heading back the way they had come.

Lieutenant Lyle Bouck jumped up onto one of the tanks.

The road skirted a forest and then began to climb up a steep hillside. It led to a semicircular clearing on a small plateau, skirted by deep forest to the west and north. Bouck's tank stopped near a stone barn.

It was announced that Task Force Baum would regroup here before trying to break out once more shortly after daylight. Baum's men quickly set about draining and transferring gasoline, in some cases cutting the rubber lines and emptying the Shermans' fuel directly into jerricans to save precious time.

Colonel Paul Goode, who had remained at the rear of the probe with the majority of the Kriegies, now learned that Baum still intended to fight his way out.

Goode climbed onto a tank near the stone barn. His fellow POWs gathered in the darkness.

'We have to face it,' said Goode. 'Most of us can't keep going. We should go back to the camp. We have tried our best. If we stick with the task force now, we'll weigh them down. We'll follow the road back toward the Oflag. Those of you who are able to go on and are prepared to fight can stay with the column.'

Bouck turned to Reid.

'What do you want to do?'

'Let's stay with them,' said Reid.

Only a dozen other Kriegies wanted to stay with Baum and fight their way to freedom at daybreak.

Back at the Hammelburg officers' Oflag, dispirited Kriegies, including Father Cavanaugh, watched forlornly as German guards escorted American wounded and other Kriegies back into the camp. It was obvious now that the raid to liberate them had failed miserably.

'We are not free yet, Father,' one of the returning Kriegies told Cavanaugh.

'Well, let's get some sleep anyway,' Cavanaugh replied.

In the noncoms' camp, a German soldier entered forward

artillery observer Sergeant Peter Gacki's barracks and demanded volunteers to help dig graves. Gacki and his fellow observer, Willard Wibben, volunteered. 'They took us out to the cemetery, and we dug several graves,' recalled Gacki. 'It was very, very sad.' Two bodies of Americans were unloaded and placed in the graves.

Gacki and Wibben returned to the camp, deeply depressed. The barracks was deathly silent. A cloud of despair had fallen over Hammelburg.

On Hill 427, Lyle Bouck could sense that daylight was approaching. He could make out a red cross that had been painted on the stone barn where the wounded lay moaning.

Bouck looked on as all but a dozen of his fellow Kriegies formed a column with Colonel Goode, carrying a white flag, at its head. Forlornly, the men walked back toward the camp. Bouck watched them go, knowing they were probably doing the sensible thing. But he had made his decision. He was going to fight on, come what may. He had been taken prisoner once. He could not bear to walk into captivity under his own volition.

Around 8:00 A.M., Baum called his surviving officers to him.

'We're not stopping for any roadblocks this time,' he told them. 'We take them out. If we hit a defensive position, we overrun it. If we meet Tigers, we fight them. If we hit a wide stream, I want a half-track to go in as a bridge for the tanks. We go like a straight arrow until we run out of gas. . . . Remember, we've got to bowl over the Krauts. Mount up.'

Baum's officers and men boarded the remaining half-tracks and tanks. Baum got in his jeep and then drove to the edge of the clearing and faced south.

'Turn 'em over,' Baum shouted, making the hand signal to move out.

The tanks and half-tracks cranked up. Then, suddenly, a 'hellfire' of artillery, machine gun, and mortar fire descended from all directions.

The whole clearing seemed to erupt in flames. Every tank and half-track appeared to be hit. The aim was incredibly accurate: the Germans had surrounded them during the night and waited for the first signal of movement before launching their attack.

Abe Baum saw one of his radio operators in a nearby half-track. He was oblivious to the explosions and screams of wounded as he tapped out furiously in Morse code: 'Task Force Baum surrounded. Under heavy fire. Request air support.'

It was Task Force Baum's last communication.

Lyle Bouck could see Germans in all directions.

'Every man for himself,' shouted Baum.

Machine gun fire roared.

Bouck and Reid jumped from a half-track, fired at random, and ducked into a wooded area.

Perhaps eighty men also made it to the tree line; most were unarmed.

'Fan out,' Baum ordered as terrified men scrambled into undergrowth. 'Don't follow me. Break up into groups of twos or threes and go your own way.'

The men took off in different directions. There was the sound of barking. Germans approached with sniffer dogs.

Baum hid with Major Stiller and a radio operator called John Sidles.

They were suddenly spotted.

'*Raus! Raus!*' cried a German.

Baum quickly threw away his dog tags – they would have

revealed that he was Jewish. Sometime later, he saw a horse and carriage carrying two members of the German Army of the Interior. One of them noticed Baum and lifted his rifle.

'I had a mackinaw over my clothes, and it hid my .45,' recalled Baum. 'I tried to get my .45 out, but my hand was so wet I couldn't shoot it.'

The German put down his rifle, stepped toward Baum, took out a P38 Luger, and fired.

Baum fell: the bullet had hit him in the groin, 'greasing [his] left nut.' The German told Stiller and Sidles to help Baum walk. They set off in the direction of Hammelburg.

'Let me get close to him and I'll hit him with my fucking helmet,' Baum told Stiller.

'No, no, no.'

'Please. Let me do it.'

Stiller grabbed Baum's arm to hold him back.

As they neared a wooded area, the Germans took Sidles and Stiller away and left Baum lying by the side of the road. He would soon be picked up by camp guards and taken to the Serbian hospital in Hammelburg, where he would be liberated with seventy remaining Oflag POWs, including Waters, by the 14th Armored Division of the Seventh Army on April 5, 1945 – barely a week later.[58]

Bouck and Reid were also quickly surrounded. The sniffer dogs yelped and barked, smelling *Amerikaner* everywhere they turned. There was no choice but to put their hands in the air. They were sent to join the other tankers and Kriegies.

Then they were all lined up. Some of the tankers had wisely thrown away their greasy overalls and anything else that might distinguish them as part of the task force. But it was no use. Bouck watched a German officer go along the line of Americans, pinching their cheeks. It was obvious who had some meat left on them. The men from Task Force Baum were easily identified, separated, and marched off.

It was not long before Lieutenants Bouck and Reid were trudging, utterly dejected and exhausted, back towards Hammelburg. As they neared the camp, Bouck noticed that many of the Serbs had fled their compound. Then he was marched beside Reid into the equestrian arena where they had been processed back in January. The Germans took Bouck's name and his POW number and handed him some boiled potatoes and a piece of pork sausage. A few hours later, around 3:00 P.M., it was announced that every American POW in the Hammelburg Oflag would be evacuated farther south. Bouck and the other Oflag Kriegies were given a Red Cross parcel to share between four men; they were then ordered into columns and marched out of Hammelburg.

The noncom Kriegies in the Lager three miles away were also told to move out. Only the wounded would be left behind to be treated in the Lager's hospital. Corporal Aubrey McGehee once again helped Corporal Sam Jenkins hobble along on his bad feet. They had finally started to improve with the warmer weather but were still too tender for him to walk unaided for more than a few hundred yards. Two other members of the platoon who still had some strength – Private First Class Robert Preston and radio operator James Fort – took turns with McGehee in helping Jenkins.

Failure littered the journey toward the Hammelburg railway station. Wreckage from Task Force Baum – every vehicle had been captured or destroyed – and spent ammunition lay around bends in the road, as did the inert bodies of Baum's men and the German defenders of Hammelburg.

Thanks to General George S. Patton's reckless arrogance, the 4th Armored Division had suffered its greatest loss of the war: 4 officers and 73 men missing in action. The 10th Armored had lost 6 officers; 209 men were listed as MIAs. The eventual death toll from Task Force Baum, calculated at war's end, would be 25 men. There is no accurate figure for how many Kriegies died, but the most conservative estimate is a dozen. Just 15 of Baum's approximately 300 men managed to get back to American lines, most of them several days after the raid – which was, of course, immediately hushed up. 'I can say this,' Patton would later write, 'that throughout the campaign in Europe I know of no error I made except that of failing to send a Combat Command to take Hammelburg.'

The Kriegies finally arrived at the Hammelburg train station. Among the bewildered ranks were Colonel Paul Goode and Major Alexander Stiller, Patton's aide. Stiller had been quickly interrogated by the Germans, who had assumed he was the task force commander because of his superior rank. He had gone along on the raid, he would later maintain, simply 'for the thrills.'

Dreaded boxcars awaited the men. Thankfully, just thirty were allotted to each car this time. They could at least lie down, and there was straw on the floor. The doors were slammed shut and locked. Guards scribbled the number of men in each car in blue chalk on the heavy oak doors.

At 6:00 P.M. on March 28, 1945, the train pulled out.

Yet again, the Kriegies did not know where they were going, when they would next be fed, and how long the journey might take. One thing was soon clear – they were headed farther south, toward the Bavarian Alps, where the SS, under the command of Otto Skorzeny, was planning to fight to the very last man.

Early the next morning, March 29, 1945 – Good Friday – the 4th Armored Division reported: 'No news of Baum.'

14. Last Days of the Reich

Germany – April 1945

By Easter Sunday, the 99th Division was assembling around the industrial town of Gemünden in the Ruhr Valley. In the previous fortnight, after establishing the Remagen bridgehead, Colonel Kriz's 2nd Battalion of the 394th Infantry Regiment had advanced more than a hundred miles, taking scores of POWs along the way. There would now be a couple of days to regroup and rest before the 99th went into action again, this time to clear the so-called Ruhr Pocket, an area of several hundred square miles stretching from Düsseldorf and Cologne in the west to Kassel in the east and from Giessen in the south to the small town of Iserlohn in the north.

The Ruhr Pocket contained an estimated four hundred thousand German troops – remnants of the Wehrmacht and SS armies that had been in more or less continual retreat since February. Cut off from reinforcement and without air support, Hitler's armies in the Ruhr were increasingly opting to surrender en masse rather than fight on pointlessly. Once they had been defeated, the total collapse of the Third Reich would be inevitable.

Kriz had little contact with the 394th's re-formed I&R platoon, which still included Private First Class Carlos Fernandez and Sergeant Robert Lambert. Kriz had been too busy leading his 2nd Battalion from the front, snatching just a few hours' sleep night after night, pushing on for week after week, barely pausing to clean up and get a hot meal, let alone catch up with his correspondence.

The journey from Lanzerath all the way to Gemünden had taken a toll on all those who had survived it. Like his fellow officers, Kriz had become hardened, but the war still had ways of burning itself anew into a man's psyche, even when he thought he had closed off his emotions for good. One haunting image in particular would stay with Kriz for fifty years: an American nurse crying as she cradled a dying SS grenadier in her arms.

It may have been in Gemünden that Kriz received an astonishing letter, dated March 30, 1945, from the badly wounded Private Bill James. It began with James relating in detail what had happened on December 16 in Lanzerath. James was unable to recall anything between falling unconscious late the night of December 16 and arriving at a German military hospital in Underach on the west bank of the Rhine on December 21. He had spent several weeks in the hospital. Each day, he had plotted the American advance until early March, when he had decided that the front lines were close enough for him to try to make a break for them.

'When I heard the Yanks were getting close,' James explained, 'I tried to escape on 4 March. I was the only American in the hospital. I managed to get out of town [but was] apprehended. The next morning they [the Germans] took me across the Rhine to Montabaour. There were one hundred wounded Yanks in a wooden barracks enclosed in barbed wire. We had an American medical Captain take care of us. Monday, 26th March, at 1:30 P.M., the 9th Armored Recons liberated us. That night our medics set up an aid station where we were. No infantry had entered the town. There was no resistance in the town, but a couple of [former] prisoners of war helped the few MPs round up German prisoners. They all were willing to part with some article, and I collected quite a few souvenirs.

'Then the nasty rumor started that about 300 SS troops were marching on the town to clean house on the population for not resisting. Rumor or no rumor I and a couple of others decided to pull out with the first section of medics that was going back with a load of frontline wounded. Two of us hopped on the tail-board of an ambulance and hung on. We went until the ambulance stopped to look over the route where a land bridge was blown. Then they let one of us ride in front on each ambulance. They took me clear back to the 102nd Evacuation Hospital and then to 48th General Hospital where I'm awaiting shipment to the States.

'Major Kriz, a luckier man than I never lived. However, I still wish I were in good enough shape to come back to you (or shall I say our outfit?). Please, Major Kriz, write to me with all our old boys' addresses, and let me know if there is any news. Give my regards to any of the old guys left, and give them hell. Yank! Good Luck, and I pray it all ends soon.'

The letter must have been a wonderful surprise for Kriz. If James, with such a critical wound, had survived, then perhaps the others who had fought so long that December day were also still alive in some POW camp, Lyle Bouck among them. Surely it was not too much to hope for?

Meanwhile, Lyle Bouck and others from the platoon traveled farther south toward the planned last redoubt of the Third Reich, the Bavarian Alps. 'We were traveling in the daytime, which was very dangerous, as we would [soon] discover,' recalled Sergeant Peter Gacki, who was on the same POW train from Hammelburg. 'As we were moving along, we heard one of the most frightening sounds we had ever heard.'

The sound was of an American P-47's eight .50-caliber machine guns firing simultaneously, stitching holes all along the train's roof with the precision and pattern of some monstrous sewing machine.

The men around Gacki clawed at their boxcar's wooden floor, frantic to escape the 'friendly' bullets. Mercifully, the train came to a stop; as soon as the doors were opened, almost every Kriegie jumped out and ran, along with the guards, into nearby fields.

Once the P-47 had passed and the guards had rounded up the Kriegies, it was learned that only one man had been killed. Then there was a long discussion; many men, including some of the guards, refused to get back on the train. They were not very far from Schweinfurt. It would be safer to walk there. Many of the POWs set off on foot. Peter Gacki's feet were still very sore from frostbite, and he opted to stay on the train. Thankfully, it was not attacked again. 'We later learned that the Germans had neglected to mark the train with the Red Cross insignia,' recalled Gacki. 'They let us travel to Schweinfurt with the doors open for their safety as well as ours. When we came into Schweinfurt we could see the town had been devastated. The factories in town had provided most all of the ball bearings and other war materials. I learned later that our Air Force paid a terrible price for those bombing raids. It was generally believed that it did help to shorten the war. At Schweinfurt, everyone got back on the train and we continued on our way.'

Early on April 5, 1945, the POW transport from Hammelburg arrived in Nuremberg. Since the platoon's previous visit in January, the city had been repeatedly bombed; some of its citizens spat on the POWs as the column filed out of the train station. Before crossing the ruined city, the men were given a bowl of soup. To their disgust, some quickly discovered that their soup contained black beetles. Those who had only recently become POWs couldn't force themselves to swallow even a spoonful. But most ate the soup without grumbling.

Then the Kriegies were marched south in a column that filed past the massive arena where Hitler and the Nazis had held huge rallies: a giant swastika still flew above the arch over the entrance to the stadium. The Kriegies trudged on. There was the odd sight of an old car powered by a wood-burning motor. Finally, by late morning, they had reached an industrial area on the southern outskirts of the city. Some factories were still operating, despite the intense bombing throughout the winter and spring.

The men paused for an hour's rest and unwrapped small bundles of food they had stored. Around midday, they heard an air-raid siren – a *Vorwarnung* – soon followed by a short series of wails indicating the imminent approach of Allied planes. The German guards looked up into the clear skies, hoping not to spot 'jabos' – fighter-bombers such as Mosquitoes and Typhoons. Suddenly, hundreds of German workers streamed out of some nearby factories and ran fast toward the prisoners.

Father Paul Cavanaugh, who had already endured the December 23 Limburg bombing, looked up and saw Allied bombers. Marker flares lit up the scene with a terrible brightness.

The Kriegies began to panic.

'My God, we're on the target,' someone screamed.

'Make the Act of Contrition,' shouted Cavanaugh as bombs began to rain down.

The priest shouted the words of the general absolution and then flung himself to the ground, pressing his head to the earth.

Men screamed and whimpered.

Finally, the bombers were gone.

'Back to their goddam ham and eggs!' someone shouted.

The shocked group of POWs was reassembled. Guards marched off the able-bodied while Cavanaugh, other chaplains, and medics tended to more than a hundred wounded and dozens of dead. All of Lyle Bouck's men were unharmed.

Perhaps an hour later, after the bodies of some forty men had been neatly laid out in rows, Cavanaugh sat in silence staring at the dead Americans, killed so close to the end of the war by their own comrades after enduring so much.

Lieutenant Lyle Bouck and his fellow Kriegies from Hammelburg kept walking for days on end, and sometimes at night – Allied planes now seemed to patrol the skies by day in swarms, destroying anything that looked even remotely like a target. From Nuremberg, they walked south through the Frankische Alb – a mountain range that stretches like a hooked finger across Bavaria from the Swiss Alps – for two weeks, pilfering potatoes or any other food from farms along the way and sleeping in barns and hedgerows. In the mornings, guards would fire bursts into the hay where the men had slept to make sure no one thought of hiding and trying to escape when the column had moved on.

Corporal Sam Jenkins relied on LSU linebacker Corporal Aubrey McGehee more than ever. One morning in Hammelburg, they had slipped on some ice. Jenkins landed badly on his tailbone with McGehee sprawled on top of him. It was some time before the pain in his back eased. 'I couldn't get my boots on, my feet were so bad,' recalled Jenkins. 'I couldn't walk. So McGehee volunteered to carry me. He saved my life. By then, he must have lost 30 pounds, at least, down from 250. We knew the Americans were getting closer and the Russians were coming from the east. It didn't seem like the Germans could last out much longer.'

Then came April 12, 1945. That morning, Corporals Jenkins and McGehee passed some German civilians standing by a roadside watching the columns of prisoners pass by.

'*Roosevelt ist tot!*' (Roosevelt is dead!), shouted the Germans gleefully.

The news of Roosevelt's death plunged the men into another depression. All felt some measure of grief. Some recalled the bitter, fallow years of the Great Depression and the hope Roosevelt had personified since his election in 1933. He was more than just a president to these men, and they mourned as if a close relative had suddenly passed away.

In Berlin, by contrast, Goebbels ordered his staff to 'bring out the best champagne.' Himmler, surrounded by agitated sycophants, telephoned Hitler in his bunker near the ruins of the Reichstag. It was after midnight.

'Mein Führer,' Himmler said excitedly. 'I congratulate you! Roosevelt is dead. It is written in the stars that the second half of April will be the turning point for us. This is Friday, April thirteenth! Fate has laid low your greatest enemy. God has not abandoned us. Twice he has saved you from assassins. Death, which the enemy aimed at you in 1939 and 1944, has now struck down our most dangerous enemy. It is a miracle.'

For the next several days, the Kriegies felt the sunshine on their backs as they marched. Summer beckoned. Lice picked up in straw and elsewhere spread and grew so fast, feasting on the dirty men, that it was soon a morning and evening ritual to pick off the most bloated specimens and audibly pop them between thumb and forefinger.

Locals along the route finally seemed to have accepted that the war was now lost. Some even muttered '*Krieg is nichts gut*' (War is not good) as the ragged GIs shuffled past. One day, after crossing a river, radio operator James Fort passed an old woman standing beside her wooden garden gate: 'She opened the gate and motioned for me and a buddy to come follow her into her house. She gave us a piece of German bread with butter and jelly. Boy, that was the greatest stuff that I ever ate. And then we slipped back out and rejoined the column.'

Finally, the Kriegies from Hammelburg reached the famous Danube River, central Europe's main waterway. It was as blue as the men had imagined as it cut through limestone cliffs, a hundred yards wide, swollen with spring melt from the nearby Alps.

Lieutenants Reid and Bouck escaped when their guards' backs were turned and managed to get to a bridge across the Danube.

As they crossed, an SS guard appeared.

'Halt!'

Bouck and Reid put their hands above their heads and were quickly escorted back to the Kriegie column. A few days later, they reached a small railroad station where they were loaded onto trains and taken to a nearby concentration camp called Dachau.

Tens of thousands of Jews, huddled together in boxcars, had also reached the sidings at Dachau and then been marched to their deaths. Would the Kriegies meet the same fate as countless other undesirables for whom the camp's main gates, bearing the wrought-iron Nazi lie *Arbeit Macht Frei* (Work Makes One Free), had marked the last stop on their terrible journeys? Perhaps Hitler had decided to finish off the Kriegies.

For almost two days, the Kriegies waited in their boxcars in the sidings at Dachau. Inside the camp, the SS were still busy burning corpses and killing their final consignments of Jews, homosexuals, communists, gypsies, and the last of the traitors connected to the July 1944 bomb plot. Then the train rumbled to life, and they were moving again – not into the camp, but farther south toward Munich, where at last the men were given some bread and 'soup.'

In his hospital ward in Gotha, Major Abe Baum waited impatiently.

A few days after the 4th Armored Division had occupied Hammelburg on April 5, 1945, Baum had discharged himself from the Serbian camp's hospital. He had jumped on the foot-rail of an ambulance, headed out of the camp, and then hitched lifts to the 34th Evacuation Hospital in Gotha, where Lieutenant Colonel John Waters was also now being treated.

Baum knew that sooner or later General Patton would arrive in Gotha to check on his son-in-law. Patton could hardly visit Waters without also looking in on Baum, who had a few questions he wanted to ask the Third Army's commander in chief.

Sure enough, Baum didn't have to wait long.

When Patton arrived at Gotha, he hurried through the hospital with two aides, found Waters's room, checked that he was recovering well, placed a Distinguished Service Cross around his neck, shook his hand, and left. Patton then toured the hospital and finally entered Baum's room.

Patton found Baum sitting up in bed.

'At ease,' ordered Patton.

One of Patton's aides walked to Baum's bedside and read out a citation for 'extraordinary heroism.'

As Baum listened to the citation, he wondered what he should do.

'Do I call him on this?' thought Baum. 'If I do, I'll be shafted. No, I'll leave it. If what happened becomes public, there would be a court-martial – a massive scandal.'

The aide pinned the Distinguished Service Cross to Baum's chest. Patton had promised Baum the Medal of Honor if he carried out the mission. But to receive a Medal of Honor, there must be a prior investigation into the circumstances in which the award was earned. Obviously, Patton did not want any such investigation.

There was some small talk about tactical use of armor in the field. Baum addressed Patton as if he were a fellow middle-ranking officer, not the legendary 'Old Blood and Guts' who had stormed across Western Europe.

Patton finally asked: 'Well, what do you want to do now?'

'I want to go back with my troops.'

'You can't. You're a [former] POW. You can't go back. The Geneva Convention forbids it. You can't return to fight in the same theater. You can only fight in Japan.'

'No. I want to go back with the troops.'

Baum continued to plead his case, growing more and more frustrated.

'You're George S. Patton, aren't you?' Baum said.

'Yes.'

'Well, I want to go back with the troops.'

Baum knew he was in the 'driver's seat.'

Patton looked over to his aide: 'Get the hospital commanding officer in here.'

The colonel in charge of the hospital appeared a few seconds later.

'No paperwork,' Patton told him. 'I'm going to send somebody to pick up Abe.'

Patton left the room. His aide leaned closer to Baum: 'You know that Task Force Baum has been classified Top Secret. Use discretion in discussing it.'

'That goes without saying.'

It was late afternoon on April 16, 1945, by the time twenty-eight-year-old Lieutenant Colonel Robert Kriz and his men had surrounded the town of Iserlohn, the last objective in the 99th Division's drive to clear the Ruhr Pocket. In all, some 350,000 Germans had surrendered or been captured in the pocket in less than a fortnight. Few had put up serious resistance as the inevitability of their defeat had dawned on even the most ardent Nazis. In the last villages Kriz had seized, the occupants had flown any piece of fabric they could find to indicate their surrender: table linens, shirts, bed sheets – anything that was white and could be seen by trigger-happy, victorious GIs hunting for souvenirs, schnapps, and in some cases vengeance.

Earlier on April 16, at 11:05 A.M., all German garrisons in the 99th section had laid down their arms. Only the defenders of Iserlohn had yet to give up. Among them was Lieutenant Albert Ernst, a fiercely proud commander of the remnants of Panzerjager Abteilung 512, a tank-destroyer battalion. Ernst and his last remaining officers – dubbed 'aces' because each had destroyed at least twenty-five American tanks – still controlled formidable weapons: seventy-ton Jagdtigers equipped with 128mm cannon.

Colonel Kriz had already had dealings with Ernst that morning. 'The first time I met Ernst was under a white flag,' he recalled. 'He didn't believe I was in charge and he thought I was pulling his leg since I had no insignia, except on my helmet – which was covered up by mud intentionally. I recall taking off my GI jacket to show my rank before he would talk through his interpreter. He requested two hours to evacuate. We had skirmished with his Jagdtigers for several days as we advanced into the Ruhr Pocket. I had never seen this type of tank before. Our tanks were unable to knock them out of action. . . . I wanted to save lives, so I gave [Ernst] two hours to evacuate. I didn't know where he would go, but I didn't want any part of these tanks again.

'[That afternoon] we approached the outskirts of Iserlohn,' Kriz continued, 'where several thousand German soldiers had surrendered, including many generals – but not Albert Ernst and his Jagdtigers. This was the only city in the Ruhr Pocket that remained in German hands. I took my jeep, put two German generals in the backseat with a white flag and entered Iserlohn. In the city square I found Ernst with three of his tanks. I talked to him about avoiding needless bloodshed and told him that the German ground troops and officers had all surrendered. He requested a formal surrender ceremony on the condition that only his tanks participate. Request was granted which concluded the Ruhr Pocket campaign.'

Later that afternoon, Kriz stood proudly and watched a score of hardened German troops, headed by Ernst, form up in the square before him, their tanks lined up in perfect order behind them. Ernst made a brief speech to his men, turned on his heel toward Kriz, and snapped him a salute. It was a rare honor, one that only a couple of American officers as tenacious as Kriz experienced in the Ruhr Pocket that spring.

With the Ruhr Pocket finally mopped up, Kriz knew he and his men would soon head south to join Patton's massive spearhead as it tore through Bavaria toward Munich and then the Nazis' last redoubt – the Alps. Would the last remaining Nazis surrender as Ernst had, with their rectitude and a certain measure of honor intact, or would they fight to the final man? If they chose to make a last stand in significant numbers, Kriz knew that one thing was guaranteed: yet more good men under his command would lose their lives before the Third Reich was at an end.

PART FOUR

Last Battles

15. Moosberg

Moosberg, Germany – Mid-April 1945

After a grueling three-week trek, Lyle Bouck and his fellow Hammelburg Kriegies finally arrived at the sprawling Stalag VIIA near Moosberg, forty miles to the north of Munich. Moosberg was the end of the line. Stalag VIIA was the worst camp in what was left of the Third Reich.

The new arrivals were sent to a decontamination shower. Some POWs, who had learned of the Final Solution through harrowing BBC radio reports that April, thought they were going to be gassed. To their relief, the shower heads did not emit Cyclon B gas, used in Auschwitz and other death camps to kill millions of Jews, but warm water.

As they looked at other men who had arrived at Moosberg from camps across Germany, some of the Kriegies were astonished by their physical state. One man gave a sound from his throat like an animal and pointed to his mouth. He had no tongue; the Germans had cut it out. Others were horrifically thin. The flesh on their arms had fallen down below the elbows, and all the skin from their thighs hung below their knees.

When Bouck and his fellow Hammelburg evacuees emerged from the showers, they were escorted to barracks or tents hastily erected to accommodate wave after wave of Kriegies arriving from Lagers all over Germany. By April 18, 1945, there were an estimated one hundred thousand Allied prisoners in a camp that had been designed to hold ten thousand. More than a third were French. Fourteen thousand were American and British.

Bouck and Reid were marched all the way to the farthest end of the camp from the main gate and assigned a bunk in a flimsy wooden barracks. Twelve other men squeezed into the room, which had just one three-tier bunk. Almost every piece of wood, even slats from the bunks, had been cut up to fuel the Kriegies' Klim-can cookers, crafted from old tins and ration containers.

At dusk, the camp took on a surreal, ghoulish atmosphere as emaciated, dirty men crowded around their Klim cans and small fires and bartered whatever they could find for a morsel of food. A primitive jungle law prevailed, with Kriegies doling out savage punishment to food thieves and every man forced to look after himself. The German guards turned their backs as men did whatever they deemed necessary to stay alive. The two roll calls each day were ineffective – no one, not even the Germans, knew how many men were exactly in the camp.[59]

A few days after Bouck and the Hammelburg contingent arrived at Moosberg, a rumor spread that the Allied POWs held throughout Bavaria were finally going to be moved to Berchtesgarten and used as hostages. American Lieutenant Joe Lovoi had been shot down in a B-17 bomber in December 1944 and had moved from camp to camp like Bouck and his platoon before finally arriving in Moosberg around the same time. 'Because we had a radio we knew what was going on and we knew we were going to win the war,' he recalled. 'The question now was, were they going to machine-gun us before then? We weren't sure what they were going to do. But we knew the moment was coming when it would either be: "OK, guys, it's over, you're free," or "Here's a bullet in your head." We knew we had to face it sooner or later.'

Fallingbostel, Germany – April 18, 1945

At Fallingbostel, James Silvola and Louis Kalil also waited nervously for liberation. Some days the Germans issued no food at all. But there was now little physical cruelty. The guards seemed afraid of being handed over to the fast-approaching Russians. If they behaved themselves, and if the British arrived first, as seemed more and more likely from news reports of Montgomery's cautious advance, then they would probably be treated fairly.

But then, just as Fallingbostel's 'canary' – secret radio – indicated that the British were only a few days away, it seemed that the endless wait for liberation had been in vain: more than a hundred SS troops arrived at the main gates. The Kriegies watched, terrified as the camp's Army of the Interior 'goons' and the SS troops conferred. The SS wanted to come into the camp and shoot Silvola, Kalil, and all the other POWs who had not been marched away to points south. Most were fanatical teenagers, culled from the Hitler Youth, and they carried Schmeiser machine guns, ideally suited to mowing down defenseless men at close range. For about twenty minutes, SS officers and the Army of the Interior argued about the POWs' fate. Finally, much to the Kriegies' relief, the SS teenagers left.

In the following days, anarchy ruled. More and more POWs poured into the camp, herded west by Germans determined to escape 'Ivan.' The hospital was soon overflowing with men suffering from severe exhaustion and so many illnesses caused by prolonged malnutrition and exposure that the doctors could no longer cope. Those without life-threatening wounds or illnesses had to sleep on the cold concrete floors of the camp's delousing shower rooms.

Some Kriegies were so desperate for food that they risked being shot to go forage in nearby fields and on farms. When the guards started to ignore such trips beyond the perimeter fence, scores more prisoners simply cut holes in the wire and left the camp, often in organized groups, to find whatever they could to keep themselves alive. Rotten peas and moldy old potatoes now became many men's sole sustenance.

One night, an RAF Hawker Typhoon fired rockets into the camp, killing at least thirty-five Russian POWs who may have left a small light burning. Hastily, white crosses were painted on top of barracks throughout Fallingbostel to indicate that they were part of a POW camp, not an enemy base.

Long German columns marched past the camp every day, oblivious to the POWs, intent on saving their skins. More British fighters flew over and did barrel rolls. Gradually, the Army of the Interior guards began to disappear. Then an immense explosion rocked the camp – the ammunition dump was blown, and more guards fled. According to some accounts, others chose to surrender and were herded into one area of the compound as Allied noncoms took over control, seizing the Germans' weapons and then organizing parties of men to maintain some semblance of order and distribute food.

Foraging was suddenly made very difficult when the surviving Russian prisoners who had been treated with untold brutality – thousands are thought to have died in Fallingbostel – left the camp and cleaned out every local farm, raping and looting their way east toward the advancing Red

Army. They had seen their fellows beaten to death, starved to skeletons, and shot for no reason and were now hell-bent on revenge.

On April 16, 1945, Privates Louis Kalil and James Silvola heard sounds of fighting in the distance. Men rushed outside their barracks and watched as a tank from the British Second Army drove through the front gate, closely followed by Bren-gun carriers. In the camp hospital, Louis Kalil's ward erupted in joy. Kalil, Robbie, and Roy Burke all still bunked beside each other. They hugged with enormous relief and joy and then staggered into the fresh air.

British soldiers were throwing rations and cartons of cigarettes into the throngs of POWs. Some of the Kriegies were strangely quiet after the initial elation of liberation; several kneeled in the open and prayed, tears dripping onto clasped hands. Then every POW was ordered to delousing points. James Silvola vividly recalled disappearing in a cloud of DDT powder after a nozzle was placed up each of his trouser legs.

After they had been deloused, the men spent their first day of liberation roaming around the camp and its surrounds, glorying in their ability to step where they pleased without the risk of being shot.

On April 18, 1945, Kalil heard a British officer address his fellow wounded: 'We're going to fly you to Brussels tomorrow.' Kalil was issued a new uniform. It felt wonderful after wearing his old one for almost four months. The weakest were stretchered to trucks, and others walked to a nearby clearing camp to be flown to Belgium. Some would later recall arriving in a muddy field that had been filled with large British army tents. In some of the tents, there were long tables; cooks ladled out dishes of nonmoldy potatoes and real beef. The men could not believe their eyes. But just as they were about to tuck in, doctors arrived and ordered that the meals were far too much for the men's digestive systems to cope with. The men had to make do with just a couple of spoonfuls of gravy and mashed potatoes instead.

Kalil and Silvola and their fellow Kriegies were finally helped onto British Lancaster bombers, which had just returned from raids over Berlin and other cities, and then flown to several hospitals in Brussels. Whether he could walk or not, each man was placed on a stretcher in Brussels and carried to immaculate wards where young nurses awaited them with broad smiles. Kalil enjoyed being carried around and was delighted when his turn came to be scrubbed down in a bath by a particularly attractive British nurse. He had never been washed by a woman, and her firm but gentle scrubbing finally made him feel clean. It was almost as joyous an experience to then lie on a mattress in fresh mustard-brown hospital fatigues. Kalil joked with Robbie that their new clothes made them look just like English schoolboys.

Kalil did not yet know that his Lebanese-born parents back in Indiana had been informed just two weeks before his liberation that he was a POW. They had been overjoyed but then quickly disturbed by the added news that he had been wounded. Kalil hoped he would soon be able to telephone them and reassure them that he was doing well. He had already resolved never to tell them in detail what had happened to him — that would be too much for them to bear.

For Louis Kalil and James Silvola, the war was finally over. Now a long campaign would begin to regain weight (Silvola had lost thirty-seven pounds) and to recover from their wounds. Kalil needed major reconstructive surgery on his jaw; the flesh wound in Silvola's left arm had healed, but the muscles in the area hurt when he used his arm and would require intensive physical therapy. As he recuperated in Brussels, Silvola sent a postcard to his parents in Minnesota. 'That was the first time they knew I was alive,' he recalled. 'They were convinced I had been dead for four months.'

Moosberg, Germany – April 18, 1945

Back at Moosberg, April 18, 1945, was a particularly balmy day. Spring had truly arrived, and as the temperatures rose rapidly so did the camp's already vast armies of body lice. 'It started getting real warm,' recalled radio operator James Fort. 'Soon the guys were stood outside the barracks picking lice off one another like monkeys.'

Corporal Sam Jenkins, now severely anemic, shared a bunk in Moosberg with Corporal Aubrey McGehee. One day, he saw a 'goon' deliver food to another guard. 'There was maybe a sardine, that was it,' recalled Jenkins. 'The German started to cry because he was so hungry. . . . We didn't blame guards like him for starving us. But we did blame their superiors. We were sure they were eating high on the hog.'

Conditions in the camp were now unbearable. There were simply far too many men for the Germans to cope with. The latrine could not be pumped out, apparently because of a lack of gasoline for the pumps. The men feared a serious epidemic of typhus, and it was decided that no one would attend roll call until the Germans emptied the latrines. The guards tried to force the Kriegies out of their barracks the next morning, but they slipped back in as soon as they had been pushed out. Then Alsatian dogs were brought in by the Luger-waving 'goons.' There was a standoff. Finally, the

German commandant ordered his men to withdraw, and
that night a 'honey wagon' arrived and started to clean out
the latrines.

The men knew from several camp canaries that Nuremberg was in American hands. American Mustangs and
Typhoons began to buzz the camp; some waggled their
wings to cheer the men. One flew so low over the camp
that it sent the POWs sprinting for cover. Men who had so
far contained their emotions became edgy, snapping at each
other, unable to bear the anticipation. And still the question
lingered: Would the Germans kill them?

In his barracks, Lieutenant Lyle Bouck lay listlessly, knowing now he was beginning to die. There were days when he
felt nothing but lethargy. His skin had turned yellow. Some
mornings, he felt so weak that he could barely make it to
the communal soup-can.

On April 29, 1945, Bouck was woken around 8:30 A.M.
by the sound of small-arms fire. He had been liberated once
before. Was this finally the real thing? Before long, a furious
firefight raged between SS troops, well dug in by a nearby
river, and American soldiers. Throughout Moosberg, men
ran for cover, many crowding into the barracks to avoid the
crackling bullets. Then Bouck heard silence. With a group
of fellow Kriegies from his barracks, he ventured into the
compound, curiosity getting the better of his fear.

'The Germans have left!' someone shouted. 'The Americans are almost in the camp – it's the front lines!'

In another corner of the camp, Private First Class Risto
Milosevich joined hundreds of other men peering into the
far distance. He could see a group of tanks on a hill perhaps
two miles away. The tanks moved closer, and men began to
cheer as they recognized the American stars on the sides of
the tanks.

Radio operator James Fort and others from the platoon joined Milosevich in cheering on the American advance toward the camp. 'We could see a ridge in the distance and American tanks on it,' recalled Fort. 'I heard a German machine gun firing not too far away, and an American one answered it. And then that was it – the fighting stopped. Then we saw the tanks. They broke through the fence and started down through the rows of tents. We tried to jump on the tanks, but we weren't allowed to. I was real close to crying.'

Lieutenant Lyle Bouck did not want to jump on any more tanks after his experience in Hammelburg. Instead, he walked over to the perimeter wire. He saw some American troops. One of them wore a 99th Division checkerboard patch. He couldn't believe it – his own division was liberating the camp. He called out to the GI with the shoulder patch. What regiment was the man with?

'The three ninety-fifth.'

'Do you know Major Robert L. Kriz? Is the 394th near here?' asked Bouck.

The GI had never heard of Kriz.

The long months of desperation began to overwhelm Bouck. He feared that because there were so many thousands of POWs it might be several weeks before everyone could be processed out of the camp. He knew he would not live that long.

'Oh Jesus,' Bouck said, emotion cracking his voice. 'If you've ever done anything for anyone, will you promise me you'll do one thing for me?'

The GI nodded from the other side of the fence.

'If I can do it, I will.'

'Do you have anything to write with?' asked Bouck.

The GI tore a piece of cardboard from a K ration box. Then he pulled a pencil from his pack.

'Major Robert L. Kriz, 394th Regiment,' wrote Bouck and then scratched a map directing Kriz to the rear of the camp. He signed the scrap 'Bouck.'

'[I'm] as far from the main gate as you can get,' said Bouck. 'Get this to the 394th regiment HQ.'

Bouck handed the scrap through the fence and then reached farther through the wire and shook the GI's hand.

'Will you promise to do this?'

Bouck was close to tears.

'It's a different regiment,' said the GI. 'But, yeah, I'll do this. You have my word.'

The GI turned and walked away.

Bouck returned to his barracks. It was true after all – finally, he was free. The previous night, he hadn't believed the rumors of impending rescue. Even when Kriegies throughout the camp had lit bonfires to draw the advancing Americans' attention, he had remained skeptical. Now all he could do, yet again, was lie in his bunk and wait. As he climbed into it, he realized he had very little strength left. Maybe he could last another day or two, or perhaps it would be all over for him in just a few hours. Kriz was his last hope.

Some of the men saw a jeep speed toward the camp gates. An American flag fluttered from it, and a tall man was distinguishable, standing with his back as straight as a board. The jeep got closer. Some men recognized the figure – it was General Patton, looking like a cowboy with his pearl-handled six-shooters strapped to his sides.

The jeep skidded to a halt just inside the camp.

Patton was immediately rushed by a mass of thin, weeping men. The most senior officer pushed through the throng, stood stiffly before Patton, and saluted him.

Patton solemnly returned the salute.

'It is we who salute you and all these brave men,' said Patton.

As Patton and the officer embraced, men throughout the camp did likewise. There were screams, yells, and uncontrollable, often hysterical tears of relief. No man was ashamed to reveal his pent-up feelings.

Patton then pointed to the German flag flying from a nearby flagpole and shouted in his high-pitched voice: 'I want that son-of-a-bitch cut down, and the man that cuts it down, I want him to wipe his ass with it!'

A Kriegie grabbed the American flag from Patton's jeep and began to replace the swastika on the camp's main flagpole with it. It is not known whether he then carried out the remainder of Patton's order.

As the flag reached the top of the pole, recalled one POW, a 'thunderous cheer erupted that could surely be heard as far west as New York City. Thousands of young men looked up at the American flag as tears streamed unashamedly down their grimy youthful faces.'

Patton then made his way through the camp, shaking as many men's hands as he could. He vowed to one that he would 'whip the bastards all the way to Berlin.' A short time later, the hungriest of the men watched in delirious silence as trucks arrived and began to disgorge the stuff of their nightly dreams – meat loaf, pasta, donuts – that would be served by Red Cross nurses. To most of the men, who had not seen an American female for well over a year, if not several, the nurses looked like goddesses. Even to look at them was too much for some, who were suddenly as desperate to hold their wives and sweethearts as they were to eat.

Freedom tasted heavenly, as did the Lucky Strikes and other American cigarettes that Patton's men threw like confetti into the throngs of men. One of Bouck's men, Private

John Creger, now weighing a little more than a hundred pounds, was amazed when an American soldier handed him cigars. Creger was standing beside a tough Kriegie from Kentucky when they noticed a small, particularly unpleasant German guard whom the men had made fun of throughout their captivity. The Kentuckian grabbed the guard, forced him to smoke the cigar, and then stuffed it into the German's mouth with the butt of his hand, making him choke.

Platoon Sergeant Bill Slape watched as another sadistic guard handed his machine gun and pistol to a Kriegie, who then immediately shot to death his former captor at point-blank range.

Lyle Bouck felt weaker than ever as he lay on a mattress in his barracks.

'This is finally getting to me,' he said to himself, his last reserves of adrenaline fast ebbing away.

It was shortly before midnight when Bouck thought he heard someone call his name. Then he heard it. He struggled to his feet, a skin-and-bones 114 pounds, and walked in a daze out of the barracks.

'Bouck, someone wants you out here.'

Bouck walked out into the darkness. He could see a man beside a jeep.

It was Kriz.

'Jesus Christ, Bouck, you're alive!' said an overjoyed Kriz.

They saluted each other and then shook hands. Bouck had never seen Kriz look so excited, so pleased. 'It was a very emotional experience,' recalled Bouck. 'Without question, it was for me the high point of the entire war.'

The man he respected more than any other, who had been something of a father figure as well as his first mentor, had arrived at the eleventh hour to save his life.

Seeing how far gone Bouck was, Kriz was suddenly all business. He turned to the jeep driver.

'Unhook that trailer.'

Kriz then looked toward a former prisoner.

'Tell your guys there's food in here but use your noodle.' Kriz didn't want the men to gorge themselves on hard food, knowing their bodies could not yet process it.

In the confusion of liberation, Bouck had lost Lieutenant Matthew Reid. He now tried to find him, not wanting to leave without at least thanking him for helping him survive.

Meanwhile, Kriz attended to other members of the platoon.

Milosevich lay beside one of the camp's woefully inadequate kitchens, where liberating GIs were now dropping off more emergency supplies for the worst cases of malnutrition. He was in the same advanced state of hepatitis as Bouck and had not eaten for almost three weeks. 'I probably could have lasted another week, but by then I would have been dead.'

Milosevich tried to eat but threw up the food almost as soon as he had swallowed it.

Suddenly, he saw Kriz approach.

'What's the matter, Milosevich?'

'I don't know, sir. I feel like I've got an iron ball in my stomach.'

'Don't move. Just stay right there.'

'I'm not going anyplace.'

Kriz arranged help for Milosevich and then returned to Bouck's barracks. He handed Bouck a helmet liner, a helmet, a pistol belt, a .45, and some clips.

'Get your ass in the jeep – the backseat.'

A few seconds later, the jeep pulled out very fast.

Bouck felt torn. He didn't want to leave without Reid,

but if he stayed behind he would die waiting to be officially processed out of the camp. Kriz's jeep passed through mobs of men singing at the tops of their voices, hugging, banging their metal spoons on cups, celebrating the end of their war. There were tens of thousands of them. Then the jeep sped through the main gate and out into the dark countryside, headed toward the 394th's latest headquarters in Landshut, a dozen miles away.

Kriz had a detailed map of the area, but after half an hour they were lost so he ordered his driver to pull into a farmhouse on top of a nearby hill.

Kriz knocked on the front door and two elderly, frightened Germans appeared.

'I'm not going to hurt you,' said Kriz. 'I need some help.'

They went inside. Kriz pulled out his map. The couple couldn't speak English, but Kriz spoke enough German to make himself understood and get directions to Landshut.

Suddenly, there was a violent knocking on the door. The war wasn't over yet.

Kriz told Bouck and the couple to stay out of sight and then went to the door, pulling out his loaded carbine.

The unexpected visitors were two black GIs.

'Colonel!' said one of them. 'There's thousands of Germans coming down the hill!'

Kriz angrily pointed the carbine at them.

'Get back to your units!'

The men took off.

Kriz and Bouck set off again in the darkness. Sometime around dawn, as they approached Landshut, Kriz picked up his radio telephone and contacted headquarters: 'I've got Bouck.'

They arrived in Landshut around 7:00 A.M.

'Get Bouck some food,' Kriz ordered. 'And some hot tea, some milk and coffee.'

Bouck lay down in a sick bay to get some sleep. Meanwhile, Kriz arranged for a transport plane to land as close as possible to Moosberg and for Milosevich and other severely ill men from the 394th to be flown to France. Because of Kriz's prompt intervention, Milosevich was then taken to Military Hospital 36 in Rheims, where he would make a rapid recovery.

Those in Bouck's platoon who were still able to stand – Platoon Sergeant William Slape, radio operator James Fort, Corporal Sam Jenkins, and Southerners Private John Creger and Corporal Aubrey McGehee – gathered in their barracks in Moosberg and awaited orders to be shipped home. It was not long before they were told to form up outside hastily erected shower units. 'We went in there together, and boy, that was something,' recalled Fort. 'We'd not been clean for so long, and we were so weak that hot water was almost too much to bear. But everybody was happy, at last, and making jokes again.' When they finally scrubbed off months of dirt, some were amazed at how pale their skin was. Then they were given clean clothes.

Meanwhile, platoon members Sergeant Robert Lambert and Private First Class Carlos Fernandez learned that Lieutenant Lyle Bouck had been picked up in Moosberg, and they decided to visit the camp to look for other captured buddies who might still be alive. 'One late night in early May, 1945, some of our 99th men sent us word that they had liberated a prisoner-of-war camp located in Moosberg and that some of our boys were there,' recalled Fernandez. 'I got a jeep and headed for that camp. I remember how bad a night it was. It was snowing hard and the wind was blowing strongly. Extremely slow driving was necessary due to the darkness and snow. It was getting to be daylight when we arrived in Moosberg.'

Fernandez searched all over Moosberg for his buddies. When he finally found them, he almost cried: 'McGehee had shrunk down to 120 pounds. He was just skin and bones.'

Fernandez pulled out some hard army bread and handed it to his fellow Texan, Sam Jenkins.

Jenkins took a bite and grinned.

'This tastes just like angel bread.'

The next day, the survivors from the I&R platoon were trucked to the nearest airstrip where DC-3 airplanes waited to fly them home. 'There were planes landing all the time and lined up to take us out,' recalled Fort. 'I got on a plane and someone gave me a K ration – just a tin of food and crackers. It was the first real meal I'd had since December 15, 1944, and it tasted great.'

Landshut, Germany – April 1945

In the sick bay in Landshut, Lieutenant Lyle Bouck got weaker. His spirits soared for a few hours, however, when he too was visited by Lambert and Fernandez, who handed him chicken soup and orange juice in two canteen cups. It was wonderful to see them again, but he barely had the energy to greet them.

'Bouck was quite obviously seriously ill,' recalled Lambert. 'For a while I thought he was about to die as he became so weak while we talked that he had to lie down rather than sit. At the time by his color I thought he might have yellow jaundice and he could not have weighed much more than 100 pounds.'

Bouck tried to eat but immediately threw up. 'He was a skeleton of his former self,' recalled Kriz. 'I had one of the men cook a couple of chickens that we had picked up, along with some small potatoes that we fried. Lieutenant Bouck, after eating a very little, started vomiting, and I noticed his color was not good. I summoned the doctor, the battalion surgeon.'

Major Steven Gillespie, the 394th's chief surgeon, looked carefully into Bouck's eyes.

'You don't feel too good, do you?'

'No sir. I really don't. I'm so excited.'

'Give me your hands.'

Gillespie pinched Bouck's fingernails.

'Get him in an ambulance,' he ordered a nearby soldier, and then turned back to Bouck. 'You're going to look like a Chinaman in a few days. You have hepatitis and must be evacuated without delay.'

Bouck protested. He wanted to stay with the 394th. But the Geneva Convention forbade POWs from rejoining their former units after release, and in any case Kriz could not accommodate him. 'Bouck, we're getting ready to [move out], you have to get out of here.'

Bouck was carried on a stretcher and then taken by ambulance to a vast field hospital. Medics soon had an IV started, and he began receiving his first true nourishment in five months.

Bouck would later come to feel enormous guilt about the rapid evacuation that saved his life. There had been no time for him to make an official report on his platoon's actions even if he had been physically capable of doing so. And so the extraordinary achievement in Lanzerath of the 394th

Regiment's I&R platoon, let alone its subsequent psychological and physical battle for survival, was never officially recorded. Without an official report, no medals would be issued and Bouck and his men would, like so many other small units that had held and fought against all odds, become yet another forgotten platoon.[60] Their valiant stand on the slopes above Lanzerath, which had helped seal the fate of the Third Reich, seemed destined to not even be recorded as a footnote in the story of the greatest battle in U.S. military history – the Battle of the Bulge.

Adolf Hitler's Bunker, the Chancellery, Berlin – April 30, 1945

It was around 6:00 A.M. when Adolf Hitler, his hair gray, his face waxy and deeply lined with stress, called for General Wilhelm Mohnke, the SS general charged with defending Hitler's last command post – the cavernous bunker beneath the ruins of the Reichstag. Mohnke reported that the Soviet front lines were less than half a mile away. Advance elements of the huge Red Army, pressing in on all sides, had already seized the Tiergarten. There was now no escape – the tunnel used by members of Hitler's inner circle in recent days was blocked at one end by fanatical Soviet troops who were now vying for the ultimate honor of storming the Reichstag. Mohnke's men – aided by teenaged Hitler Youth – could perhaps hold off Stalin's 'Slavic hordes,' as Hitler called them, for another twenty-four hours. It was inevitable that on May 1, 1945, the most important Soviet holiday, 'Ivan' would make a concerted effort to seize Hitler's underground refuge and undoubtedly succeed.

Hitler listened to Mohnke's report without showing any

emotion and then, around 2:00 P.M., sat down to his final meal: spaghetti and a tossed salad. There was little conversation. Then Hitler and his longtime lover, Eva Braun, whom he had married shortly after midnight on the 29th, shook hands with the last occupants of the bunker: the ever-faithful Goebbels and a handful of aides and secretaries.

That morning, Hitler had ordered that two hundred liters of gasoline be massed in the chancellery garden. Now it was time for the final act. Eva Braun and Hitler returned to their rooms in the bunker. They each placed a capsule of cyanide in their mouths. Braun bit down on hers and fell back dead over the armrest of a couch. At 3:30 P.M., Hitler took one of his two Walther pistols, sat down at a table, placed the barrel in his mouth, and squeezed the trigger. On the wall behind him was an oil painting of Frederick the Great, whose great military feats Hitler had invoked to inspire his generals in the buildup to his last desperate gamble: the Battle of the Bulge.

A few minutes later, Artur Axmann, head of the Hitler Youth, arrived on the scene. He examined Hitler's and Braun's corpses, talked with Goebbels, and then left. Throughout the chancellery, the news spread fast: '*Der Chef ist tot!*' (The Chief is dead!).

Meanwhile, in the chancellery garden, Hitler's aides prepared a fitting send-off for the founder of the thousand-year Reich: a Norse inferno. But there would be no Viking longship to symbolize the transport of Hitler's and Braun's spirits to Valhalla; a shallow ditch among the rubble beside a concrete mixer would have to do. Two SS officers carried Hitler's bloody corpse, concealed by a blanket, up four flights of stairs and into the garden.

Frau Hitler and the Führer were laid beside each other and doused with several jerricans of gasoline. The climax of the Battle of Berlin raged ever louder in the near distance; suddenly, a nearby Soviet bombardment gave the events in the chancellery garden a fittingly apocalyptic feel. Shrapnel filled the air. Between artillery bursts, SS adjutant Otto Günsche dipped a rag in the gasoline, lit it, and then tossed it onto the Führer's corpse. Flames jumped into the gray sky, quickly roasting Hitler and Braun beyond recognition.

The last of the faithful made the 'Heil Hitler!' salute, stood motionless by the gaseous flames for several seconds, and then fell back to the relative safety of the bunker. All afternoon, as the Soviets edged closer and closer, Günsche continually doused the bodies, and the high priest of the most savage cult in modern history slowly turned to ashes. 'I don't want to be put on exhibition in a Russian *panoptikon* [war museum],' Hitler had told Günsche that morning.

Darkness fell as the last orange flames from Hitler's corpse sent an eerie flicker across the shell-holed walls of the chancellery garden. Just as Germany lay in ashes, its finest cities burnt beyond recognition, so now did the architect of its ruin.

Geisenhausen, Bavaria – May 7, 1945

Since liberating Moosberg on April 29, 1945 – the day before Hitler's suicide – the 99th Division had advanced twenty miles south toward the Austrian border. Colonel Robert Kriz and his men from the 2nd Battalion had been instructed on May 2 to halt their advance at the Alpine town of Geisenhausen and await further orders. Those orders finally came on May 7. Operational Instruction No. 43 informed every man in the 99th Division that 'A representative of the German High Command signed the unconditional surrender of all German land, sea, and air forces in Europe to the

Allied Expeditionary Force and simultaneously to the Soviet High Command 0141 hours, Central European Time, 7 May, under which all forces will cease active operations.'

It was finally all over.

'My sincerest congratulations to each and every one of you on this historic occasion,' announced General Lauer. 'Every member of the 99th Division can be proud of his combat record in having aided materially in defeating the Nazi beast, and gaining this victory.'

For the first time, Kriz was able to drive with headlights through the cold rain that evening. Throughout the 394th's command post, officers sat down to dinners of venison with french fries followed by fresh coffee. Veteran noncoms cracked open bottles of beer and schnapps, got drunk, and settled down to their first truly undisturbed night of sleep for almost seven months.

The 99th Division had formally entered combat on November 9, 1944. It had been in action for 151 days, suffering 6,103 battle casualties and 5,884 nonbattle casualties – mostly due to trench foot and combat fatigue. There had been an 85.1 percent turnover in men: only a couple of stalwarts in each platoon who had arrived in Le Havre that cold autumn day in 1944 remained.

As his fellow 99ers celebrated the end of the most destructive war in human history, Lyle Bouck was transported from a field hospital in Bavaria to Army General Hospital Number One in Paris. Bouck's hospital ward was crowded with other men who had fallen prey to a hepatitis epidemic that eventually killed hundreds of released POWs. For the remainder of that May, Bouck slowly began to regain some strength on a fat-free diet of vegetables and fruit. In July, he was flown back to New York and then went by train to O'Riley General Hospital in Springfield, Missouri.

Bouck had been granted a brief furlough stop in St. Louis. He didn't contact his parents earlier, not wanting his mother to come to the station and see him limp off the train because of the leg wound sustained in Lanzerath. At St. Louis's Union Station, Bouck called an aunt instead. His parents did not have a telephone, so she alerted them. Then he climbed into a cab, which took him twenty-five miles out to his parents' home in the country. Upon arrival he lugged his duffle bag out of the cab and handed over three dollars. Suddenly, a neighbor's fox terrier ran over and sank its teeth into his behind.

Lyle Bouck was home at last.

16. Summer of '45

Jochen Peiper's war ended as it had begun – with unflinching arrogance. In early March 1945, he had again led a desperate Panzer attack, this time aimed at splintering the Russian advance in Hungary. Lacking adequate support, Peiper and his Leibstandarte stalwarts – 'old hares' – had successfully pierced the Soviet lines but then been forced into retreat, just as they had during the Battle of the Bulge.

By the time Bouck and his platoon were liberated, Peiper was fighting a desperate rearguard action in Prague against both Czech patriots and a Russian division. The 'Imperial Guard' of the Third Reich was finally falling apart.

The Führer himself had sounded its death knell only weeks before his suicide. After a report that some SS men had fled the enemy in Prague, Hitler had shouted at a top general: 'If my own Leibstandarte can't hold their ground, they aren't worthy of carrying my personal emblem.' An order had then gone out to Sepp Dietrich that the men under his command be stripped of their armbands.

For Peiper, Hitler's edict was the ultimate betrayal. He had immediately called his officers to him and told them to place their medals in a chamber pot. It would be sent to Berlin. Peiper's officers had eventually managed to calm him down, and the potful of medals was never sent.

After pulling back from Prague, most of the Leibstandarte Adolf Hitler surrendered piecemeal to Patton's Third Army in southern Germany. But not Peiper. He would never surrender. In the chaotic final days of the war, he set off with a couple of trusted aides, determined to get to his home in Bavaria and finally see his wife and three children. Just twelve miles from their doorstep, Peiper was apprehended and placed in a 'cage,' as the massive holding areas for German POWs were called. He knew the *Amerikaner* would soon seek vengeance – the massacre at Malmedy and many other atrocities committed by the Liebstandarte Adolf Hitler would not go unpunished. And so he began to steel himself for the hangman's noose.

Otto Skorzeny's final mission had been to organize a hold-out in the Bavarian Alps where Hitler would make a last stand with twenty divisions dug in around a mountain retreat. But then, the day after Bouck's liberation, Hitler had committed suicide, and Skorzeny had found himself without orders for the first time in five years of unrelenting war.

For ten days after war's end, Skorzeny watched the May sun melt the snow and ice high up in the Alps.

Three times, Skorzeny contacted Allied authorities in nearby villages. Meanwhile, one newspaper reported, 'The most diabolically clever man in Germany is still free. He is being hunted everywhere by the top brains of Allied intelligence.' But the Allies in the Alpine region on the Austro-German border obviously thought the offer of surrender from Skorzeny was a ruse and did not contact him.

Finally, Skorzeny drove down from the mountains and tried to surrender at a nearby American supply depot. The sergeant on duty had never heard of Skorzeny and was too busy to deal with yet another surrendering German, so he ordered a Texan jeep driver to take Skorzeny to a divisional headquarters in Salzburg. An American major there sent Skorzeny under guard to a villa outside Salzburg, where he was strip-searched and then taken to prison in a jeep, tailed by an armored car mounted with a machine gun. An MP kept his gun pressed to Skorzeny's heart all the way.

While Peiper languished in his 'cage' and Skorzeny began a seemingly endless round of interrogations, several members of Lyle Bouck's I&R platoon awaited news of when they would return home. Their new address was a barracks in a new camp: a 'fattening center' called Camp Lucky Strike near the French port of Le Havre, where they had arrived less than a year before. They were no longer Kriegies but RAMPs – Recovered Allied Military Personnel.

Private Kurt Vonnegut vividly recalled his time in Lucky Strike: 'We were fed cheeseburgers and milkshakes and could call home. When I was captured I weighed 180 pounds. When I was liberated I weighed 132. When I got to Camp Lucky Strike, a lot of my muscles had atrophied. I finally arrived home wearing an overcoat of fat.'

Sergeant Peter Gacki, from Lieutenant Warren Springer's forward observation team, spent a fortnight in Camp Lucky Strike. 'The chow lines were very long,' he recalled. 'After eating you could get back in line and by the time you got to the head of the line you would be hungry again. You can be sure no one complained about the food. It was like being in heaven.'

Finally, the day came for the platoon to leave Camp Lucky Strike. 'We boarded trucks and headed through Le Havre,' recalled Sam Jenkins. 'There were some guys from New Mexico with us – they were Hispanic. Suddenly one of them saw this French gal walking down the road. He jumped out of the truck. "See you guys later!" he cried. We never saw him again. He might still be over there.'

*

That summer of 1945, it seemed as if a miracle had saved the 394th Infantry Regiment's platoon. What else could explain how every member, who had fought so long and hard that December day and killed so many of the enemy, had survived?

As they recuperated, many of them no longer felt bitterness that they had been given suicidal orders, sacrificed to buy others time, and reduced to physical wrecks because of the monumental intelligence failures leading up to the Battle of the Bulge. As they learned what had happened to their fellow 99ers, how fierce and fatal the final push toward the Rhine and across it had been, they were mostly just grateful to be able to soon put the war behind them, especially the POW experience. Now they could reclaim their interrupted lives.

Platoon Sergeant William Slape was first among the platoon to get home that summer from Camp Lucky Strike. Along with several hundred fellow GIs, he crossed the Atlantic on a liberty ship.

For many returning RAMPs, their first sight of America was the Statue of Liberty. 'When we caught sight of [it],' recalled a former Kriegie, 'it was the greatest thrill in the world for all of us. The Port Authority fire boats shot water into the sky as they came alongside, and ahead on the dock a band was playing Sousa.'

The evening Slape arrived in New York, he had the 'most fabulous steak dinner' he had ever seen, and then, within twelve hours of arriving in the States, boarded a train and headed for Fort Sam Houston in San Antonio, Texas, his home state. People lined the tracks, waving and bringing food and beer to the soldiers. As the train pulled into Little Rock, Arkansas, a soldier pointed out of the window.

'That's my house!'

At a road crossing, the soldier suddenly spotted his wife sitting in a waiting car. 'Out the window he went,' recalled Slape. 'She saw him and almost fainted. When we got to Fort Sam Houston, they were both standing there waiting for us.'

Slape returned home and then reenlisted in the U.S. Army, eventually serving thirty years and seeing combat in both Korea and Vietnam. By the time he retired, he had earned the rare honor of being Sergeant Major of the U.S. Army – the highest position a noncommissioned man can attain.

Risto Milosevich arrived back in the States via Norfolk, Virginia, and boarded a train bound for his native California. It took twenty days to cross America. 'Every little town we'd stop in, the bands would come out and play and all that crap,' he recalled. 'We'd lose at least half a dozen guys in every town. Their girls would be waiting and would grab them and take them home. Only a handful of us got to California. Then we were given ninety-day furloughs. Guys who'd jumped the train would straggle back, and they were still given ninety days.'

After the atomic bombs were dropped on Hiroshima and Nagasaki that August and the Pacific war finally ended, Milosevich was given a desk job discharging ground forces at Fort MacArthur near Los Angeles; he had learned to type during his time in the ASTP and was assigned the night shift: 'It was the easiest job I ever had in my life.'

One night, of all people, Major Kriz appeared in the processing line.

'Okay, Milosevich, I want to be out of here in a couple hours.'

'What? Are you kidding?' said Milosevich. 'It takes seven days for officers. Three days for enlisted men.'

Milosevich was joking. He managed to discharge Kriz in

just seven hours. But, he later quipped, 'I got myself out a lot faster – an hour and three-quarters.'

Milosevich then returned to work with his father in the construction business. Eventually, he would set up his own firm and prosper as California boomed.

Thirty-eight-year-old Private First Class Jordan 'Pop' Robinson, the man who had won the draw to see Marlene Dietrich that fateful December of 1944, tried to go back to the coal mines where he had worked before going into the army but found that he was still too weak. So he turned to tobacco farming and settled down in Blaine, Tennessee.

By contrast, the 'quiz kids' in the platoon took advantage of the GI Bill and went on to highly successful careers. Former ASTPer Private First Class Carlos Fernandez realized his prewar ambition and became a respected doctor in his home city of El Paso. His close friend, Minnesotan Robert Lambert, won many notable cases as a meticulous lawyer in California and passed away in early 2003.

Others were destined for tragedy.

Corporal Aubrey 'Schnoz' McGehee, who had done so much to save Corporal Sam Jenkins, never managed to readjust fully to civilian life. Suffering from chronic schizophrenia, he would die alone in the 1980s in a boardinghouse within sight of his beloved University of Louisiana's football field, where he had spent by far the happiest afternoons of his life.

The most seriously wounded man from the platoon, Private Bill James, arrived back in the States on a hospital plane in June 1945. From Brooklyn, he called his family in White Plains, New York, to tell them he was being sent to Cleveland for plastic surgery. Sixty years later, his younger sister, Anna Tsakanikas, remembered the call vividly: 'We cried. Everybody was crying. . . . Only my mother went to

Cleveland to see him. She had almost given him up for dead during his time as a POW but had prayed he might come home. I was very jealous that I couldn't go with her. She came back and told us how badly he was wounded. It was very painful for her to see her son like that.'

The last of the platoon to set foot on American soil that year was Private Joseph McConnell, who arrived back on November 19, 1945. He had lost about forty pounds since entering the army, and his body was covered with boils. 'The day I came home there were no mobs or celebration,' he said. 'It was just like anyone else getting off a plane.' After his discharge from the army, McConnell began driving a bus for Greyhound in 1948. In 1966, he moved his family to Phoenix. McConnell and his wife, Treva, now have three children and three grandchildren.

By war's end, Private Louis Kalil had been moved to England along with his two POW buddies, Roy Burke and the British parachutist, Robbie, who was then assigned for transfer to a hospital for British troops. It was hard for the three men to part after such intense experiences as POWs. By now, they felt irrevocably bonded, as close to each other as they had been to anyone in their lives.

'Well, if things work out maybe I'll come to England and see you,' Kalil told Robbie. 'And if you ever come to the United States, you're more than welcome. You've got an open invitation.'

'I'll probably never come to the United States.'

Robbie was right. They would never see each other again.

Burke and Kalil spent another month in England recuperating. They were then taken to Scotland and finally given departure dates.

The two sat beside each other on a converted C-54 plane

that would take them home. They were almost across the Atlantic when Burke nudged Kalil.

'Louis, look at that damn engine.'

Kalil looked through the window. The motor was leaking oil. Soon it was on fire.

'We're never going to get home. We're going to crash.'

Thankfully, the pilot cut the engine. The flames disappeared and the plane managed to get to Newfoundland, where it was repaired. The next day, Burke and Kalil took off again. This time, the plane flew right into an electrical storm. They were soon being bounced around as the plane creaked loudly.

'We're never going to get home. We're never going to get home.'

The plane was forced down at Bradley Field in Connecticut. At least they were now on American soil. They then flew to Mitchell Field in New York. On the way into Manhattan from the airport, their bus driver got lost.

'We'll never get home.'

But they finally did get home. For Kalil, however, it was only after fourteen months of extensive surgery in Cleveland. Kalil was happy to be sent to yet another hospital; he didn't want his family to see his badly disfigured face.

In Cleveland, Kalil was amazed to again find Roy Burke. They passed the rest of their rehabilitation together and would remain lifelong friends.

After six operations to repair his face, twenty-three-year-old Louis Kalil left the hospital in early 1946 a profoundly changed man. He would take one day at a time and play things safe; he felt he had been blessed to make it home when so many others had not. Like every other returning member of his platoon, Kalil had a newfound appreciation for family and was determined to spend as much time with his loved ones as possible.

When Kalil finally returned to Mishawaka, Indiana, he found his father waiting for him on the front stoop.

'We didn't know if we were going to have you anymore or not,' he said, a look of immense joy and relief on his face.

His father dropped to his knees and kissed the ground.

17. Justice

In late 1945, Jochen Peiper was moved from his 'cage' and interned as an alleged war criminal at Dachau, the death camp that Lyle Bouck's POW transport had briefly visited earlier that year. Investigators quickly followed, eager to discover from Peiper himself what had happened on December 17, 1944, at the Baugnez crossroads. The Malmedy massacre had by now received massive publicity, becoming the most notorious atrocity committed against Americans in the European Theater of Operations.

Peiper and others in his Kampfgruppe were soon formally accused of being responsible for the massacre and scores of other killings, mainly of defenseless Belgian civilians. In May 1946, Peiper was one of seventy men who took their seats in a military courtroom with numbers dangling from their necks. Peiper was number 42; Sepp Dietrich, 11. They were portrayed by the prosecution as heartless SS fanatics who had stopped at nothing, however barbarous, to achieve Hitler's last desperate counterattack. To some eyewitnesses, it seemed as if unalloyed evil was on trial. Newspapers around the globe cited gruesome details from autopsy reports: GIs had been mutilated, shot point-blank in the face, cut down mercilessly as they held their hands in the air. In Peiper's defense, it was stressed that he had never joined the Nazi Party and had simply fought for the Fatherland and the Führer.

American survivors from the Malmedy massacre recounted their experiences, testifying that the Germans had mowed their group down without provocation. Under intense cross-examination, several of Peiper's men admitted to killing POWs and helpless, wounded Americans. The chief American prosecutor, Lieutenant Colonel Burton Ellis, told the court that 'some [German] troops were told to excel in the killing of prisoners of war as well as in fighting. Others were told to make plenty of *Rabatz*, which in SS parlance means to have plenty of fun by killing everything that comes into sight.'

Peiper's commanding officer, Sepp Dietrich, tried to wriggle off the hook by passing ultimate responsibility to his men. 'I ordered that every resistance is to be broken by terror,' he admitted. 'However, I certainly did not order that POWs should be shot.'

Under interrogation at Dachau, Jochen Peiper was characteristically forthright. In the heat of battle, with so much at stake, POWs' safety could never be absolutely guaranteed – true combatants on both sides knew that.

When the verdicts finally came in, just one of the defendants was acquitted. Forty-three men were sentenced to death by hanging and made to wear a red jacket, as was the German tradition for condemned men. They included Jochen Peiper. Dietrich was sentenced to life in prison.

Peiper asked that as an officer he be shot by firing squad, not hanged like some common murderer. Appeals soon followed, and then Peiper's fate became politicized. It emerged that Jewish guards had abused Peiper and others. Key trial confessions had been made in dubious circumstances. Defendants had even endured mock executions and beatings.

The cold war had now begun, and American authorities, some have argued, were as interested in maintaining Germany as a bulwark against communism as they were in seeking revenge or, as victims of Kampfgruppe Peiper saw it, true justice. Peiper's defense counsel publicly decried the trial. There followed a Senate Armed Services Committee investigation. During the hearings, a young senator from Wisconsin, Joseph McCarthy, who had faked his own war record, spoke out on behalf of Peiper, accusing Peiper's prosecutors of a witch-hunt. McCarthy also exaggerated and lied about the abusive behavior of the guards at his jail. After accusing the prime interrogator of Peiper, and others, of physical brutality and perjury, McCarthy stormed out of the hearings. The U.S. Army had used 'Gestapo tactics,' raged McCarthy, who would soon head a virulent and ultimately discredited witch-hunt of his own.

Meanwhile, Peiper sat on death row in Landsberg prison, where Hitler had written *Mein Kampf*, expecting to be called before a firing squad any day. 'Nothing that happens to oneself is unbearable,' he wrote from his cell. 'I have seen too much of life not to be able to laugh at it; for the thinking man it is a comedy.'

The comedy was about to have a happy ending, or so it then seemed. Peiper and his fellow SS men were spared the firing squad and hangman's noose – all death sentences were to be commuted to life imprisonment. Survivors of the massacre and many veterans of the Bulge were outraged.

Many of the condemned were soon released. Sepp Dietrich, one of the most ruthless of Hitler's SS generals, walked out of prison a free man as early as 1955. Peiper left Landsberg prison in time to celebrate Christmas 1956 with his family.

'When my father was released,' Peiper's daughter Elke recalled, 'he came back to a family in which mother and half-grown children already formed a firm community. Papa was known to us solely through letters and the occasional visit to Landsberg. It wasn't easy to become accustomed to him and it took some time before he was finally accepted really into the family.'

Shortly after his release, Peiper went to work for Porsche in Stuttgart. Porsche had built the Panther tanks in which he and his men had stormed across the Russian steppe. Before long, Peiper was working his way toward senior management, his brilliance as a tactician and decisive leader once again making its mark. A new phoenix had arisen. The Third Reich was now a democratic republic too absorbed in the miracle of its rebirth to dwell on the pasts of those who had so recently reduced it to ashes.

Peiper quickly rose to a white-collar position as publicity manager with Porsche and was considered for a top post with the company. But then left-wing union officials, who had to be consulted on such promotions, discovered his past and demanded his dismissal.

By the late 1960s, Peiper had had enough of 'the bankrupt state' of Germany, now the economic powerhouse of the new Europe. He decided to find peace and quiet in, of all places, rural France. In 1940, he had been enchanted by an area around the Langres Plateau in the southeast. Back then, Peiper had helped a French POW from the region, a man named Gauthier, return from Germany to his family in France.

In 1969, an ever-grateful Gauthier sold Peiper property in the village of Traves, eight miles west of the nearest town, Vesoul, and he and his wife moved there. Peiper soon discovered that he was not the only SS veteran in the tiny village. Lieutenant Colonel Erwin Ketelhut lived close by, and the two became friends as Peiper built a modest wooden cabin above the banks of a small river on the outskirts of Traves.

Little did the villagers know that their new neighbor had first visited the area in 1940 with Heinrich Himmler. Together, they had shared the dream of setting up an autonomous SS state within the Reich. It would be a Nazi Valhalla, free of Jews, populated only by pure Aryans and their super-children. Of course, the dream never came to be, but former SS men such as Peiper and Ketelhut, nostalgic for what might have been, were now at least able to make the region their home.

In the early 1970s, Peiper kept his wood stove burning and food on the table by translating military history books. 'The material is depressing,' he told his son. 'It is clear to me that these relapses in barbarity took place not just under Hitler, but have happened always. It is the human being who is at fault. He has always attempted to kill his neighbors in order to ensure the survival of himself and his family. . . . The fruit of this realization is resignation.'

Even in Traves, Peiper's reputation inevitably caught up with him. Three years after he moved there, a local journalist – tipped off by communists – reported that the notorious SS Peiper, the butcher of Malmedy, was hiding in the village. 'If I am here,' Peiper retorted arrogantly, 'it is because in 1940, the French were here without courage. There are threats to burn down my house. I thought France was a democratic country that respected human rights.'

Around the same time that Peiper left Germany, Technical Sergeant William Slape, still serving in the U.S. Army, walked into a bar near his army base in Germany. To his amazement, he recognized the barman as the very same German para-trooper who had taken him prisoner in Lanzerath in December 1944. 'I walked in the front door,' recalled Slape, 'and that old bald-headed joker came flying over the counter. I didn't get out of that damn bar until 2 the next morning. We had a ball. The man cleared people out of the bar and brought his family to meet the American soldier who he once pointed his gun at. I thought a lot of the guy. He was a damn fine man.'

'Why didn't you shoot me that day?' asked Slape.

'I had too much respect for you,' replied his former captor.

In contrast to Jochen Peiper, Otto Skorzeny's postwar career went from strength to strength. Brought to trial at Dachau a year after Peiper and his men, he was spectacularly acquitted on all charges after British wing commander Yeo Thomas, the famous 'White Rabbit,' testified that British agents acting behind German lines had, like Skorzeny's men, dressed up in enemy uniform. If Skorzeny was to be hanged for ordering his men to do the same, then Yeo Thomas and many others should also meet the same fate. Prosecutors had dug long and deep to try to pin a specific atrocity on Skorzeny but had failed.

Facing possible deportation to Czechoslovakia, which by the late 1940s was under rigid Soviet influence, Skorzeny slipped out of Europe to Argentina, another favored destination of SS luminaries. According to some sources, he was heartily welcomed by fellow fascist Colonel Juan Peron, whom Skorzeny advised, and by the dictator's legendary wife, Eva, whom Skorzeny later claimed to have seduced after foiling an attempt on her life. In Buenos Aires, Skorzeny may also have succeeded in secretly repatriating to former Nazis some of the hundreds of millions of dollars of Nazi gold that had been shipped to Argentina in the last months of the Third Reich.

In 1952, Skorzeny went to work for another colonel,

Gamal Abdul Nasser, who had seized power in Egypt. Skorzeny and dozens of other former SS men helped Nasser, a staunch admirer of Hitler, to set up and train a secret service. Skorzeny was also said to have trained Palestinian terrorists, helped other Arab nations in their struggle against the nascent Israel, and smuggled arms into Egypt. Indirectly, he also worked for the CIA through the murky Gehlen organization, a network of Nazis headed by General Reinhard Gehlen, former head of intelligence on the eastern front. The cold war was by now white-hot, and men such as Skorzeny, with excellent links to anticommunists throughout Eastern Germany, made ideal operatives. Skorzeny was even rumored to have been connected to CIA-sponsored attempts in the late 1960s to assassinate Fidel Castro.

By the 1970s, 'The Most Dangerous Man in Europe' was reputed to be running guns to Africa and was living in fascist Spain. The country was still ruled by Generalissimo Francisco Franco, who had crushed Spanish democracy in the late 1930s with Hitler's help. On July 7, 1975, after reportedly ensuring the safe return of Eva Peron's corpse from Europe to Colonel Peron in Argentina, Otto Skorzeny died peacefully of old age in his bed, an unrepentant Nazi and anti-Semite to the very end.

18. Reunion

Though still only in his twenties, for several years after his return to St. Louis Lyle Bouck was a shadow of his former self. He suffered the lingering effects of hepatitis and started to experience almost constant aches. It was only after he visited a chiropractor that he began to regain his health.

Bouck intended to stay in the army and filed papers to secure the permanent rank of first lieutenant. To his dismay, he received a letter notifying him that he had been accepted into the regular army but as a second lieutenant. 'That same day, there was a second letter,' he recalled. 'It contained my leave pay and it was much less than I anticipated. I called up and was informed that regulations stated that if you were an enlisted man for any period of time, you'd be compensated at that pay scale. I was so pissed off that I said to hell with it [and] tore up my commission.' Bouck then considered becoming a lawyer, but after meeting a chiropractor at a party and recalling how the profession had helped heal him, he decided to study to become a chiropractor instead. He struggled at first to build up a client base but after several years was recognized as one of the best practitioners in St. Louis.

Over the next two decades there was little contact between Bouck and his former platoon. But Bouck did visit Lieutenant Colonel Kriz in Grand Island, Nebraska, where his former mentor had become a successful businessman and then the town's mayor.

In December 1965, Bouck received a letter from Bill

James regarding the official U.S. Army history *The Ardennes: Battle of the Bulge*, by Hugh M. Cole. James had arresting news: 'Bouck – we were responsible for blunting the main spearhead of the whole German offensive for that whole first twenty-four-hour period. However, you would never know it without having been there and then reading the account from the American position and the German position. Listen, Bouck, I would like to see our unit cited, but more importantly, I want the world to know, but for your calm determination, it could have been another story. . . . Remember when you used to say "Fuck the torpedoes, straight ahead?" What are your orders this time?'

Bouck had no orders. By now he had a very busy practice in St. Louis and three children to support. There seemed little to be gained from stirring up the past. But Bouck still felt responsible for James's wounds and now also wondered whether he had failed in his duties as an officer in May 1945. His men had fought with extraordinary valor. If James was right about the significance of their actions, surely it was now his duty to bring them some recognition? Bouck set about trying to contact former members of the platoon and corresponding with others from the 99th Division, including General Walter Lauer.

'I feel most strongly just the way you do,' replied Lauer, 'that the 99th Infantry Division did not by a long shot receive the credit due it for its most heroic stand during the first three days of the Battle of the Bulge. . . . It was the do or die order, the "hold at all costs" order that I issued that was carried out to the letter by all units of the Division, even to such small elements as your own, that saved the destruction of the North shoulder of the Bulge. Had we failed, there would have been no Bastogne and the entire complexion of the War could have changed most drastically.'

With James, the desire for recognition quickly became an obsession, and perhaps a way of coming to terms with the severe face wounds that had left him horrifically disfigured and deaf in one ear.

James was now married and raising four sons. He had met his wife, Lucille 'Peg' Cassell, a pretty young army nurse from West Virginia, in 1945 at the Valley Forge Veterans Hospital outside Philadelphia. James had asked Cassell to bring him something to eat. When she returned with a large sandwich, James had mumbled through his sewed-up mouth, 'What am I supposed to do with that?'

The couple had laughed, and Cassell had broken the sandwich into small pieces. Several weeks later, they had been married at the hospital. 'He often laughed about the wedding,' recalled his son, Ed, 'calling it a gathering of the cripples. There he was with his damaged face, a few others with missing limbs. But what wasn't missing was his luck in his choice of a bride. My mother ought to get a medal too. Since she was a nurse she was able to take care of dad's extensive needs.'

The couple settled in White Plains, New York. James went back to college and studied law at Cornell, but his injuries forced him to quit. Then he began a series of jobs selling insurance, which ended when his pain got too great. 'He depended on painkillers, painkillers, painkillers,' recalled his sister, Anna. 'It got to the point where he would come to my house every day, sick as a dog and begging for painkillers; I had been in a car accident, and I had plenty of them around. He was in pain every hour, every day.' It seemed the only time he was happy when he was playing with his four sons.

Gone was the handsome live wire whom Anna had grown up with. Now, James was often depressed. He wore an eye patch, and he was excruciatingly aware of his face. People could not help but stare or wince. For spiritual support, he turned more and more to the Greek Orthodox Church and even considered joining the clergy. He also became politically active, serving as the Republican chairman of Rye, New York, with a reputation as an outspoken patriot.

The pain got worse and worse. Some nights, his neighbors could not sleep because of his cries. 'Before they started the plastic surgery it was possible to put your fist into his cheek cavity,' recalled James's son, Edward. 'They sewed the sightless eye back in, and it would open and close through the years. But towards the end it became too much of a painful bother, so they sewed it shut for good. The pain was always so great that he had to use painkilling drugs increasingly, so the doctors tried deadening the area by cutting the nerves. This caused him to lose feeling there, as you do when the dentist injects novocaine. When we ate, at home or out, he would never know when food was dripping down his chin, and we would have to tell him so he could wipe it.'

In June 1966, Lyle Bouck received a letter informing him that he had been awarded a Silver Star by the 99th Division commander, General Lauer, in 1945. 'Ordered to protect the right flank during the enemy counter offensive, Lieutenant Bouck . . . by directing and laying down murderous volumes of fire inflicting heavy casualties on the enemy, repelled the initial attack of the hostile forces,' read the citation. 'It was not until all ammunition had been expended and further resistance was impossible that he was forced to surrender at the point of an enemy weapon.'

Bouck had received the medal after requesting his military records in order to help the writer John Eisenhower, son of the former president, with research for a book about the Battle of the Bulge. 'I should have done more to get recognition for the I&R platoon but [in 1945] I felt we hadn't done any more than anyone else,' Bouck recalled. 'But now I knew differently. It eventually became a personal crusade with me to see that [my men] received the recognition for what they had done as youngsters.'

John Eisenhower asked Bouck to return to Lanzerath with him. But Bouck was unable to leave his chiropractic business, so instead he paid for Bill James to accompany Eisenhower to the scene of their bloody stand. James and Eisenhower walked the hilltop, scouted out the old position, and even visited the Café Scholzen. The cuckoo clock was still there. James took it home and put it above the mantel as a souvenir. Bouck soon heard from Eisenhower about the trip: 'When [Bill] got up there on the hill and reenacted what happened, running back and forth, John was afraid he'd have to ship him home as a corpse.'

To further aid Eisenhower, Bouck agreed to write to Jochen Peiper, asking him to comment on what had happened at Lanzerath. 'I know you faced charges of having your men shoot prisoners of war at Honsfeld, Büllingen and Malmedy,' wrote Bouck. 'Because we were not molested after a day of severe battle with the best German troops, I have always thought you had been accused of something for which you had no control. It is well known that in the heat of battle tempers flare and men will do things they normally would not do. Many situations like this happened also with our troops.'

Peiper replied quickly in fluent English, explaining that he had been delayed that day because of a jam in tanks and traffic. He then described his impressions on arriving in Lanzerath: 'No shots rang out. . . . The [Café Scholzen] was full of soldiers, mostly officers, a great number of them asleep. . . . I fully appreciate your honest attempt to correct the ruling "historic" version. . . . But we lost the war, are outcasts and pretty much disillusioned. However, though we have other problems and no time to again delve into our military past, we still have an ear for the language of front line soldiers. Therefore, once more: thank you for the outstretched hand. Good luck and best wishes, Jochen Peiper.'

In January 1967, Lyle Bouck was contacted by a German veteran, former Private First Class Rudi Fruehbeisser, of the German 3rd Parachute Regiment, who had fought at Lanzerath. Fruehbeisser, now police commissioner for Nuremberg, was organizing a reunion of his unit for the twenty-fifth anniversary of the Battle of Bulge. Would any of his comrades' former adversaries, men of the 99th Division, be interested in meeting with the paratroopers in Belgium?

Bouck spread the word through the 99th Division Association and even wrote to Peiper, asking if he would like to join the anniversary celebrations.

Peiper replied immediately: 'Public opinion and certain forces behind the press and propaganda would not tolerate such a "cease fire" as too many people still live on the unsettled past and prosper on wounds artificially kept open. . . . It would be naïve not to realize that the world still today is strongly influenced by certain organizations you had better not provoke, at least not openly.'

Finally, in early December 1969, a party of 99th Division veterans left America for Belgium. Accompanied by his wife Lucy, who had been a grade school classmate in the 1930s, Lyle Bouck joined other veterans in Brussels on December 11 at a formal reception, where they were praised and welcomed back to Europe by senior generals from several Allied nations. They were then driven to the American Embassy. The ambassador was, of all people, John Eisenhower. His book on the Battle of the Bulge, *The Bitter Woods*, had been published earlier that year. Recalling the words of his father, Eisenhower told Bouck and his fellow Checkerboard veterans that what the 99th Division had done in the Battle of the Bulge was the most outstanding tactical maneuver in World War II.

The next day, the group met with its former enemies in Junkerath, Germany, where Bouck and his men had been loaded onto trains twenty-five years before. After a welcome address and a few drinks, the Germans told the Americans to get their hats and coats. 'We are going to take you on a secret journey,' a German host explained.

The Americans and their wives were driven to Stadtkyll, Germany, where they walked, led by torchbearers, about half a mile through the snow up a hill. 'This was really something for the women because they had their high heels on,' recalled Bouck. 'At the top they had a huge bonfire and silhouetted against this was a monument shaped just like the Arch of Triumph.'

The Germans stood on one side and the Americans on the other. A band played the German and American national anthems. Then Rudi Fruehbeisser made a short speech, dedicating the ceremony to the Germans and Americans killed and wounded in the Battle of the Bulge.

During a formal banquet held that evening by the Germans, a former paratrooper approached Bouck.

'Lyle, we haven't talked since that day,' the man said. 'Do you remember someone who asked, "Who is the commandant?" It was me.'

The man was Sergeant Vinz Kuhlbach. He was now an accountant.

Kuhlbach placed his hand on Bouck's shoulder.

'Lyle, we weren't told you were here . . . what tremendous courage the American soldier had that day.'

On December 13, the Americans and Germans stood together in a graveyard just outside the village of Stadtkyll. 'A priest offered prayers,' recalled one of the 99th Division veterans. 'Wreaths were placed by the American and German parties followed by the trumpeter playing "*Ich hatt einen Kamerad*" [I had a comrade], used where we blow "Taps."'

The Germans then lingered in the graveyard, wiping snow from the graves of several of their fallen comrades, calling long-forgotten names to each other and then gathering in silence to pay their respects.

Before returning to America, Bouck and his wife Lucy visited the position on the hillside above Lanzerath. The foxholes were still there. The woods nearby had been cut down and replanted. Suddenly, Bouck was twenty years old again. The place had exactly the same feel as it had all those years before.

Now forty-six, Lyle Bouck realized that perhaps one factor above all – their youth – had explained why he and his men had stood and held, knowing they would probably pay for their obstinacy with their lives. They had been so terribly young, so inexperienced in so many ways. Older men – fathers, wiser and more cautious adults – would surely have retreated as soon as the Germans appeared in such superior numbers.

None of the other platoon members returned to Belgium that December. 'I've already seen enough of that place,' said Jordan 'Pop' Robinson. 'I didn't leave anything over there, except for a little piece of my leg, and I sure couldn't find it again anyway.'

On June 11, 1976, sixty-year-old Jochen Peiper, gray-haired but still handsome, walked into his local hardware store in Vesoul looking for some wire with which to build a kennel for one of his beloved Alsatian dogs. Little did he know that the man behind the counter, Paul Cacheux, was a Communist Party member. Cacheux heard Peiper's German accent and asked if Peiper had been in France during the war. Peiper avoided the question and paid for the wire with a check.

The check had his name and address on it.

Recognizing Peiper's name, Cacheux consulted the so-called brown list, issued by the East German government, that gave the names of all German war criminals. Cacheux soon discovered that he had sold chicken wire to one of the most notorious SS officers of the Third Reich, and a convicted war criminal to boot. He quickly passed on Peiper's details and address to contacts who had been in the French Resistance.

Less than a fortnight after Peiper had entered Cacheux's shop, on June 22, 1976, the French communist newspaper *L'Humanité* broke the story of Peiper's presence in France. Within days, posters portraying Peiper as a war criminal and Nazi were distributed in Traves. Threats that revenge would be delivered on July 14 were daubed on walls.

July 14 was Bastille Day, the annual celebration of the 1789 French Revolution and similar in its patriotic significance to July 4 in America.

The morning before Bastille Day, Peiper sent his wife, Sigurd, who was suffering from cancer, back to Germany. He refused to leave their home beside the Saône River even though he now fully expected his house to be attacked. His SS neighbor, Ketelhut, suggested Peiper spend the night of the fourteenth with him. Peiper declined. 'He was absolutely calm and at ease,' Ketelhut recalled. 'I offered to stay and help him, but he refused. His last words to me were, "I won't be bullied! They can shoot me if they wish, but I'm not going to allow them to beat me into a cripple. If they come, I'm going to defend my home."'

That night, it has been claimed, Peiper waited on the veranda of his house from where he could observe the Saône River. Erwin Ketelhut had lent him his rifle.

As fireworks lit up the sky, local teenagers approached Peiper's home, intent on torching it with Molotov cocktails.

What happened next can only be told by Jochen Peiper's murderers.

The following morning, among the smoldering remains of Peiper's last refuge, the police found spent pistol bullets and, in his bedroom, the charred corpse of Jochen Peiper. The fire had been so intense that it had shrunk his body to around a meter in length. It was later assumed that Peiper had escaped the initial torching of his home. Intent on saving his signed copy of *Mein Kampf* and other personal items, he had run into the blazing house and a ceiling had collapsed, trapping him in the flames.

The French police investigated the murder for six months. Local communists from Vesoul and Resistance members were questioned. Most villagers knew only too well the teenagers who had actually torched Peiper's home. But for political reasons – France and Germany did not want an embarrassing trial – the French police did not bring a single prosecution, and the case was finally closed. To this day, the killers of Jochen Peiper remain at large.

*

On June 27, 1977, Bill James died, possibly from an overdose of painkillers, shortly after returning home from his thirty-sixth operation. He was just fifty-two. The cuckoo clock from the Café Scholzen still hung above the mantel in his living room. According to his widow, Peg, it stopped chiming soon after he passed away.

Ironically, James's sister Anna was in Belgium at the time of his death, on her way to the very hillside where he had been wounded. She quickly returned to New York for his funeral, which was covered by the New York press. 'On the way to the Queens cemetery,' a Greek journalist reported, 'the funeral passed the gas station where he had often lingered in his idle time. The staff, all lined up in clean pressed uniforms, dipped the flag as James went by. It was not until the procession reached the cemetery that they received word that President Carter's office had given permission for James to be buried at Arlington.' The proceedings were stopped, and his burial was rescheduled for Arlington.

Along with James's family Lyle Bouck and others from the platoon were at the graveside in Washington. The last time Bouck had visited James in New York, they had sat up late talking and drinking after watching a Memorial Day parade. Finally, their conversation had gotten around to the burp gun incident that had destroyed James's face. Bouck had apologized, saying he had always wished the bullets had hit him instead. James had told Bouck he was being ridiculous. How could he blame himself for an instinctive reaction? Besides, if he hadn't pushed the barrel to one side, they could both be dead.

Private Vernon Leopold, now a Harvard-educated immigration lawyer, was enjoying a vacation from the harsh winter in Michigan when he picked up *Parade* magazine in the local Sunday newspaper. To his astonishment, the cover story was titled 'Why Private Tsakanikas Should Get the Medal of Honor.' Bill James's death had prompted columnist Jack Anderson to compile an in-depth report for the magazine; several surviving platoon members were quoted. Leopold's former platoon commander, Lyle Bouck, was described as a chiropractor now working in St. Louis.

The following morning, Leopold called Bouck's office number.

'Is that Lyle, Lyle Bouck?' asked Leopold.

'Yes,' replied Bouck.

'It's Vernon Leopold. Do you remember me?'

'Of course. How are your feet?'

Leopold was soon near tears as he reminisced with Bouck. 'These guys were like brothers to me,' he later explained. 'And now I knew they were alive.'

After Leopold's call, Bouck heard from Sam Jenkins and Carlos Fernandez in El Paso. It was agreed that they should try to organize a reunion.

Long before the article appeared in *Parade* magazine, New York Yankees owner George Steinbrenner had called for James, a Yankees fan, to be awarded the Congressional Medal of Honor. When Steinbrenner learned from *Parade* that there were fourteen surviving members of the platoon, he invited them all to New York. Just a week later, with Steinbrenner footing the bill, ten were flown first class to Manhattan with their wives and put up in suites at the Mayfair House Hotel.

The visit was to climax with James's widow, Peg, tossing the first ball of the new season while survivors of the platoon formed up behind the Yankees' home plate. Lyle Bouck began to worry that the fans would be less hospitable than their team's owner. At the sight of a widow and a bunch of middle-aged men, they would surely start to shout, 'Get those old farts out of there and play ball!'

When Lyle Bouck and his men, accompanied by their families, arrived at Yankee Stadium on April 5, 1979, they found the ballpark crammed to capacity for the opening game of the season.

Vernon Leopold and his wife Shirley had flown in at the last moment from Detroit. As he entered a hospitality suite, Leopold heard familiar voices and then started to recognize his old platoon buddies. It had been thirty-four years since he'd last set eyes on them. 'Of course,' he recalled, 'we had all gotten older. But everybody looked pretty much the same. We shook hands, and then we embraced. One of the men came over and asked me if I'd brought foot powder along. I realized it was John Creger. We all began to bond again.'

James Silvola's wife, Jean, watched as her husband and fellow platoon members began to reminisce. 'They were like a bunch of kids again. Lots of hugging, teary eyes, and when they got to talking it was like watching fireworks. So much emotion.' Risto Milosevich had not seen some of his platoon buddies since the war. 'We must have hugged each other for ten minutes,' recalled Milosevich. 'It was a hell of a reunion.'[61]

The reunion was particularly moving for the men's commanding officer, Lyle Bouck. 'After the experiences we all shared training at Camp Maxey in Texas and then to England, France, Belgium and Germany in combat and prison camps,' he later wrote, 'the reunion in the Stadium Club at Yankee Stadium on April 5th was packed with controlled emotion. After a few cocktails and an attempt at lunch, we were led to the field box next to the dugout.'

Nervously, Lyle Bouck took his seat behind the dugout.

'Ladies and gentlemen, your attention please,' said an announcer.

The ballpark quieted down.

'Undoubtedly, the most underpublicized, yet one of the most valiant episodes of World War II, the Lanzerath incident, was brought to light by renowned columnist Jack Anderson in *Parade* magazine last month,' continued the announcer. 'In December 1944, eighteen brave Americans of the 99th Army Division, halted a vast column of German tanks, paratroopers and SS troops in a fierce 18-hour battle which ended in hand-to-hand combat in the Belgian village of Lanzerath. These eighteen, sent out only as a reconnaissance patrol, thus blunted a massive surprise Nazi attack that could have changed the entire outcome of the Battle of the Bulge. Miraculously, the Americans suffered only two casualties. . . . On this opening day, the New York Yankees are remembering the survivors of Lanzerath, and hope they will not be forgotten by the country they so bravely defended. . . . Ladies and gentlemen, we would like to introduce to you members of this heroic group.'

The announcer read out the men's names as the scoreboard lit up:

Robert D. Adams, Akron, Ohio
Dr. Lyle Bouck, St. Louis, Missouri
John Creger, Richmond, Virginia
Dr. Carlos A. Fernandez, El Paso, Texas
Samuel Jenkins, El Paso, Texas
Louis Kalil, Mishawaka, Indiana
Robert Lambert, Fullerton, California
Vernon Leopold, Detroit, Michigan
Aubrey P. McGehee, Summitt, Mississippi
James Silvola, Ocala, Florida

'And the widow of one of these brave men, Mrs. Lucille James of Port Chester, New York,' added the announcer. 'The Yankees would respectfully ask you to rise and applaud and show our deep appreciation – though some 35 years late – to these gallant Americans.'

Yankee Stadium stood and applauded – much to Lieutenant Lyle Bouck's relief. That night, the platoon was taken to the famous 21 Club, where the men caught up after three decades. Around 4:00 A.M., after closing the bar at the 21 Club, the platoon called it a night in Corporal Sam Jenkins's suite and headed to bed.[62]

Later that season, on July 11, 1979, the campaign to award James the Congressional Medal of Honor reached Congress. Federal statutes for the submission of award recommendations from World War II had expired on May 2, 1952, so only by changing the law could the statute of limitations be waived and a medal awarded. In an attempt to lift the waiver, three of the platoon members – Carlos Fernandez, Robert Lambert, and Lyle Bouck – testified before Congress about the platoon and James's actions. 'I don't want a damn thing for myself,' Bouck told reporters following the hearings. 'But I hope the Defense Department sees fit to give credit where credit is due. James paid a heavy price. I'm just happy to be alive and well.'

Others were not so sure that James deserved the Medal of Honor. Platoon Sergeant Bill Slape had not attended the Yankee Stadium event, nor had he testified before Congress. Like Risto Milosevich and others in the platoon, he did not believe that James had done more than others that day. In his eyes, it would be unfair to single out any one individual for such an exceptional award: every platoon member had played his part.

When interviewed by his local newspaper, Lieutenant Colonel Robert Kriz didn't hesitate to call all the platoon members heroes. But he echoed Slape's reservations about singling out any one individual, saying he didn't believe medals made heroes any more than a court-martial made a coward. Kriz could remember one man in his command who was wrongfully court-martialed on grounds of cowardice. Kriz had seen that same man climb onto an enemy tank to throw a grenade through its hatch. Official commendations or condemnations didn't impress him. It was enough to say that the platoon members did their jobs: 'They gave a good accounting of themselves.'

The congressional hearings finally resulted in a recommendation that the Secretary of Defense award the Congressional Medal of Honor to Bill James. The U.S. Army and Air Force both supported the award, but after review by the U.S. Marines it was denied because James had shown insufficient 'intrepidity.' The James family refused to give up, eventually sending more than a thousand letters to congressmen and even President Reagan. 'We're Greeks. We're fighters,' explained Peter Tsakanikas, one of James's brothers, adding that the family name, Tsakanikas, meant 'champion of fighters.'

Sadly, their efforts were in vain. But Bill James did not go unrecognized. On December 14, 1979, the congressional hearings culminated in President Carter signing Public Law 96–145, waiving the time limitation for awards exclusively for members of the I&R platoon. Two days later, former Lieutenant Colonel Robert Kriz submitted a recommendation that the platoon receive a Presidential Unit Citation and that Lyle Bouck be awarded a Distinguished Service Cross, the U.S. Army's second highest award. The next day, Lyle

Bouck submitted awards recommendations for all members of his former platoon.

At last, Lyle Bouck and his men were formally recognized.

On July 2, 1980, the U.S. Army awarded five Silver Stars and nine Bronze Star medals with a 'V' [for valor] device. On August 12, it approved a posthumous Distinguished Service Cross for Bill James and a Distinguished Service Cross for Risto Milosevich. 'Firing from point blank range with a grease gun,' read James's citation, 'and from an exposed machine gun position, he is credited with inflicting heavy casualties on the enemy.' Milosevich was also commended for 'extraordinary heroism . . . Milosevich's dauntless efforts and sustained weapons fire throughout the day contributed immensely to the platoon's ability to stop three frontal attacks.'[63] On November 13, Lyle Bouck and Bill Slape were also awarded the Distinguished Service Cross.

The good news kept getting better. On January 15, 1981, President Carter approved a Presidential Unit Citation for 'extraordinary heroism.' The I&R platoon had through its 'valorous actions provided crucial time for the American forces to prepare to defend against the massive German offensive. The extraordinary gallantry, determination and esprit de corps of the Intelligence and Reconnaissance Platoon in close combat against a numerically superior enemy force are in keeping with the highest traditions of the United States Army and reflect great credit upon the Unit and the Armed Forces of the United States.'

Bill Slape had retired from the U.S. Army only thirteen years before, having ended his military service as a sergeant major. With enormous pride, he now stood in his uniform once more, this time surrounded by his family, in a hotel foyer in

Maryland. They were headed to Fort Meyer and to a special awards ceremony attended by Army Secretary John O. Marsh Jr. 'I put on my uniform and went to that ceremony,' recalled Slape. 'They had elements of 3rd Infantry, the old guard, some of the sharpest young troops in the world – and it was as if thirteen years had been completely wiped out of my life. It was just as natural as could be. And I loved it.'

Their intelligence commander also went to Washington. It was the first time Kriz had seen the platoon as a group since World War II. 'Chuckling, Kriz said a lot of the platoon members were amazed he was so young. Kriz noted he was only twenty-eight when he trained the unit at Camp Maxey. . . . The clean-shaven Kriz said he wore a moustache back in those days just so he would look older.'

A writer from the *Washington Post* watched as the men received their awards. 'In contrast, perhaps, with a cross section of Vietnam veterans,' he reported, 'there was a matter of factness, a calm about these men, an absence of introspection, a presence of self-definition as soldiers, patriots and citizens.'[64]

Louis Kalil, John Creger, James Silvola, Jordan Robinson, and Aubrey McGehee were presented with Silver Stars. George Redmond – Kalil's foxhole buddy – Sam Jenkins, Carlos Fernandez, Robert Lambert, and Vernon Leopold had Bronze Stars pinned to their chests. From a gallery, their proud families watched in glee. Then the colors were posted and the United States Army Band played 'Grand Old Flag.'

After the ceremony, the men gathered for photographs and celebrated with each other's families at a special banquet held at the Crystal City Marriott Hotel. Slape spoke with James's sons. 'It was apparent from the number of enemy dead in front of your dad's position when the fight was over,' said Slape, 'that he had done an outstanding job with no concern for his personal safety.'

Former 2nd Division company commander and celebrated historian Charles MacDonald, who had fought alongside the 99th Division during the Battle of the Bulge, was invited to make a short speech at the banquet. 'Ladies and gentlemen,' MacDonald concluded, lifting his glass, 'I give you the gallant men of the I&R platoon, 394th Infantry, 99th Infantry Division, and the high honors – however belated – now bestowed upon them.'

All stood and joined MacDonald in his toast.

Thirty-seven years had passed since they had fought for one another on a snow-covered hillside above a small Belgian village called Lanzerath. Now Lyle Bouck and his men belonged to what was thought to be the most decorated American platoon for a single action of the entire Second World War.

Notes

1. 'Everything passes,
   everything goes by.
   After every December,
   there is always a May.'
2. The plot to kill Hitler had been forming since 1942 and had the tacit support of von Rundstedt and Rommel, among other senior generals. It was hoped that after removing Hitler, and possibly Göring and Himmler, democracy would be restored, peace could be negotiated with the Western Allies, and a successful war could be pursued against the Russians.
3. The name 'ninety-day wonder' was a somewhat derogatory term for the young men who had passed through officer training school in a matter of a few months.
4. The ASTP program was designed to provide the continuous and accelerated flow of high-grade technicians and specialists needed by the army. To this end, soldiers were sent to select colleges to receive specialized training. Although attending college, they were under military discipline and formally on active duty. They received regular army pay. The last thing they expected was to be sent to regular infantry units as privates.
5. Many infantry regiments had an Intelligence and Reconnaissance platoon. The twenty-five men in the 394th's I&R platoon comprised two nine-man reconnaissance squads and a seven-man headquarters section that worked directly under the supervision of Major Kriz, the 394th's intelligence officer.
6. The ASTP shoulder patch was a blue lamp of knowledge.
7. When Leopold became a U.S. citizen during his stint as an

ASTP student at the University of Arkansas, he changed his name because he feared that in the event of possible capture the Nazis would kill him. He therefore took Gerald for a new first name but, not intending to be called by it, he wanted to use only the initial 'G.' and then go by his middle name that he had adapted to Vernon. As it turned out, the army didn't go for first-initial and middle-name designations on identification (dog) tags and issued him new tags that identified him as Gerald V. Leopold, the name by which he remains designated in all army and veteran records.

8. White Anglo-Saxon Protestant.

9. Risto had worked for his father as soon as he was physically capable of the long, hard hours on construction sites and had inherited his father's strict work ethic, rigid moral code, and propensity for violence. As a boy, Risto had seen a Mexican laborer threaten his father with a pickax. Risto had run toward his father's assailant, determined to 'tackle the son of a bitch.' 'You stay out of this!' his father had shouted. Risto's father had taken the pickax off the Mexican, removed the metal head, and beaten him with the wooden handle. Another time, at a church meeting, he had been called a liar in front of the congregation. Risto's father had simply walked across the crowded church and punched his accuser in the face, knocking him out. 'If you called my father a liar,' recalled Risto, 'that's what he would do. Hell, that guy was out for a long time.'

10. Two other former ASTP men who had been transferred into the platoon, Privates Rueter and Vic Adams, also knew some German. But neither of them was natively fluent in the language because they both came from second- or third-generation German immigrant families and could only speak American-accented German. Shortly after the platoon had been reconstituted, Rueter was transferred to the Office of Strategic Service (OSS).

11. Like his father, who had come to America in 1905, Kalil had

worked at a local rubber plant after high school. He had played baseball avidly and applied to go to Notre Dame before being drafted in 1942 at age nineteen.

12. There was another Adams in the platoon – a former ASTP man named Robert Adams.

13. One hot summer night, Adams recalled, he had been involved in a divisional reconnaissance exercise. Other German-speaking privates, including Leopold, were ordered to dress up in hot woolen Afrika Corps uniforms and try to confuse the night maneuvers. 'We kept popping up in the area speaking German. Finally, towards morning we allowed ourselves to be "captured." They were utterly confused and didn't know what to do. Their officers really got mad when we finally said in English we were tired and hungry and would they give us a lift back to our outfit. They knew they'd been "had."' One of the few surviving photographs of the platoon members during their time in Camp Maxey shows Private Adams and Private Leopold grinning sheepishly in their German uniforms.

14. Bill James was born William Tsakanikas and would change his name to James after the war. His name is given as James throughout the book to avoid confusion. He was known as 'Tsak' to other platoon members who had trouble pronouncing his second name. The platoon knew that James was fiercely proud of his Greek heritage and that he had three brothers in service and seven sisters.

15. While with the 60th Regiment of the 9th Division in the fighting near Mknassey, Kriz suffered a shrapnel wound from mortar fire and spent several weeks going from hospital to hospital. On his recovery Kriz rejoined his unit in the midst of its campaign against Bizerte. Soon afterward Kriz volunteered for a dangerous mission to find a platoon that had lost contact with its battalion and was thought to be lost very near enemy positions. With two linemen from the regiment and a field phone, Kriz started out in search of the lost

platoon. During the search he came upon a company that was trapped by a field of antipersonnel mines. Kriz was placed in command of the company and led the men safely through the minefield and to their objective. For this heroic action and exceptional courage, Kriz was awarded the Silver Star. Kriz would later explain his appointment as S-2 with typical modesty, saying that after he had recuperated from his leg wound, 'they [the army] didn't know what the hell to do with me so they made me into an intelligence officer.'

16. To Lieutenant Lyle Bouck's surprise, his train went through his hometown of St. Louis, Missouri. Sadly, he was not allowed off the train. As the train pulled out of St. Louis, he must have been full of thoughts of his family and the childhood haunts he might not see again. And if he did come home, he would make something of himself.

17. The United Service Organization looked after the morale and welfare of U.S. troops overseas.

18. 'At night the "Piccadilly Commandos" come out into the blackout and innocents like me have to fight for their honor,' wrote fellow 99er, Sergeant Dick Byers, an ardent Anglophile who had listened with his family back in Cleveland, Ohio, to BBC reports of the Battle of Britain in 1940. 'The sidewalks are crowded with "Commandos" accosting soldiers and trying to proposition them. Five pounds ($25) to spend the night; two pounds to go in a taxi; one pound to go into the alley. You damn near have to knock them away. Several times I was grabbed by the arm and had to fight like hell to save myself from a "fate worse than death!" At first it was amusing but eventually the novelty of their brazenness wears off. Some of them are quite nice-looking and that makes it seem even more revolting. Most GIs forget the beauty of England and the suffering and terror the English have gone through and remember only the whores in Piccadilly Circus. It is unfortunate.'

19. Jenkins and Fernandez had attended the same high school

but had not met each other until joining the platoon. Jenkins also thought of his father, who had worked long hours in the 1930s to put food on the table. Jenkins's mother had died, along with most of her family, from tuberculosis in the mid-1930s, leaving his father to cope alone with two boisterous boys.

20. Shortly after their first patrol, Bouck and several others in the platoon were among the first in the 394th to earn the Combat Infantryman badge, valued by veterans because it signifies participation in dangerous frontline action.

21. That fall, Eisenhower had bet with Montgomery that the war would be over by Christmas.

22. Adams would be honorably discharged in September 1945 after several months in military hospitals.

23. The document was relayed to General Bradley's headquarters that morning, providing crucial early evidence of the scale of the attack and thereby allowing Bradley to act quickly in informing Eisenhower that as many American divisions as possible should be brought into the battle. Lambert would later write: 'It is a matter of history that the 99th Division captured that document and many years later when I met General of the Army Omar Bradley on an airplane flight from Los Angeles to Washington, D.C., he confirmed to me that he had been informed of the contents of that document in a timely manner.'

24. Some of the platoon were angered by the order to hold at all costs. But not one refused to carry it out. Private Joseph McConnell was one of those who was convinced that the platoon would be wiped out, but nevertheless he readied his M-1 and grenades, trying to calm his nerves. 'I thought that was a stupid order. We were up there with just eighteen men. We were just going to be sacrificed. No doubt about it. It was a stupid goddamned order. "Hold at all costs" – against so many Germans.'

25. Billy Queen was left where he lay. His frozen corpse was

discovered weeks later when the Americans retook Lanzerath. It has been claimed that Queen was shot in the back after abandoning the dugout as he tried to make a run for cover. Understandably, the surviving members of the artillery obser-vation group resent the implication that Queen lost his life in such ignoble circumstances. Joseph McConnell, who was in the dugout with Queen, recalls, 'I told Queen to stay down. But he couldn't do that. He had to get up and see what he was shooting at. Then a shot got him in the chest. They say he was shot in the back. That's a lot of baloney. I saw him die. He got shot in the chest and dropped down.' As his fellow artillery observers saw it, Queen should never have been on the hillside or for that matter anywhere near combat. Sergeant Peter Gacki believed Queen would 'have been better suited somewhere where he could use his education. He was very intelligent, always had a slide rule with him, and you could give him any kind of puzzle and he'd figure it out. He looked so harmless, wore spectacles, had curly hair, and was just this chubby, nice guy.'

26. Slape explained: 'I think human nature makes you feel it may happen to the guy next to you, but it's not going to happen to you.'

27. Lambert later recalled, 'I have often wondered if that soldier that came running into the command post might have been a German in an American uniform.'

28. Robert Lambert would later maintain: 'The time bought for the American forces by the 394th I&R Platoon must have been more valuable than the capture at Remagen of the Ludendorff Bridge across the Rhine River by a unit of an American Armored Division in March 1945. General of the Army Eisenhower, I believe, was supposed to have said that bridge was worth its weight in gold to the allied forces.'

29. After the war, when some of the platoon learned about Skorzeny's men, they believed the Germans did this to provide these men with false identities. Milosevich wasn't

bothered when his dog tags were taken: 'They had better use for them than I did. But any of [Skorzeny's men] would have had a hell of a time convincing the Americans that Milosevich was American.'

30. Leopold is convinced that had Lyle Bouck not ordered him out of the outpost for medical attention the evening before the German onslaught, he most likely would have been part of this column of POWs. And he believes that these SS officers would not simply have made him a 'packhorse' – as a German Jew in an American uniform, he would have been shot on the spot or sent to a death camp.

31. The names of individuals and description of their actions in the initial phase of the massacre are based on evidence presented at the Malmedy Massacre war trial of 1947.

32. As Kriz's assistant Lieutenant Buegner ran down a road toward a schoolhouse where hot chow was being served, shells came in so close that he had to dive into the snow and mud for cover. When he finally found the schoolhouse, 88s again exploded nearby, shattering the schoolhouse's windows and spraying shards of glass. Dropping his mess kit, he and others hoping for a hot meal scrambled down to the basement where they sat in utter darkness for thirty minutes until the shelling ended. There was no telling when they would get another chance to eat.

33. Many men from the 394th Regiment did not make it to Krinkelt. 'Our regiment did suffer some casualties across the countryside and were mistaken to be attacking Germans,' recalled Buegner. 'In a similar way, some of our soldiers were killed or wounded as they retreated through 2nd Division positions [toward Krinkelt] and were shot without being challenged – the general rule that was followed in front line foxholes. It was in this way that a Sergeant of Lt. Melford's Interrogators of Prisoners of War (IPW) team [which had translated Lambert's captured document on the 16th] was killed, shortly after he abandoned his vehicle in the motor

column on the road from Mürringen to Krinkelt when the command "every man for himself" was given.'

34. According to the official history of the 99th Division: 'The losses of the 99th Division, fighting its first major action under circumstances far more difficult than was the lot of most American infantry divisions in the European Theater of Operations, [were] compiled only as a total for the whole month of December. Nine-tenths or more of the following represents the cost of four days in battle [December 16–20, 1944]: 14 officers and 119 men confirmed dead; 53 officers and 1,341 men missing in action (many were later determined to be dead, but most were prisoners of war); 51 officers and 864 men wounded in action. About 600 officers and men passed through the division clearing station before 20 December as non-battle casualties; half were trench foot cases.'

35. Robert Lambert recalled what it was like on Elsenborn Ridge. 'We occupied a foxhole for about the next forty days. We were just behind a few rifle companies. If anyone would sneak through, our sentry had to get them. One morning I woke up and found a German body outside my foxhole. Somebody killed him during the night. I don't know how it happened or what happened. . . . I think that we only had maybe a thousand people left in our regiment after the first three days.'

36. Eventually, on December 26, 1944, elements of the 4th Armored Division would return to Bastogne as the first Americans to relieve the heavily battered 101st Airborne. But Abraham Baum would not be among them, his unit having by then been placed in reserve.

37. The 99th Division lost 3,000 in four days – a stunning loss for such a battle-green division. But it regrouped magnificently. The 1st Battalion, 394th Regiment, for example, went back on line by December 19 but with only 139 of its original 700 men.

38. After the war, Leopold remembered that one of his I&R buddies, John Creger, came from a small Virginia town.

Perhaps, he thought, the town was small enough that a letter to him might not need a street address. He wrote to Creger to find out what had happened to him and the rest of his platoon buddies. When he didn't receive a reply, he concluded that none of them had survived.

39. 'I was worried about what my parents would go through when they found out I was missing in action,' said Kalil. 'They finally received a telegram on New Year's Eve saying I was MIA, and it was, of course, terrible for them.'

40. 'The flash and roar of exploding shells was incessant,' recalled Captain Charles Roland, a battalion executive officer with the 99th's 394th Infantry. 'In all directions the landscape was a Dante's inferno of burning towns and villages. Everyone was aware that there would be no further withdrawal, whatever the cost. Moreover, I could sense in the demeanor of the troops at all ranks that this resolution was written in their hearts. A few men broke under the strain, wetting themselves repeatedly, weeping, vomiting.'

41. The exact toll in American casualties was 80,987. By January 2, 1945, when the American counteroffensive began in earnest, more than 4,000 men had been killed and 17,000 taken prisoner.

42. Matters were not helped by the infrequency of Red Cross parcel deliveries. Many of the Red Cross parcels containing medical supplies were diverted for German use or simply remained embargoed. That the Allied governments placed the welfare of more than two hundred thousand of their men solely in the hands of the Red Cross, which was faced with insurmountable logistical challenges, is still a matter of bitterness among some survivors. In general, the fate of Allied POWs in Germany in 1945 remains one of the great untold tragedies of World War II. In the popular imagination, the POW experience has been mythologized in movies such as *The Great Escape* and *Colditz*. But, in reality, the unbowed, phlegmatic captive hell-bent on escape was a rare individual.

For the vast majority of Hitler's 'guests' during that winter of 1944–45, it was a case of simply trying to stay alive, knowing that the war could not last too much longer. For thousands, the end did not come soon enough: they died in pain and were buried in knocked-together wooden boxes in desolate graveyards dotted around the Third Reich.

43. At Joseph McConnell's wood-cutting camp, the Americans soon found ways to get the best of their German commandant. 'He got pissed off a lot,' recalled McConnell. 'We told him we weren't going to work anymore until we got our Red Cross packages. Christ! He got so mad. He brought in a platoon of soldiers to watch over us. . . . He'd go along the roll call lines with his dagger, waving it around, screaming curses in German. We didn't know what the hell he was saying. And we didn't care. We refused to work and finally got our packages.'

44. The Stammlager was a hellhole but heaven compared to a boxcar. Most of the new arrivals were grateful to have a bunk and finally a roof over their heads that was daubed with the letters 'P-O-W' to prevent attacks from Allied planes. 'We were put into an old cavalry stable,' recalled a relieved Sergeant Peter Gacki, the forward artillery observer captured along with the I&R platoon. 'The ground floor had two- or three-tiered bunk beds; they had put in a ceiling, and some of us were put up in the attic. The lower bunks were infested with lice, but upstairs we slept on the floor; we weren't bothered much by lice.'

45. By January 23, 1945, there were 453 officers, all of whom had been captured in the Ardennes between December 16 and December 22, 1944. By late March, there would be 1,291. These included 423 officers who arrived in the camp from Oflag 64 in Poland.

46. Every morning at eight and every evening at five, the Germans would count the men no matter the weather. 'There were times when we felt the cold wind blowing through our

thinning arms and limbs and were chilled to the marrow while the camp was searched for some missing Kriegie,' recalled Father Paul Cavanaugh, who had arrived the same day as Bouck and Reid. 'On warmer days we prolonged the counting in bright sunshine when out of mere devilment little men hid behind big men to make the number fall short of the total, or spaces were left vacant in the ranks to step up the count beyond the reported number. Smiles of mischievous delight rippled the files as back and back again came the guards to count the spoils of war, each time arriving at a variant figure until they were so confused as to call one another nasty names in sharp sounding phrases in the very presence of their captives.'

47. By 1945, prisoners from most Allied countries were incarcerated at Hammelburg, including the son of Soviet leader Joseph Stalin. Captain Stalin was as brutish and morose as his father, according to fellow Kriegies. Shortly after a fistfight with a British POW, he was reportedly shot to death by a guard after being warned to move away from the perimeter wire.

48. During the breakout from the Ardennes, Kriz again won acclaim for his bravery and professionalism. In an after-battle report describing the action of Kriz's battalion in the breakout, he was cited for his 'heroic deeds, outstanding courage and leadership.'

49. 'The officers of the 106th Infantry Division were at a bit of a disadvantage from the morale point of view,' recalled Major Albert Berndt, a surgeon who ran the Oflag's American infirmary. 'In the first few days of the Battle of the Bulge, Manteuffel's Fifth Panzer Army [had] flowed around the Schnee Eiffel and surrounded the 422nd and 423rd Infantry Regiments, which surrendered with personnel almost intact.' Individually they were fine people, but collectively they bore a cross that haunted them throughout their period of captivity. 'In particular, the onus of surrender lay heavily

upon the shoulders of Colonel Charles Cavender, who was, by virtue of his age and grade, the senior American officer present in the prison camp. Throughout his stay in the camp Cavender was distraught and tense. He could think only of the fact that he had capitulated with an intact regiment. He anticipated almost certain court-martial if he survived his captivity. Colonel Cavender's trepidation was obvious to the Germans as well as to the American officers in the camp. He lacked firm control over the Americans and his relations with the German Commanding General were not of the best.'

50. Milosevich also reflected bitterly on the German POWs he had seen while based at Camp Maxey in Texas. By this stage in the war, many German POWs held in America were writing to their relatives asking them not to waste their precious food and other resources by sending care packages to them – they were far from short of sustenance. 'I remember seeing those German POWs,' recalled Milosevich. 'They were big, fat sons-of-bitches. We fed them like they were on gourmet diets.' There were widespread complaints about the lenient treatment of German POWs in America, with many relatives of POWs such as Milosevich arguing bitterly that the enemy was eating better in some cases than ordinary Americans. However, the U.S. government continued to treat the Germans well, knowing that rumors had spread to German combat units that being a POW was actually something to look forward to, certainly as compared with being captured by the Russians, who treated German POWs with complete brutality, shooting and starving hundreds of thousands to death in the first months of 1945. The authorities also hoped that their POWs would be better treated by the Germans if German POWs were treated well. It didn't make any difference, as Lyle Bouck and his men were now learning only too well.

51. The bombing of Dresden has become perhaps the most controversial action of the Allies in Europe. 'Bomber' Arthur

Harris, head of RAF Bomber Command, was the only British senior military commander not to be knighted after the war. As early as March 1945, Churchill himself was trying to distance himself from Operation Thunderclap, sensing the eventual fallout from the terror raid that he too believed had gone too far, though of course he had ordered it. Among some pilots on the raid, there were also mixed feelings. But American Flight Lieutenant John Morris, with the American Eighth Air Force, was one of many who had no regrets whatsoever. 'I'm hardly ashamed of having gone to Dresden that day,' he recalled. 'It was sound strategy to prevent the Wehrmacht from falling back to regroup and be lethal again. So we bombed the hell out of the railroad marshaling yards and road hubs along the Wehrmacht's line of retreat, up and down Germany's eastern border. I don't rejoice at the 35,000 Germans killed there. I doubt there were many Jews in that number. The good burghers of Dresden had shipped them all off to Auschwitz. . . . It is true that the RAF purposely started a firestorm, causing many of the casualties. It was a tactic they frequently tried. But they, and we, killed more people in other cities, on other days. So did the Russians. So did the Japanese. So did the Germans. Dresden was not unique.' As a POW laborer, Private Kurt Vonnegut famously witnessed the fire-bombing of Dresden, which had been perhaps the most beautiful of all central European cities. 'It was just one huge flame. . . . There wasn't anything organic left after it.' Vonnegut and other American POWs were forced to dispose of some of the bodies. Private Jim Mills, from Company I, 423rd Regiment of the 106th, joined Vonnegut in a work party removing bodies from the basement of slaughterhouses. In one room in the basement, Mills saw a card table with bottles of liquor beside a pile of burnt bodies. One of the bodies was particularly badly disfigured. 'The guard pointed at the corpse as one I should remove,' recalled Mills. 'He indicated I take a belt off another body and put it around the one I was to remove. It's surprising how much could be communicated by hand motions. I put a belt around the neck of this man and started to drag it towards the ramp, but [the body] broke in half. That was too much for me. I sort of lost it for a bit. I began to scream, yell and dance around. I tried to go out but they wouldn't let me. They got me quieted down, pointed to one of the bottles on the table and insisted I have a few swallows. That was the first I ever tasted liquor of any kind.'

52. By now, Kriz had earned a nickname among his troops: 'Crazy, Crazy Kriz.' His men used it respectfully, though, because above all Kriz was admired for his ability to minimize their casualties. But it was his penchant for dogfighting that added to his reputation as a colorful character. After breaking out of the Ardennes, Kriz had taken a German shepherd dog from a captured German unit. The dog was a giant female, and Kriz would have his dog fight any and all comers, on one condition – the other dog had to be male. Whenever the dogfights took place, the male would pause to sniff Kriz's beloved mascot – a lethal mistake, for in that split second Kriz's dog pounced. Kriz won a small fortune and was heartbroken when he had to give the dog away at war's end.

53. Three days earlier, on March 7, 1945, men of the 27th Armored Infantry Battalion had fought their way to the western end of the bridge. After several failed attempts to blow the bridge behind them, a German sergeant had dashed out under heavy fire and lit a primer cord attached to a massive explosive charge on the bridge itself. There had been a huge roar, and timber and masonry had flown through the air. But when the dust had settled, to both the Germans' and Americans' astonishment, the bridge still stood. Immediately, GIs had begun to cross, supported by fire from Pershing tanks. The first American to set foot on the eastern bank of the Rhine was an assistant squad leader, Sergeant Alex Drabnik. The news that Drabnik and others had taken the

Ludendorff bridge soon reached senior Allied commanders. For General Eisenhower, it was the most pleasing news of the entire war. Along with General Hodges of the U.S. First Army and General Bradley, he had ordered every available infantry division to exploit the crossing – first among them the 99th Division.

54. Later that night, one of the German doctors working in the Hammelburg Lager, a Major Seisser, rushed back to the city to find his home office and all his medical equipment destroyed and his father seriously injured. He returned the next morning and told Berndt that he would no longer help with extra medical supplies as he had before.

55. Cabanatuan was a prison camp recently liberated by MacArthur's men in the Philippines. Five hundred men had been freed. The escapade had made international headlines.

56. Goode kept his word, later submitting a secret report to Swiss authorities about the shooting.

57. Thanks to the skill and speed of Colonel Radovan Danich, a Serbian doctor of great renown before the war in Belgrade, Waters's life would be saved. Danich only had paper bandages and a table knife to work with.

58. When the camp was liberated, Patton immediately sent his Third Army's assistant chief surgeon, Colonel Charles B. Odom, to Hammelburg. On reaching Hammelburg, he ordered two Piper Cub planes to take him and Waters to the 34th Evacuation Hospital at Frankfurt. Baum and the other wounded Kriegies were stunned and embittered by such flagrant favoritism, which only deepened their suspicions that Task Force Baum had been sent to rescue above all just one man, Bea Waters's husband – Patton's son-in-law.

59. Dysentery was rampant, and fear of an outbreak of typhus was widespread. The queues for the open-air latrines sometimes stretched for fifty yards; using them felt like being tortured. The men's diet did not help the multiple digestive and intestinal diseases that now afflicted thousands of

inmates. Most days, there was not much more than sauerkraut – often rancid – ladled out of huge barrels. Most men vomited if they ate more than a couple of spoonfuls, and all first-time tasters, such as Lyle Bouck and his platoon, struggled to keep the sometimes maggot-infested stuff down. Anything that moved in Moosberg, other than humans, was killed to eat. In the Russian sector of the camp, where conditions were even worse, there were rumors that some men had resorted to cannibalism – corpses would later be found with bite marks. One day shortly after his arrival, Peter Gacki watched as two men tried to capture a cat: 'I'm not sure if they wanted a pet or a meal. The cat obviously had been around the camp for some time because it stayed out of reach. We were not a friendly group. Everyone had a friend or two, and they stayed together.'

60. By contrast, another 99er liberated from Moosberg, Staff Sergeant Vernon McGarity, a squad leader with Company L, 393rd Infantry Regiment, was fit enough to be fully debriefed. He would become the only Checkerboard man to receive the Medal of Honor. During December 16–17, despite being badly injured, he had wiped out machine gun nests, saved fellow 99ers under intense fire, and then finally been taken prisoner but only after his squad had fired its last bullet. General Orders #6, War Department, Washington, D.C., January 11, 1946. Twenty-four Distinguished Service Crosses were awarded to the 99th Division.

61. The platoon joked now about even their worst experiences. There was one incident, which Slape recalled, that prompted raucous laughter. 'A German in a trench coat ran along the barbed wire fence in front of their position, afraid he would get shot if he stopped to climb over it. Everyone fired at him, but nobody hit him. Then someone put a tracer round in his rifle. The tracer round sped towards the German and went right across the cheeks of his butt. The guy just flat-foot jumped that fence, and the platoon never saw him again.'

62. The following evening, Vernon Leopold arranged for the platoon to see a Broadway musical, *Sweeney Todd.* 'A barber with his shop on a second floor,' recalled Bouck, 'slit the throat of his customers and dropped the corpse through the trap door. Below, the barber's girlfriend would grind the bodies three times and serve the remains as meat pies in her beer garden. Wow! How about that for class in New York.'

63. Because Lieutenant Warren Springer was fit enough upon liberation from Moosberg to make a report to a senior officer on his unit's actions on December 16, every man in the four-man unit received a Silver Star in 1945.

64. The *Washington Post* reporter had asked several men how they felt about the awards. 'Ours was a patriotic war, Vietnam was a political one,' said Private James Silvola. 'I was just in the wrong place at the wrong time,' Corporal Sam Jenkins told his local El Paso newspaper. Jenkins added that his wife was thinking of hanging the Bronze Star on display. He preferred to put it in a drawer: 'Don't call Samuel Jenkins a hero. Please don't use that word. Too many other people did a lot more than I did who were never recognized.' Private Joseph McConnell was equally self-effacing. A German slug lodged in his left shoulder and his bullet-torn jacket were the only war souvenirs the quiet, soft-spoken bus driver kept. 'I'm no hero. I just did what I had to do. I've never talked about it or lost any sleep. Different people react in different ways.' McConnell placed the Bronze Star in a drawer alongside his Purple Heart and the army jacket he was wearing when he was shot.

List of Awards

Intelligence and Reconnaissance Platoon, 394th Infantry Regiment, 99th Infantry Division, and 394th I&R Presidential Unit Citation

First Lieutenant Lyle J. Bouck Jr.   Distinguished Service Cross, Silver Star

Private William James (Tsakanikas)   Distinguished Service Cross
Private First Class Risto Milosevich   Distinguished Service Cross
Sergeant William L. Slape   Distinguished Service Cross

Private John B. Creger   Silver Star
Private Louis J. Kalil   Silver Star
Corporal Aubrey P. McGehee, Jr.   Silver Star
Private First Class Jordan H. Robinson   Silver Star
Private James R. Silvola   Silver Star

Private Robert D. Adams   Bronze Star with Valor Device
Private Robert J. Baasch   Bronze Star with Valor Device
Sergeant William R. Dustman   Bronze Star with Valor Device
Private Clifford R. Fansher   Bronze Star with Valor Device
Technician Fourth Class James Fort   Bronze Star with Valor Device
Corporal Samuel L. Jenkins   Bronze Star with Valor Device
Private Joseph A. McConnell   Bronze Star with Valor Device
Private First Class Robert H. Preston   Bronze Star with Valor Device
Sergeant George H. Redmond   Bronze Star with Valor Device

Private First Class Carlos A. Fernandez   Presidential Unit Citation
Private First Class John P. Frankovitch   Presidential Unit Citation
Technician Fifth Class Robert L. Lambert   Presidential Unit Citation

List of Awards

Private Vernon G. Leopold	Presidential Unit Citation
Private First Class Elmer J. Nowacki	Presidential Unit Citation
Private Samuel J. Oakley	Presidential Unit Citation

All members of the platoon who received individual awards also received the Presidential Unit Citation. Lyle Bouck's Silver Star was awarded in 1945 and is superseded by his DSC award.

Sources

Interviews and personal files

Vic Adams
Barbara Anderson
Abe Baum
Lyle Bouck
Edward Buegner
Will Cavanagh
Paul Cavanaugh
John Creger Jr.
John Creger Sr.
Delfina Fernanadez

Carlos Fernandez
James Fort
Peter Gacki
Bill James
Sam Jenkins
Louis Kalil
Robert L. Kriz
Robert Lambert
Vernon Leopold
Agnes McGehee

Bill Merricken
Risto Milosevich
William Nutto
Jochen Peiper
James Silvola
Bill Slape
Warren Springer
Robert Thompson
Anna Tsakanikas
Kurt Vonnegut

Journals and websites

Birmingham News
Checkerboard
Daily Independent (Grand Island, Neb.)
El Paso Times
Fairfax Journal
Fayetteville Observer
Knoxville News-Sentinel
Phoenix Gazette
Roanoke Times & World-News
Saddleback Valley News
Senior Circuit (St. Louis)
Shreveport Times

Sources

South Bend Tribune
St. Louis Post-Dispatch
St. Louis Star-Bulletin
Tempe Daily News
Times (Shreveport)
Washington Post
www.chuckallan.com
www.raf.mod.uk/bombercommand/diary/dec44.html
www.raf.mod.uk/bombercommand/diary/jan45.html
www.raf.mod.uk/bombercommand/diary/feb45.html

Bibliography

Ambrose, Stephen. *Citizen Soldiers.* New York: Touchstone, 1997.
———. *The Supreme Commander: The War Years of General Dwight D. Eisenhower.* Garden City, NY: Doubleday, 1970.
Angolia, John R., and Adolf Schlicht. *Uniforms and Traditions of the German Army, 1933–1945.* Vol. 3. San Jose, CA: R. James Bender Publishing, 1987.
Arnold, James R. *Ardennes 1944: Hitler's Last Gamble in the West.* Osprey Campaign Series. Number 5. London: Osprey Publishing Ltd., 1990.
Astor, Gerald. *A Blood-Dimmed Tide: The Battle of the Bulge by the Men Who Fought It.* New York: Donald I. Fine, 1992.
———. *The Mighty Eighth: The Air War in Europe as Told by the Men Who Fought It.* New York: Donald Fine Books, 1997.
Ayer, Frederick. *Before the Colors Fade.* New York: Houghton Mifflin, 1964.
Baldwin, Hanson. *Battles Lost and Won: Great Campaigns of World War II.* New York: Harper & Row, 1966.
Baron, Richard, Abe Baum, and Richard Goldhurst. *Raid!* New York: G. P. Putnam's Sons, 1981.
Bennett, Ralph. *Ultra in the West: The Normandy Campaign of 1944–45.* New York: Charles Scribner's Sons, 1980.

Blumenson, Martin. *The Hammelburg Affair.* Army 15 (October 1965).

——. *Patton.* New York: Morrow, 1985.

——. *The Patton Papers, 1940–45.* Boston: Houghton Mifflin, 1974.

Bradley, Omar. *A Soldier's Story.* New York: Henry Holt and Co., 1951.

Brett-Smith, Richard. *Hitler's Generals.* San Rafael, CA: Presidio Press, 1977.

Bryant, Arthur. *Triumph in the West: A History of the War Years Based on the Diaries of Field-Marshal Lord Alan Brooke, Chief of the Imperial General Staff.* Garden City, NY: Doubleday, 1959.

Butcher, Harry Cecil. *My Three Years with Eisenhower.* New York: Simon and Schuster, 1946.

Calvocoressi, Peter. *Top Secret Ultra.* London: Cassell, 1980.

Cavanagh, William. *Krinkelt-Rocherath: The Battle for the Twin Villages.* Norwell, MA: Christopher Publishing House, 1986.

Chandler, Alfred D., Jr., ed. *The Papers of Dwight David Eisenhower,* Vol. IV, *The War Years.* Baltimore: Johns Hopkins University Press, 1970.

Chernitsky, Dorothy. *Voices from the Foxholes.* Uniontown, PA: Dorothy Chernitsky, 1991.

Codman, Charles. *Drive.* Boston: Little, Brown, 1957.

Cole, Hugh M. *The Ardennes: Battle of the Bulge, US Army in World War II.* Washington, D.C.: Government Printing Office, 1965.

Downing, David. *The Devil's Virtuosos: German Generals at War 1940–5.* New York: St. Martin's Press, 1977.

Eisenhower, Dwight D. *Crusade in Europe.* Garden City, NY: Doubleday, 1948.

——. *Eisenhower at War, 1943–45.* New York: Random House, 1986.

Eisenhower, John. *The Bitter Woods.* New York: G. P. Putnam's Sons, 1969.

Ellis, Maj. L. F., with Lt. Col. A. E. Warhurst. *Victory in the West,* Vol. II, *The Defeat of Germany.* London: Her Majesty's Stationery Office, 1968.

Elstob, Peter. *Hitler's Last Offensive*. London: Secker & Warburg, 1971.

Erickson, John. *The Road to Berlin*. London: Weidenfeld & Nicolson, 1983.

Essame, H. *Patton: Study in Command*. New York: Scribners, 1974.

Farago, L. *Patton: Ordeal and Triumph*. New York: Obolensky, 1964.

Farrar, Walton T. 1/LT. *The Combat History of the 394th Infantry Regiment*, ed. PFC James L. Haseltine. Privately published, 1945.

Fest, Joachim C. *Hitler*. London: Weidenfeld & Nicolson, 1974.

Foley, Charles. *Commando Extraordinary*. Costa Mesa, CA: Noontide Press, 1988.

Forty, George. *Patton's Third Army at War*. London: Arms and Armour Press, 1976.

Frischauer, Willi. *Himmler: Evil Genius of the Third Reich*. London: Odhams, 1953.

Garlinski, Josef. *The Enigma War*. New York: Charles Scribner's Sons, 1980.

Gilbert, Felix, ed. *Hitler Directs His War*. New York: Oxford University Press, 1950.

Giles, Janet Holt. *The Damned Engineers*. Boston: Houghton Mifflin, 1970.

Gorlitz, Walter. *The German General Staff: Its History and Structure, 1657–1945*. London: Hollis & Carter, 1953.

Graber, C. S. *History of the SS*. London: Hale, 1978.

Grunberger, Richard. *A Social History of the Third Reich*. London: Weidenfeld & Nicolson, 1971.

Hart, B. H. Liddell. *The German Generals Talk*. New York: Quill, 1979.

Hoffmann, Peter. *The History of the German Resistance 1933–1945*. London: Macdonald & Jane's, 1977.

Hogg, Ian V., and John Weeks. *Military Small Arms of the 20th Century*. Northbrook, IL: DBI Books, 1985.

Hohne, Heinz. *The Order of the Death's Head: The Story of Hitler's SS*. London: Secker & Warburg, 1969.

Infeld, Glenn B. *Skorzeny, Hitler's Commando.* New York: St. Martin's Press, 1981.

Irving, David. *The War between the Generals: Inside the Allied High Command.* New York: Congdon & Lanes, 1981.

Keegan, John. *The Face of Battle.* New York: Viking, 1976.

——. *Waffen-SS: The Asphalt Soldiers.* New York: Ballantine Books, 1970.

Kesselring, Albert. *The Memoirs of Field-Marshal Kesselring.* London: W. Kimber, 1953.

Kessler, Leo. *SS Peiper.* London: Leo Cooper in Association with Secker & Warburg, 1986.

Koehl, Robert Louis. *The Black Corps: The Structure and Power Struggles of the Nazi SS.* Madison: University of Wisconsin Press, 1983.

Koyen, Kenneth A. *The Fourth Armored Division from the Beach to Bavaria.* Munich: Privately published, 1946.

Lauer, Walter. *Battle Babies: The Story of the 99th Infantry Division in World War II.* Baton Rouge: Military Press of Louisiana, 1951.

Legare, Ben W. *The Operations of the 2nd Battalion, 394th Infantry (99th Infantry Division) in the German Counteroffensive, Vicinity of Losheimergraben, Germany. 16–19 December 1944 (Personal Experience of a Battalion Executive Officer) (Ardennes Campaign).* Unpublished monograph (Advanced Infantry Officers Course, 1949–1950). U.S. Army Infantry School, Fort Benning, Georgia.

Lehmann, Rudolf. *Die Leibstandarte.* 3 vols. Osnabruck: Munin Verlag, 1977–1982.

Leinbaugh, Harold P., and John D. Campbell. *The Men of Company K.* New York: William Morrow, 1985.

Lucas, James, and Matthew Cooper. *Hitler's Elite: Leibstandarte SS.* London: Macdonald & Jane's, 1975.

MacDonald, Charles B. *The Mighty Endeavor: American Armed Forces in the European Theater in World War II.* New York: Oxford University Press, 1969.

——. *A Time for Trumpets.* New York: William Morrow, 1985.

Manvell, Roger, and Heinrich Fraenkel. *Heinrich Himmler.* London: Heinemann, 1965.

Marshall, S. L. A. *Night Drop.* Boston: Little, Brown, 1962.

McMillan, Richard. *Miracle before Berlin.* London: Jarrolds, 1946.

Merriam, Robert. *Dark December.* Chicago: Ziff-Davis, 1947.

Mitcham, Samuel W., Jr. *Hitler's Legions: The German Army Order of Battle, World War II.* New York: Stein and Day, 1985.

Mollo, Andrew. *The Armed Forces of World War II.* New York: Military Press, 1987.

Montgomery, Bernard L. *The Memoirs of Field-Marshal the Viscount Montgomery of Alamein, K. G.* Cleveland: World, 1958.

Niedermayer, Walter. *Into the Deep Misty Woods of the Ardennes.* Indiana, PA: A. G. Halldin Publishing Company, 1990.

Nobecourt, Jacques. *Hitler's Last Gamble: The Battle of the Bulge.* New York: Schocken Books, 1967.

Pallud, Jean-Paul. *Ardennes 1944: Peiper and Skorzerny.* Osprey Elite Series No. 11. London: Osprey Publishing, 1987.

Parker, Danny S. *Battle of the Bulge: Hitler's Ardennes Offensive, 1944–1945.* Philadelphia: Combined Books, 1991.

Parrish, Thomas, ed. *The Simon and Schuster Encyclopedia of World War II.* New York: Simon and Schuster, 1978.

Patton, George Smith. *War as I Knew It.* New York: Houghton Mifflin, 1947.

Pogue, Forrest C. *The Supreme Command: US Army in World War II.* Washington, D.C.: Government Printing Office, 1954.

Reimann, Viktor. *Joseph Goebbels: The Man Who Created Hitler.* London: Sphere paperback edition, 1979.

Reitlinger, Gerald. *The SS: Alibi of a Nation, 1922–1945.* London: Arms & Armour, 1985.

Richardson, William, and Seymour Freidin, eds. *The Fatal Decisions.* London: Michael Joseph, 1956.

Ridgway, Matthew B., and Harold H. Martin. *Soldier: The Memoirs of Matthew B. Ridgway.* New York: Harper & Bros., 1956.

Robichon, Jacques. *The Second D-Day.* New York: Walker & Co., 1969.

Ryan, Cornelius. *The Last Battle*. New York: Simon & Schuster, 1966.

Schramm, Wilhelm von. *Conspiracy among the Generals*. London: Allen & Unwin, 1956.

Seaton, Albert. *The German Army, 1933–45*. London: Weidenfeld & Nicolson, 1982.

Shirer, William. *The Rise and Fall of the Third Reich*. London: Book Club Associates edition, 1971.

Shulman, Milton. *Defeat in the West*. London: Mercury Books, 1963.

Smith, Bradley F. *The Road to Nuremberg*. London: André Deutsch, 1981.

Snyder, Louis L. *Encyclopaedia of the Third Reich*. London: Hall, 1976.

Speer, Albert. *Inside the Third Reich*. London: Weidenfeld & Nicolson, 1970.

Stanton, Shelby L. *World War II Order of Battle*. New York: Galahad Books, 1991.

Stein, George H. *The Waffen-SS: Hitler's Elite Guard at War, 1939–1945*. Ithaca, NY: Cornell University Press paperback edition, 1984.

Sydnor, Charles W., Jr. *Soldiers of Destruction: The SS Death's Head Division, 1933–1945*. Princeton: Princeton University Press, 1977.

Taylor, Fred, ed. *The Goebbels Diaries, 1939–1941*. London: Hamish Hamilton, 1982.

Toland, John. *Adolf Hitler*. New York: Doubleday, 1976.

———. *Battle: The Story of the Bulge*. New York: Random House, 1959.

———. *The Last 100 Days*. New York: Random House, 1966.

Trevor-Roper, Hugh, ed. *The Goebbels Diaries: The Last Days*. London: Pan paperback edition, 1979.

Warlimont, Walter. *Inside Hitler's Headquarters, 1939–45*. London: Weidenfeld & Nicolson, 1964.

Weigley, Russell E. *Eisenhower's Lieutenants*. Bloomington: Indiana University Press, 1981.

Weingartner, James J. *Crossroads of Death*. Berkeley: University of California Press, 1979.

Wellard, James Howard. *General George S. Patton, Jr.: Man under Mars*. New York: Dodd, Mead & Co., 1946.

Whiting, Charles. *The Battle of Hürtgen Forest*. New York: Pocket Books, 1989.

——. *Death of a Division*. New York: Stein and Day, 1980.

——. *48 Hours to Hammelburg*. New York: Jove Books, 1984.

——. *Massacre at Malmedy*. London: Leo Cooper, 1971.

——. *Patton*. New York: Ballantine, 1970.

Wilmot, Chester. *The Struggle for Europe*. New York: Harper & Bros., 1952.

Windrow, Martin, and Francis K. A. Mason. *Concise Dictionary of Military Biography*. London: Purnell, 1975.

Wistrich, Robert. *Who's Who in Nazi Germany*. London: Weidenfeld & Nicolson, 1982.

Index